NONBINARY

NONBINARY

Memoirs of Gender and Identity

EDITED BY
MICAH RAJUNOV
AND SCOTT DUANE

Columbia University Press
New York

Columbia University Press
Publishers Since 1893
New York   Chichester, West Sussex
cup.columbia.edu
Copyright © 2019 Columbia University Press
All rights reserved
Library of Congress Cataloging-in-Publication Data
Names: Rajunov, Micah, editor. | Duane, A. Scott, editor.
Title: Nonbinary : memoirs of gender and identity / edited by Micah Rajunov
and A. Scott Duane.
Description: New York : Columbia University Press, [2018] | Includes
bibliographical references and index.
Identifiers: LCCN 2018033719 (print) | LCCN 2018036460 (ebook) |
ISBN 9780231546102 (e-book) | ISBN 9780231185325 (cloth)
| ISBN 9780231185332 (pbk.)
Subjects: LCSH: Gender nonconformity. | Gender nonconforming people. |
Sexual minorities—Identity. | Gender identity.
Classification: LCC HQ77.9 (ebook) | LCC HQ77.9 .N645 2018 (print) |
DDC 305.3—dc23
LC record available at https://lccn.loc.gov/2018033719

Contents

PART FIVE
Redefining Dualities: Paradoxes and Possibilities of Gender

Foreword

From Genderqueer to Nonbinary to . . .

RIKI WILCHINS

BACK IN THE 1990s, I started using the term "genderqueer" in an effort to glue together two nouns which seemed to me to describe an excluded middle: those of us who were not just trans, but also queer: the kind of gendertrash that transgressed the natural boundaries of transgender, those whom society couldn't digest. A prominent gay columnist promptly attacked me for "ruining a perfectly good word like 'queer.'"

Then Joan Nestle, Clare Howell, and I used the word for the title of our anthology of emerging young writers. And there it sat. I don't recall anyone actually picking it up or using it. Eight years later at Creating Change—an LGBTQ leadership conference—I saw a sticker someone has posted that read, "A Genderqueer Was Here!" I thought, "Well that's interesting. Someone is actually using it." And so it begins.

Fast forward about ten years and I was reading Matt Bernstein's anthology *Nobody Passes*. In it writer Rocko Bulldagger bemoans the term's very existence, declaring, "I am sick to death of hearing it." Such is the arc of new ideas.

I suspect the same thing is about to happen with nonbinary.

For the public, that arc probably began in a town hall in London, when a twenty-year-old student came out to President Obama as nonbinary: "I'm about to do something terrifying, which is I'm coming out to you as a nonbinary person. . . . In the UK we don't recognize nonbinary people under the Equality Act, so we literally have no rights," Maria Munir said. Obama, one of our most hip and cosmopolitan presidents ever, still had no idea what Munir was talking about. Befuddled, if well intentioned, he relapsed into his LGBTQ talking points, which really had very little to do with it.

He is not alone in his confusion. As nonbinary comes to the fore, it will challenge everything we currently think about bodies, sexual orientation, and gender, almost all of which depends implicitly or explicitly on the binary. One can only hope almost none of it survives. If I am nonbinary, can feminism—the politics of women—still represent me? Can I enter women-only spaces, or men-only meetings? Can I be gay, straight, or bisexual? Here language fails, the entire discourse on gayness and sexual orientation collapses.

The same thing is going to happen with transgender. The "trans" in transsexual was always about moving from one thing to another. A person was going *from* male to female, or vice versa. This conception was more or less grafted onto the newer term "transgender."

It's an overused truism that "transgender" was intended as a broad "umbrella term" for all those who are gender nonconforming. Yet there are limits: transgender itself is interpreted by some in terms of two binary genders that one is traveling between or else not conforming to. For others (especially transsexuals), being transgender implies a sense of conflict between one's inner gender identity and birth sex as male or female. In this way, transgender often unintentionally reinforced and reified the same binary of sexes and genders that makes outcasts of transpeople in the first place.

But what if one is not traveling anywhere? Or is entirely off the map of intelligible binary genders?

Familiar transgender concerns get scrambled quickly. For instance, we now accept that transgender women are women and can use the women's bathroom. But what bathroom do we want nonbinary people to have the right to use: Both? Neither? And what sex marker do we want them to be able to put on their ID? Both? Neither? A new one?

You can see where this is going. Neither our language nor our politics is suited to accommodate this, and we're going to have to do a lot of rethinking.

All of which is long overdue. Binary gender regimes maintained themselves with a few rules: everyone must be in a box; there are only two boxes; no one can change boxes; no one is allowed between the boxes. Since no one really fits the perfect masculine or feminine ideals, these rules end up being terribly oppressive to almost everyone, and more so to those who are genderqueer. One can only hope the emergence of a nonbinary movement is the first step in finally retiring it.

Munir was actually way ahead of a curve that is only now coming into view. It's not that nonbinary people have no rights (although they don't and they must), it's that—like Obama—most people have no idea that they exist or what they are.

What comes next, what takes its place, is going to be very interesting. It will be years before even something as simple as the use of the pronouns *they, them,* and *their* works its way through our language and our brain-pans and become standard. It will be even longer before people like Munir feeling emboldened, coming out, and stepping off the binary become widespread and commonplace.

And that deeper social change that really opens a profound and enduring space for those who are nonbinary to live fully with rights, dignity, and understanding will take even longer.

Fortunately, until then, we will have this excellent new anthology to guide us.

Introduction

MICAH RAJUNOV AND SCOTT DUANE

GENDER is a slippery illusion. Like the flat outline of a cube, you can perceive its shape as either concave or convex, extruding or withdrawn. If you're especially adept, you can see both simultaneously, or perhaps, even for a moment, neither at all. Upon deeper inspection, you might deduce the truth at the heart of it all: there is no one "correct" form. Yet all of them are real.

Most of us were raised to believe that gender is a dichotomy: male and female. But underneath this foundational "fact" lies a complexity we've been trying to untangle. The modern discourse on transgender people and on gender more broadly has already been elevated beyond duality. But, what *is* gender? Rather than having an answer for this basic question, we are left with even more questions. What is a man? What is a woman? And, central to the essays contained within this book, why does this matter?

Communities are blossoming around the experience of being something other than *man* or *woman*. While still new to many, the rise of nonbinary identities is another step built upon the work and accelerating progress of our LGBTQ predecessors. As gender diversity is increasingly embraced, more people and their allies are emerging and finding one another. They, in turn, extend the fight toward a deeper understanding and acceptance not only of the complexity of gender, but of the complexity of the individual.

This anthology faces the foundational questions of gender head-on. Through a personal examination of their own lives, thirty authors grant us a glimpse into the process of discovering, defining, constructing, creating, and *experiencing* gender in a unique way. Today, the world is finally ready to hear their stories.

PART I: WHAT IS GENDER?

"Is it a boy or a girl?"
   "It's a dog."
   "But is it a boy dog or a girl dog?"
People are never shy to ask about a dog's gender, and are quick to apologize when they get it wrong. Yet when it comes to the human species, directly inquiring about a person's gender is often considered egregiously offensive. Regarded almost as insulting is the act of accidental misgendering, like calling someone *sir* when it should be *ma'am*. In this situation, a casual apology is not the norm; instead, the guilty party usually fumbles through a fix, thoroughly embarrassed by this transgression.

As far as we know, dogs do not have a gender identity—they don't mind being called he or she, as long as there's a treat involved. The question of "boy" dog or "girl" dog is merely an articulation of the most familiar and fundamental schema of gender: genitals. Humans, on the other hand, have a gender—an internal sense of who we are at our core that transcends body parts.

Across cultures and millennia, people have blurred the bounds of gender.[1] Although embodied in different words, meanings, and belief systems, their experience was as real then as it is today. In contemporary Western society, only in the last few decades has the realization that gender is not a simple male/female dichotomy come to the fore. But traditions die hard and cultural inertia runs deep. Before a child can form complete sentences, they learn that gender is a (if not *the*) primary characteristic that defines a human being. Personhood is contingent on the immediate categorization into a sex. Once the doctor takes a cursory look at a newly born infant's genitals, officially proclaiming it to be male or female, the baby is marked for life.

Yet even this simple act of examining external reproductive organs leads to gray areas. While in most babies sex is as straightforward as penis or vagina, in as many as 1.7 percent of births this is not the case.[2] Medical literature possibly underestimates incidence rates, given that many people do not find out they are intersex or have a difference in sexual development (DSD) until adulthood. This happens either because only nonvisible features such as their internal organs or chromosomes exhibit this divergence, or because their parents were pressured into silence due to continued stigmatization. If you argue that biological variations in sexual dimorphism are too rare to be of much importance, then consider that roughly one in a hundred people have bodies that differ from the "standard" male or female[3]—a rate that mirrors that of people with red hair.[4] Surely you know someone with red hair.

Biological diversity is only the first crack in the precarious male/female binary. Historically, societies have afforded gender expression varying degrees of flexibility that shift across time. As an example from our own modern culture, up until the 1940s pink was considered a masculine color for its proximity to the more "vigorous" red.[5] But due to a combination of gender normative panic and marketing, pink is now exclusively reserved for the feminine.[6] Another strikingly recent gender crossover is the mundanity with which we regard women who wear pants. Clearly, the porous boundary around gender expression is not new. Rather, what has permeated our contemporary awareness is the acknowledgment that gender runs deeper than appearance, behavior, or preferences.

Gender is gradually being understood to be a holistic experience of ourselves, inside and out. Gender *identity* is regarded as separate from our *biology*—genitals, reproductive organs, chromosomes, hormones, secondary sex characteristics. It is also distinct from our gender *expression*—hair length, clothing, mannerisms, makeup.[7] For most folks, their biology, expression, and identity are all in alignment. But for an estimated 1.4 million Americans, there is a mismatch.[8] Framing gender identity as self-determined and independent from our body[9] and external presentation has allowed increased recognition and acceptance of transgender people.

Despite this promising reconceptualization, our grasp of gender hinges upon the words we use to describe it. Language, unfortunately, remains steeped in binary constructions. Try describing your gender without using the terms male/female, masculine/feminine, girl/boy, woman/man, or any variation thereof—you are likely to come up blank. Similarly, it's nearly impossible to talk about someone else without assigning a gender to them. In many cases you cannot escape gendering even yourself. For instance, in romance languages like Spanish or

French, nouns and adjectives indicate gender, which can often be your own. In English, the paltry offering of two gendered pronouns poses limitations to properly address nonbinary people. Just as we don't say "she" when referring to a man, using either "he" or "she" is incorrect when referring to someone who is not male or female.

One way of working around these constraints is by repurposing existing solutions. Because our language has been using "singular they" for centuries, this has become the most common pronoun for referring to anyone whose gender is not known, not specified, or not in the male/female binary. As of 2017, the official stylebook for the *Associated Press* now recommends using the "singular they/them" for nonbinary individuals.[10] The trans community has further spurred the proliferation of new pronouns: s/he, zie/hir, xe/xem, ey/em—the list is innumerable, with comprehensive guides,[11] apps,[12] and games[13] to help illustrate their usage. Best practices include specifying pronouns in email signatures and business cards, mentioning a person's pronoun alongside their name when introducing them, and *always* asking for someone's pronoun.

Words shape our world, and finding the right ones—or inventing new ones—gives us the power to expand what we already know. More importantly, words grant us the ability to communicate with others. At the same time, words can box us in, labeling everyone and everything, inevitably homogenizing differences. As liberating as it can be to find a word that describes your gender, it can also be limiting. Labels place boundaries on what we are as well as what we are not.

"Nonbinary" simply means *not* binary; when applied to gender, it means not exclusively male or female. Nonbinary is defined by what it's not. Even the word "genderqueer,"[14] derived from a reclaiming of the word "queer," encompasses any form of gender that is *not* normative.[15] The problem of terminology goes beyond one of social cohesion and agreement: it is philosophical. How can a group of people whose genders are largely illegible to the world translate their existence to the men and women around them? Often, the language of the nonbinary community reflects the frustrating but necessary process of defining oneself only in opposition to what is already defined. Demiboy, transfeminine, androgynous, bigender, even the word "nonbinary" itself—all of these incorporate the existing binary to one extent or another.

Gender nonconforming, gender variant, gender diverse, gender expansive, gender creative—many of the terms are quite new, and as such haven't settled firmly into the lexicon. What all of them fail to capture is the nuanced humanity of those whose gender ventures into the unknown. Nonbinary individuals are more than simply both, neither, or in between. Stepping beyond male and female leads us into the infinite universe of gender.

In this book, nonbinary people finally get a chance to define themselves by who they *are*, rather than by the negative space of what is missing. The narratives in the first part highlight how those whose gender cannot be described as simply male or female are creating a positive space for their existence.

PART II: VISIBILITY

Standing Up and Standing Out

Shared identities serve as an imperfect proxy to quickly ascertain and understand another's experience. In addition to gender, we are born into, create, adopt, and self-proclaim ourselves into further categories based on race, religion, nationality, sexuality, profession, socioeconomic status, disability; we are trauma survivors, cancer patients, Californians, parents, veterans, vegetarians, artists, athletes, and more. Not only is gender highly unique and individualized, so is the intersection of all our other identities.

We all carry visible and invisible identities. Like gender, some of our identities are immediately evident to strangers, while others are misinterpreted, misconstrued, or hidden. Some identities elicit pride; others shame. Most of them are accompanied by an inherited or chosen community of others with similar stories, uniting us through common characteristics or experiences.[16] The solidarity that arises affords support, but also demarcates *us* from *them*. When it's unclear whether someone is an "us" or a "them," outsiders tend to react unpredictably—with confusion, curiosity, desire, ridicule, anger, or even violence.

Being openly transgender still invites danger. Trans people are seven times more likely than the cisgender population to experience physical violence from law enforcement. Trans women are almost twice as likely to experience sexual violence compared to other survivors. Perhaps most worrisome, two-thirds of the victims of hate-motivated homicides are trans women of color.[17] Aside from hate crimes and harassment, trans people face alarmingly high rates of poverty, unemployment, homelessness, and HIV, with scarce legal protections.[18] Consequently many trans people, especially those who "pass" or are consistently perceived as cisgender men or women, avoid disclosing that they are transgender in the majority of their social and professional spheres.[19] Opting out of being out was the norm in the past; transition was accompanied by the presumption that one would go "stealth" and never reveal a transsexual history for fear of being ostracized, fired, arrested, or worse.[20]

Our understanding of disclosure has since evolved to encompass—like everything else—a spectrum. Reasons for disclosing are as varied as people; some feel safe sharing their trans identity to a select few, others unabashedly announce it to the world. Even *what* someone discloses and *how* vary by individual and circumstance. But choice in disclosure assumes not only safety; it is also contingent on the ability to be consistently perceived as one of the two readily available genders. So what does "passing" mean for nonbinary people? In the *2015 U.S. Transgender Survey*, only 3 percent of nonbinary respondents "always told others" that they were nonbinary.[21] When it is impossible for your external appearance to accurately reflect your inner gender—when the general public is missing the mental model that represents your gender—you will never be truly seen.

Visibility of transgender people has gained significant traction in the last decade. In 2014, *Time* magazine declared a "transgender tipping point" when Laverne Cox graced the cover. Celebrities like Jazz Jennings, Janet Mock, Chaz Bono, and Caitlyn Jenner have taken over reality TV, along with portrayals of trans characters in numerous movies, books, TV programs, and other media.[22] However, the overwhelming majority of these depictions reinforce the prototypical transgender narrative, centered on milestones related to transition from one binary gender to the other. While this template can serve as a helpful guide, it can severely limit the possibilities for anyone whose gender path does not align with it. Nonbinary experiences remain invisible to this momentum.

Mainstream portrayals of nonbinary people are scarce. In a ten-year content analysis of thirteen of the most widely circulated U.S. newspapers, only 1.2 percent of paragraphs that mentioned a transgender person were about a nonbinary individual.[23] Only a handful of global or national public figures have alluded (even tangentially) to identifying with gender in a nontraditional way.[24] In becoming one of the few nonbinary role models with far-reaching platforms, they are burdened with the unrealistic expectation of speaking for the entire genderqueer umbrella. Even when stories of nonbinary people are published, popular media tends to erase the broad range of diversity in gender communities. Left behind in the shadows are those who are nonwhite, assigned male, middle-aged or older, femme, disabled, medically transitioned, parents, religious, live in a rural area, or are part of countless other overlooked groups.

How can people understand what they don't even know exists? When a nonbinary person opens up their life to one or hundreds or millions, they contribute to rebuilding our shared mental model of gender. By speaking out and sharing their stories, each author in part 2 cultivates a new branch of gender, encouraging it to sprout and grow freely within the minds of outsiders and the spirits of their own.

PART III: COMMUNITY

Creating a Place
for the Rest of Us

We are presently witnessing an exponential rise in scientific, legal, political, educational, theoretical, and lexical advances that support the needs of gender-diverse people.[25] As transgender topics take center stage in media and in politics, so do public arguments over their rights.[26] Dinner table debates over bathroom bills[27] parallel the waning furor over gay marriage in the United States. Through that milestone, gay and queer people gained more than the right to a legal union; society's understanding of sexuality shifted from merely being about sexual acts to encompassing the complex amalgamation of romantic love, companionship, and familial structure.

Similarly, gender discourse is gradually moving from penises and vaginas and their corresponding surgeries to a conceptualization of identity that reckons with transgender people as full participants in life and society. Although widely celebrated, the consequent integration into preexisting social structures has nevertheless entailed conflict within the trans and queer population. Assimilation into the mainstream forces some to reconcile with the loss of the radicalness that once accompanied queerness by default. Meanwhile, those who do not fit the paragon of white upper-middle class respectability continue to struggle for their survival.[28]

To mitigate this ongoing marginalization of nondominant groups, the LGBTQIA+ community splinters off into countless identity-based factions. As an individual's identity shifts, so does their membership within these subgroups. This blurriness extends to the discussion itself. Within gender diverse communities, there is overlap and disagreement as to what the words we use actually mean, and who can share a given identity. For instance, do nonbinary people belong in the transgender community? Some people say yes, some no. We walk a tightrope between acknowledging these lines and finding utility within them, while claiming that such boundaries are artificial. But central to this discussion is the lived experience of the person in question.

While the dichotomy of male and female may be false, it still creates a very real bifurcation. The world remains largely divided in two—pink or blue, he or she, testosterone or estrogen, M or F—with no room for other. Nonbinary people are left out of language, paperwork, clothing stores, and bathrooms; even tea and vitamins are laden with gendered marketing. In domains segregated by gender this vulnerability is especially salient. Because they don't fully belong on any side, nonbinary people are excluded from participating in activities that define everyday life.

The Internet is sometimes the only safe platform where stigmatized or invisible groups are able to express themselves. Today, it is often the first place people go to with questions about gender. Connecting with one another can foster a sense of meaning, belonging, and fulfillment, as well as help build the resilience needed to live as an outsider. The trans community has built a thriving presence online. For genderqueer folks especially, digital life offers a plethora of identities and stories to explore.[29] Bloggers and vloggers proudly share their journey with millions of followers. On the other side of the screen is someone learning a new vocabulary, discovering possibilities, and, perhaps for the first time, seeing themselves in another person. Social media has paved the way for a self-serve model of informational resources, medical knowledge, support networks, political activism, diverse representation, and, above all, building community around themselves and their loved ones.[30]

From family, hobbies, culture, spirituality, and other shared life experiences, the authors in part 3 transition in and out of various communities throughout their lifetime. Some find, express, or announce their gender online, giving and receiving virtual validation. Like every one of us, they grapple with belonging—to multiple spaces, to no spaces, to all spaces.

PART IV: TRANS ENOUGH

Representation and Differentiation

Nonbinary people comprise over one-third of the U.S. trans population[31] (with the percentage steadily increasing with every large-scale survey),[32] yet their social and health care needs have notoriously received limited attention. Medical literature and scientific research, scant as it is for evidence-based transgender health,[33] is nearly nonexistent when it comes to serving the distinctive needs of the nonbinary population.[34] Even recent directives issued by federal medical bodies embracing trans health care do not stray from the rigid, stepwise binary model of transition.[35]

Within the largest international organization of medical professionals dedicated to transgender health, nonbinary people have been historically glossed over. The World Professional Association of Transgender Health, or WPATH, issues the Standards of Care (SOC); these are the guidelines that all providers follow to care for trans people. Only in 2012 did the updated seventh version of the Standards of Care explicitly refer to nonbinary identities. Gender is endorsed as a spectrum primarily by emphasizing individualized treatment, and by replacing the now archaic "opposite" gender with the newly introduced language of "target" gender. Even more recent articles reassessing the current SOC criteria conclude by conceding: "Perhaps the concept of gender queerness could be addressed more thoroughly in a separate paragraph."[36]

As a result of this lack of specificity, myths and misconceptions are rife among health providers. Nearly one-quarter of transgender adults, and up to half of trans young adults,[37] delay health care because of fear of mistreatment or discrimination.[38] Therapists and doctors, even those experienced in treating trans men and women, can be hesitant to care for nonbinary patients.[39] In addition to financial and structural barriers, trans people are themselves often unaware of all the options available, deterring many from self-advocacy.

Thankfully, other providers have been willing to bend the written and unwritten rules. Counselors help nonbinary people navigate coming out at work with they/them pronouns; primary care physicians prescribe low doses of hormones; doctors perform individualized surgeries using the Informed Consent model. More promising still, the as-of-yet unpublished eighth version of the WPATH Standards of Care will devote an entire chapter to nonbinary and gender-nonconforming people, as well as another robust section addressing the needs of transgender and gender-diverse children.

It seems, these days, that youth have taken center stage of our expanding notions of gender. According to GLAAD's *Accelerating Acceptance 2017* survey, one-fifth of American young adults (ages eighteen to thirty-four) identify as LGBTQ, and they are more than two times more likely to identify as LGBTQ than those over fifty. Furthermore, 12 percent do not identify with the gender they were assigned at birth, and even non-LGBTQ youth are increasingly using terminology that falls outside the male/female binary.[40] Schools across the United States are embracing gender-neutral bathrooms and LGBTQ clubs; many universities now include a field for preferred name and preferred pronoun in their application. Admittedly, groundbreaking social movements often spark from the newest generation loudly questioning the way things are. But as empowering as it sounds to lionize our young pioneers, the illusion that being genderqueer is restricted to urban white adolescents and young adults has given way to negative stereotypes that impact all nonbinary people of all ages and walks of life.[41]

Blanket dismissals of nonbinary genders are all too common. Nonbinary gender is deemed a playful fantasy, just another way for teens to get attention—as if it's suddenly cool to transgress gender. Moreover, adolescents are assumed to succumb to peer pressure, so it follows that genderqueer kids are seen as simply molding themselves after their friends. This belief is so common that there is a pejorative label for it: *transtrender.*[42] At best, they are accused of being "snowflakes" who are demanding undeserved special treatment such as obscure pronouns; at worst, they can suffer discrimination and violence at rates disproportionately higher than their cisgender or transgender peers.[43]

Even when nonbinary gender is considered valid, adults wonder, is it just a phase?[44] After all, it's normal for teenagers to be confused, to try on different labels and personas as they come of age. And as our tolerance for self-expression has expanded, gender and sexuality have become fair game for experimentation. Not to mention that every journalist feels compelled to include the oft-touted but thoroughly debunked statistic that 80 percent of children who exhibit gender variance will change their mind once they hit puberty.[45] When disregarded, nonbinary identity is seen as a passing fad. If taken seriously, nonbinary identity is viewed as a stepping-stone toward an inevitable binary transition, an assumption that can be amplified when someone takes medical steps toward gender alignment. Many well-intentioned parents and providers are simply waiting for kids to "make up their mind" or "pick a side"; they would rather their child move on with a transition that fits within established guidelines and social structures, or settle for none at all, than remain in perpetual limbo.[46] As for nonbinary adults . . . perhaps one day they will grow out of it.

Nonbinary individuals are commonly miscategorized in another way: as queer people expressing an "extreme" form of gayness, an argument that echoes back to the beginnings of the transgender movement. Aside from conflating sexual orientation, gender expression, and identity, this distorted understanding also brings to light the differential degrees of freedom for gender transgression based on birth-assigned gender. People assigned female have a wider latitude to express masculine behavior, whereas those assigned male tend to be punished for displaying any signs of femininity, even in our modern era. The words alone, "tomboy" and "sissy," respectively connote tame versus derogatory variations for gender nonconformity.[47] Given society's underlying misogyny, expressions of femininity are harshly limited, thus precluding many—especially those on the transfeminine or femme spectrum—from an authentic gender expression. As a consequence, only a narrow range of representations (often confined to transmasculine androgyny) have come to erroneously embody a genderqueer standard.

Taken together, these stereotypes lead to the harmful conclusion that nonbinary people do not deserve care. Dr. Johanna Olson-Kennedy, who has treated thousands of trans youth as a pediatrician at Children's Hospital Los Angeles, neatly counters these fallacies:[48]

What is true is that unpacking the gender binary is becoming increasingly popular, because I think youth recognize that it is not adequate for deeper human existence. Gender roles are largely archaic in many regards. So are youth experimenting with gender bending? Yes, absolutely. But they are not in distress. They are bending in solidarity with a movement to dismantle an obsolete set of gender rules, and stand in solidarity with their trans friends and the community. There are distinct differences in these youth. They are not likely to stick a needle in their body every week to be trendy. There is no reward for being trans. I can't get adolescents to finish ten days of antibiotics. It is so critical to differentiate between distress and social change.

As society's framework for gender shifts, so too do the behaviors and experiences of our youth. Undoing the biases against nonbinary people requires embracing new interpretations and expressions.

But the onus of untangling these tropes is not confined to the cisgender population. As trans men and women are being more openly embraced, there are a handful within the trans community who feel threatened by the emergence of nonbinary identities.[49] This increasingly small subset perceives genderqueer folk as facetiously toying with gender, sullying the societal attitudes toward *all* trans people, and consequently risking the incredible progress that has been made in recent years. Worries abound about continued access to hormones and surgeries, longer waitlists to get into gender clinics, and, of course, fighting for the baseline respect that all human beings deserve. These concerns are manifested in an utterly misguided vitriol that proves damaging to the entire gender community. The solution lies not in suppressing nonbinary identities, but rather in improving the system to provide adequate primary care and transition services to *everyone.*

Unfortunately, these widespread beliefs can lead anyone who questions their gender to start wondering, *Am I trans enough?* As they parse out their identity in relation to their self and society, they run into contradictory expectations and assumptions about what a transgender experience is supposed to look like.[50] Am I transitioning too little? Am I transitioning too much? Do I look too masculine? Am I perceived as a woman too often? Is it OK that I don't hate my body parts? Am I still nonbinary if I want to be called *he* and not *they*? Do I really feel gender dysphoria? What should gender dysphoria even feel like? How do I know whether I'm *really* trans?

Compounding these doubts and uncertainty are toxic narratives reinforced within the trans community itself.[51] These have been shaped by a complex interplay of cultural norms in addition to the constraints trans people face to access health and legal services.[52] Adversely impacting the community as a whole, these hierarchies are used to police who can rightly claim an "authentic" trans identity. One mark of legitimacy is physical dysphoria—the somatic misalignment between gender and body. Another sign of this supposed authentic transness is deep certainty in one's gender from a young age. Comparative taxonomies only serve to silence any trans person whose story doesn't quite align, which subsumes nearly everyone whose gender is not in the binary. Swept even further behind the curtain are trans people who come out later in life, who birth children, who retransition, or who otherwise follow a different journey.

Nonbinary people wrestle with many of the typical questions that many trans people face, such as coming out, changing their name and pronouns, opting for hormones or surgery. But the answers come in a murkier package, as there is still no paradigm for how nonbinary gender can coexist within the established male/female dichotomy. Nonbinary people reconcile with an inner gender that cannot be properly expressed and understood by the outside world; very often, their true identity can never be fully actualized. At best, transition for a nonbinary person involves a compromise: All options are inadequate, so which one will be better than nothing? Which path will be good enough?

Nonbinary people run themselves through an excruciating mental gauntlet, from pronouns to labels to physical changes. They debate not only whether medical transition is right for them, but whether their dysphoria is *enough* to warrant hormones at all, or whether they are trans *enough* to consider (let alone deserve access to) surgery. Both those who do and do not physically transition are then paradoxically challenged to demonstrate that they are *nonbinary* enough;[53] a binary appearance belies their internal gender, opening them to bias from their own community of trans siblings.

Society's reliance on science, biology, and medicine as ultimate truth[54] demotes a person's internal felt and lived experiences as illegitimate sources of self-knowledge. In an effort to "prove" their nonbinary gender really does exist, they question the very realness of it. Gender is not something we can touch. It's hard to describe—intangible, unknowable. It is also inextricably embedded in our lives. Trans people often talk of how, regardless of their current gender, their history is ingrained in who they are today. In other domains, such as religion, language, or national origin, childhood socialization is similarly given up, undone, or replaced in adulthood, whether by choice or by the involuntary outcome of circumstance. Humans also carry habits, ideologies, traumas, emotions, conditions, all of which reside to a large extent in the mind. They are difficult to unlearn, get rid of, heal, affirm. Harder still is proving they exist. Are you *actually* depressed? Are you *truly* in love? Are you *really* trans? How do you know?

Understanding the real truth lies in the individual stories of people. Representing a range of generations, genders, and journeys, every author in part 4 wrestles with the question of trans enough. Following their own path, each one found a way to reimagine their future and make themselves whole.

PART V: REDEFINING DUALITIES

Paradoxes and Possibilities of Gender

Our world is constructed on binaries that mask complexity, much like that two-dimensional rendering of the three-dimensional cube. Thin black lines against a vast white page can never wholly represent their object of imitation. At the same time, the simplicity of the outline does not detract from the intricacy of the cube. Capturing only height and width, those six lines, drawn at particular angles in particular positions, are an attempt at conveying something beyond the page: the third dimension of depth.

Our cultural consciousness is filled with binaries where an additional dimension has entered the foreground: male/female, gay/straight, black/white, cisgender/transgender, binary/nonbinary. In some cases, the process of our collective awakening feels all but complete; in others, it feels like a slogging haul of tiny steps forward and back. As an example, Americans are still forced to self-identify into one of five racial categories on nearly every form or application.[55] At the same time, the discourse around race and ethnicity has evolved to incorporate the socially constructed nature of these categories. Similarly, some people display disabled-parking placards in their car while others do not, even though the physical, mental, and emotional abilities of each body shift from year to year and moment to moment. In reconceptualizing these binaries, we deconstruct and reconstruct their definitions, their social implications, their communities, their histories, and their role in our sense of self.

Male and female are one of humanity's foundational underpinnings. Yet the creation of a new dichotomy—binary and nonbinary—ultimately proves just as limiting as the dichotomy of man and woman. At the same time, nonbinary gender is a unique concept and lived experience—separate from cisgender, and different from the mainstream understanding of transgender as a binary identity. The existence of nonbinary people shows us that gender is messy. In embracing this messiness, perhaps we can simultaneously acknowledge that the joys and struggles of nonbinary people are not the same as, yet not in opposition to, cisgender and binary transgender lives.

The narratives in part 5 illustrate the paradoxical possibilities of gender. Each author offers us a glimpse of what it would be like if our minds and bodies were met with simple curiosity, if we allowed ourselves to experience one another as the expansive, messy, uncategorizable individually unique human beings that we are.

———————

Gender is everywhere—it permeates everything we do, everyone we meet, every place we visit, every interaction we have. The benefits of expanding gender out of its neatly circumscribed discrete categories are not limited to intersex, transgender, nonbinary, or otherwise gender-diverse people.[56] Detachment from gender norms affords a man the license to reclaim pink, or ask for the soft touch of his friend when he's feeling hurt; it boosts a woman's efforts to break the glass ceiling and close the gender pay gap, or wear what she chooses without turning into the object of scorn. Freedom to explore gender means girls and boys can grow up in a world that no longer reprimands them for acting one way and not the other, a world that doesn't ridicule them for their preferences, a world that doesn't limit their authenticity. Gender constricts us. Gender can also liberate us.

It is impossible for the two boxes of "male" and "female" to capture gender's vast nuances, yet social interaction and communication necessitate constructing representations of gender, however imperfect. Perhaps we can break out of the illusion: instead of being either/or, these binaries are both/and. Accepting the paradoxical duality means it is no longer a battle between the binary and the spectrum—they coexist in the same space. Gender houses the infinite possibilities in between, adjacent to, and outside of the realm that it currently represents. Gender is static, and gender is fluid. Gender is at the core of who we are, and gender is also just one of our many identities.

NOTES

1. For a brief background on gender in other cultures, see United Nations Development Programme (UNDP), *Transgender Health and Human Rights*, www.undp.org/content/dam/undp/library/HIV-AIDS/Governance of HIV Responses/Trans Health & Human Rights.pdf.

2. Melanie Blackless, Anthony Charuvastra, Amanda Derrijck, Anne Fausto-Sterling, Karl Lauzanne, and Ellen Lee, "How Sexually Dimorphic Are We? Review and Synthesis," *American Journal of Human Biology* 12 (2000): 151–66.

3. Intersex Society of North America, "How Common Is Intersex?," www.isna.org/faq/frequency.

4. United Nations Free and Equal Campaign, "Intersex," https://unfe.org/system/unfe-65-Intersex_Factsheet_ENGLISH.pdf.

5. Susan Stamberg, "Girls Are Taught to 'Think Pink,' But That Wasn't Always So," *NPR*, April 1, 2014, www.npr.org/2014/04/01/297159948/girls-are-taught-to-think-pink-but-that-wasnt-always-so.

6. Jeanne Maglaty, "When Did Girls Start Wearing Pink?," *Smithsonian Magazine*, April 7, 2011, www.smithsonianmag.com/arts-culture/when-did-girls-start-wearing-pink-1370097.

7. For an excellent graphic explaining this, see Landyn Pan and Anna Moore, "The Gender Unicorn," *Trans Student Educational Resources*, www.transstudent.org/gender.

8. Andrew R. Flores, Jody L. Herman, Gary J. Gates, and Taylor N. T. Brown, *How Many Adults Identify as Transgender in the United States?* (Los Angeles: Williams Institute, 2016).

9. Basing gender determination on identity or biology depends on social context: Laurel Westbrook and Kristen Schilt, "Doing Gender, Determining Gender: Transgender People, Gender Panics, and the Maintenance of the Sex/Gender/Sexuality System," *Gender and Society* 28, no. 1 (2014): 32–57.

10. Kristen Hare, "AP Style Change: Singular They Is Acceptable 'in Limited Cases,'" *Poynter*, March 24, 2017, www.poynter.org/news/ap-style-change-singular-they-acceptable-limited-cases.

11. *Gender Neutral Pronoun Blog: The Search for a Polite Specific Gender-Neutral Third-Person Singular Pronoun*, www.genderneutralpronoun.word press.com/.

12. *Practice with Pronouns*, www.practicewithpronouns.com/.

13. Minus18, *Pronouns*, www.minus18.org.au/pronouns-app.

14. For the most part nonbinary and genderqueer are interchangeable, though there are nuanced differences. See Marilyn Roxie, "The Non-Binary vs. Genderqueer Quandary," *Genderqueer Identities* (blog), October 18, 2011, www.genderqueerid.com/post/11617933299/the-non-binary-vs-genderqueer-quandary.

15. Sujay Kentlyn, "Genderqueer," *Wiley Blackwell Encyclopedia of Gender and Sexuality Studies* (2016): 1–3.

16. For one framing of identities as horizontal and vertical, see Andrew Solomon, *Far from the Tree: Parents, Children and the Search for Identity* (New York: Scribner, 2012).

17. National Coalition of Anti-Violence Programs (NCAVP), *Lesbian, Gay, Bisexual, Transgender, Queer, and HIV-Affected Hate Violence in 2016* (New York: Emily Waters, 2016).

18. Sandy E. James, Jody L. Herman, Susan Rankin, Mara Keisling, Lisa Mottet, and Ma'ayan Anafi, *The Report of the 2015 U.S. Transgender Survey* (Washington, DC: National Center for Transgender Equality, 2016), www .transequality.org/sites/default/files/docs/USTS-Full-Report-FINAL.PDF.

19. Sometimes trans people who do not disclose are stigmatized within the trans community. For example, see "Stealth Shaming: What It Is, Why You Shouldn't Do It, and How Not To," *Super Mattachine Review* (blog), www.supermattachine.wordpress.com/2011/09/14/stealth-shaming-what-it -is-why-you-shouldnt-do-it-and-how-not-to/.

20. Kevin Nadal, "Transsexual Wave," in *The SAGE Encyclopedia of Psychology and Gender* (Los Angeles: Sage, 2017), 694.

21. "The Report of the 2015 U.S. Transgender Survey," 49.

22. Trey Taylor, "Why 2015 Was the Year of Trans Visibility," *Vogue*, December 29, 2015, www.vogue.com/article/2015-year-of-trans-visibility.

23. Thomas J. Billard, "Writing in the Margins: Mainstream News Media Representations of Transgenderism," *International Journal of Communication* 10 (2016): 4193–218.

24. Recent examples include Miley Cyrus, Ruby Rose, Sam Smith, Eddie Izzard, Asia Kate Dillon, and Jill Soloway.

25. Andrew R. Flores, Taylor N. T. Brown, and Andrew S. Park, *Public Support for Transgender Rights: A Twenty-Three Country Survey* (Los Angeles:

Williams Institute, 2016), https://williamsinstitute.law.ucla.edu/wp-content /uploads/23-Country-Survey.pdf.

26. United Nations Humans Rights Office of the High Commissioner, *Embrace Diversity and Protect Trans and Gender Diverse Children and Adolescents*, May 16, 2017, www.ohchr.org/EN/NewsEvents/Pages/DisplayNews .aspx?NewsID=21622.

27. In early 2016 alone, forty-four antitransgender bills were filed across sixteen U.S. states, half of which targeted children: Human Rights Campaign, *Anti-Transgender Legislation Spreads Nationwide, Bills Targeting Transgender Children Surge*, 2015, https://assets2.hrc.org/files/assets/resources/HRC -Anti-Trans-Issue-Brief-FINAL-REV2.pdf.

28. Megan Davidson, "Seeking Refuge Under the Umbrella: Inclusion, Exclusion, and Organizing Within the Category Transgender," *Sexuality Research and Social Policy* 4, no. 4 (2007): 60–80.

29. Laura E. Kuper, Robin Nussbaum, and Brian Mustanski, "Exploring the Diversity of Gender and Sexual Orientation Identities in an Online Sample of Transgender Individuals," *Journal of Sex Research* 49, nos. 2–3 (2012): 244–54.

30. Yolanda N. Evans, Samantha J. Gridley, Julia Crouch, Alicia Wang, Megan A. Moreno, Kym Ahrens, and David J. Breland, "Understanding Online Resource Use by Transgender Youth and Caregivers: A Qualitative Study," *Transgender Health* 2, no. 1 (2017): 129–39.

31. "The Report of the 2015 U.S. Transgender Survey," 45.

32. In the 2008 U.S. Transgender Survey, only 13 percent identified with "a gender not listed here." Jody L. Herman, Jack Harrison, and Jamie Grant, "A Gender Not Listed Here: Genderqueers, Gender Rebels, and OtherWise," *LGBTQ Policy Journal at the Harvard Kennedy School* 2 (2012). Compared with 35 percent for the 2015 survey: "The Report of the 2015 U.S. Transgender Survey," 60. Other studies report that upward of 40 percent of transgender participants do not consistently identify with a binary gender, e.g., S. L. Reisner, J. M. White, and E. E. Dunham, "Discrimination and Health in Massachusetts: A Statewide Survey of Transgender and Gender NonConforming Adults," *Fenway Institute* (2014).

33. Jonathon W. Wanta and Cecile A. Unger, "Review of the Transgender Literature: Where Do We Go from Here?," *Transgender Health* 2, no. 1 (2017): 119–28; Institute of Medicine, *The Health of Lesbian, Gay, Bisexual, and Transgender People: Building a Foundation for Better Understanding* (Washington, DC: National Academics Press, 2011).

34. Emmie Matsuno and Stephanie L. Budge, "Non-Binary/Genderqueer Identities: A Critical Review of the Literature," *Current Sexual Health Reports* 9, no. 3 (2017): 116–20. Christina Richards, Walter Pierre Bouman, Leighton Seal, Meg John Barker, Timo O. Nieder, and Guy T'Sjoen,

"Non-Binary or Genderqueer Genders," *International Review of Psychiatry* 28, no. 1 (2016): 95–102.

35. Kristen L. Eckstrand, Henry Ng, and Jennifer Potter, "Affirmative and Responsible Health Care for People with Nonconforming Gender Identities and Expressions," *AMA Journal of Ethics* 18, no. 11 (2016): 1107–18.

36. Britt Colebunders, Griet De Cuypere, Stan Monstrey, Britt Colebunders, and Stan Monstrey, "New Criteria for Sex Reassignment Surgery: WPATH Standards of Care, Version 7," *International Journal of Transgenderism* 16 (2015): 222–33.

37. Beth A. Clark, Jaimie F. Veale, Devon Greyson, and Elizabeth Saewyc, "Primary Care Access and Foregone Care: A Survey of Transgender Adolescents and Young Adults," *Family Practice* (2017).

38. "The Report of the 2015 U.S. Transgender Survey," 98.

39. National LGBT Health Education Center, "Providing Affirmative Care for Patients with Non-Binary Gender Identities," *Fenway Institute* (2017). Even in LGBT clinics, nonbinary patients felt misunderstood or pushed toward a binary transition. See Hannah Mogul-Adlin, "Unanticipated: Healthcare Experiences of Gender Nonbinary Patients and Suggestions For Inclusive Care," *Public Health Theses* 1197 (2015), http://elischolar.library.yale.edu /ysphtdl/1197.

40. GLAAD, "Accelerating Acceptance," 2017, www.glaad.org/files/aa /2017_GLAAD_Accelerating_Acceptance.pdf.

41. Adrian Ballou, "10 Myths About Non-Binary People It's Time to Unlearn," *Everyday Feminism*, December 6, 2014, www.everydayfeminism .com/2014/12/myths-non-binary-people. For media coverage mentioning many of these challenges, see Sarah Marsh, "The Gender-Fluid Generation: Young People on Being Male, Female or Non-Binary," *Guardian*, March 23, 2016, www.theguardian.com/commentisfree/2016/mar/23/gender -fluid-generation-young-people-male-female-trans.

42. Wiktionary, "Transtrender," www.en.wiktionary.org/wiki/transtrender.

43. J. L. Herman, J. Harrison, and J. Grant, "A Gender Not Listed Here: Genderqueers, Gender Rebels, and OtherWise," *LGBTQ Policy Journal at the Harvard Kennedy School* 2 (2012).

44. Two-thirds (63 percent) of nonbinary respondents said their identity is "often dismissed as not being a real identity or just a phase": "The Report of the 2015 U.S. Transgender Survey," 49.

45. Julia Serano, "Detransition, Desistance, and Disinformation: A Guide for Understanding Transgender Children Debates," *Medium* (blog), August 2, 2016.

46. Aidan Key, "Children," in *Trans Bodies Trans Selves*, ed. Laura Erickson-Schroth (New York: Oxford University Press, 2014), 411.

47. D'Lane Compton and Emily Knox, "Sissies and Tomboys," *International Encyclopedia of Human Sexuality* (2015): 1115–354.

48. Brittney McNamara, "Experts Answer Reddit Questions About Transgender People," *Teen Vogue*, July 28, 2017, www.teenvogue.com/story/reddit-transgender-ama-busts-myths.

49. For one example outside of online forum discussions, one subject featured in this article mentions this type of remark: Christina Capatides, "The Type of Transgender You Haven't Heard Of," *CBS News*, March 27, 2017, www.cbsnews.com/news/non-binary-transgender-you-havent-heard-of/.

50. D. Chase J. Catalano, "'Trans Enough?': The Pressures Trans Men Negotiate in Higher Education," *Transgender Studies Quarterly* 2, no. 3 (August 2015): 411–30.

51. Sierra Angel, "'Transier' Than Thou—Breaking the Transgender Hierarchy," *Rainbow Hub* (blog), August 16, 2013, www.therainbowhub.com/transier-than-thou-breaking-the-transgender-hierarchy/.

52. Devon R. Goss, "Am I Trans Enough? Experiences of Transnormativity," *Annual Meeting of the American Sociological Association*, New York City, NY, 2013.

53. For one example, see J. Latso, "Where Do I Fit In? On Being Nonbinary and Confused," *The Body Is Not An Apology* (blog), April 13, 2017.

54. Dean Spade, "Resisting Medicine, Re/Modeling Gender," *Berkeley Women's Law Journal* 63 (2003): 15–37.

55. United States Census Bureau, *Race*, www.census.gov/topics/population/race/about.html.

56. Liam Lowery, "The Transgender Rights Movement Is for Everyone," *Newsweek*, June 10, 2015, www.newsweek.com/transgender-rights-movement-everyone-341828.

NONBINARY

PART ONE

What Is Gender?

CHAPTER ONE

War Smoke Catharsis

ALEX STITT

IN 2006 I sat in the window of the Baan Siri Rama Hotel, watching smoke pour over Bangkok's jumbled power lines. A coup d'état had overthrown the prime minister, leaving him a country-less man far away at the UN summit. Leaderless, his party dissolved in favor of their own careers, yet his supporters had taken to motorcycle bombs. Behind me a dear friend lay in bed. I'd been watching her catheter for blood. She was unconscious—oblivious to the tanks outside. Her surgery was entirely irrelevant to the revolution, though it was a revolution of her own.

Queer allies in arms, she'd asked me to come with her to Thailand, and I'd agreed. She'd never left the country before, so I took her through the paces of airport etiquette. Of course, she wasn't about to dress down to match the sex on her passport, even though I did. Trans girls bound for Thailand are of no particular mystery, but to airport security a raggedy, gender-nebulous mop of curly hair and black nail polish like myself looks a tad suspicious.

I had grown up in England, but moved to the United States after my American father divorced my British mother. He had wanted me to experience U.S. high school, with all its pitfalls and milestones, though puberty for a dual citizen with dual gender bore its own brand of angst. Able to abandon the regulations of the British school uniform, which had forced me to tuck my long hair down the back of my blazer, I cycled rapidly through American fashions, as if catching up with counterculture history. I found shelter among the anarcho-hippy-goth-punks as I wasn't inherently anything, so my newfound identity was as much a surprise to me as my reflection in the mirror. I was out of the closet by the time I was out of high school.

My friend and I first met at a liberal arts college in Oregon. She was a Texan boy locked in a Texan bravado; it wasn't long after our introduction that she awakened to her own Southern belle. I take no credit for it, but the social role of pangender, ambigender, and agender individuals has always been one of catalyst.

I remember staying up late in conversation with the kind of cheap wine college students consider classy because it doesn't come from a box. My shitty apartment was our safety and our privacy, where we shared our stories on a worn-out carpet pockmarked by the cigarette burns of prior tenants. My only furniture was my bed, and if we began there we would have had nowhere to progress to. We dated for a time under the pretense of gay men, though it was a vague pretense on both our parts. I told my friend all about my crisscross life, and how I'd bounced from boy to girl to man to woman for as long as I could remember, and how I'd hid from myself in either an academic uniform or a cultural one. I told about love and sex, and how each was very dependent on my partner's conceptualization of me. I spoke at length of the liberty and imprisonment that gender allowed. And with every story his eyes grew wide, as the girl hiding therein decided she was ready.

We broke up, as I was noncommittal to anything, yet we remained steadfast friends through our bickering, aligned as we were by our need for recognition. There were so few openly queer people in our world that, even at our worst, we needed each other to steel ourselves against the blatant bigotry. Often we would find one or the other crying in a stairwell on campus; even when a pickup truck had tried to run us over in a parking lot, we rallied behind our anger, walking home with rocks in hand in case they came back. But the tiny sidelong looks? The tiny papercut glares? The tiny slashing remarks? They would eventually bleed us dry, and she and I would patch each other up, regardless of our relationship standing.

Our world, however, was not inherently harsh, though it was often lonely in a zoo-like way. People are curious, drawn by fascination to what they find most difficult to name, and for the longest time what I assumed to be judgment turned out to be catharsis. Whether I liked it or not, people sought me out, just like those Texan eyes had once watched me in class. Intrigued by my makeup, fishnets, and steel-toed boots, strangers would sidle up at parties, barrooms, bus stops, and even libraries, often to confess their own gender-bending secrets to someone who might possibly understand. They would approach me with a quiet, hopeful, skittish desperation, often rambling about how brave I was to wear what I wore. Smiling, I'd direct them to a decent boutique where the cashiers thought nothing of a man carrying a skirt to the dressing room. At this point they would either back away or up the ante, launching into how they shoplifted underwear, or daydreamed about hormones, or bought their girlfriends strap-ons. Being openly androgynous, I learned, meant that people assumed you were a pro bono sexologist.

Others approached me with a "my two cents" compulsion, throwing out obscurely irrelevant factoids about gender politics in the same way people tell the British, "I hear it rains in England," as if we didn't already know. The college kids on campus were exceptional at this, as they wanted to test their newfound knowledge on someone who might validate them. Quotes from uncited sources peppered their opinions for fear of sounding naive, and I was glad for their fumbled attempts at conversation because at least it was a conversation. Well-intentioned wannabe allies told me about what they'd read of the trans experience, their perspective on the matter reduced to percentages of suicide, violence, and self-harm. Listening, I would shake my moppish head, recalling my boyfriend-turned-girlfriend-turned-best friend's little box of razors, and the times I'd sat on the ledge of the highest tower in town for more than just a view.

When people become political they often forget, in their urgency for agency, that every sad percentage is a real-life horror show. At that point in my life I was ambling aimlessly, as I had nowhere to transition to, and sadly, nothing to be but myself. My sassy Texan friend, however, was making plans, and in the fall she announced her decision to save up for her sexual reassignment surgery. I laughed, and forbade her from buying top-of-the-line makeup, as she was terrible with money. Amazingly, through multiple jobs and a bit of budgeting on my part, she had enough saved within a year, and we were on our way to Thailand.

As a child I was always afraid of being mistaken, of being misaligned, of being excluded by all the right in the world and included by all the wrong. I assumed every eye was a cruel one. Yet as I grew older I realized that, for all the quizzical looks, more favored curiosity than disgust. This was also true on the streets of Bangkok, where being American is arguably more novel than being transsexual.

I always guarded myself emotionally when I traveled, especially through airports, as I was inevitably picked out of every line. Nevertheless, I had decided to go because, in my own way, I needed to know what it took to change it all. I needed to know if my friend's path would be a catalyst for my own. Of course I wanted to help her and support her in every way I could, but I had a vicarious stake in her transition. Call it a transsexual dry run. And in the Baan Siri Rama Hotel I had not one vicarious experience, but twenty.

The bombs had backed up traffic, which meant the nurses wouldn't be able to make their rounds on time. Typically, after three or four days in the hospital, all post-op women were transported back to their hotels to be monitored for necrosis or vaginal collapse—terrifying prospects for women who'd come so far and endured so much. The doctor had briefed us that young people are more at risk of the latter, as tight muscles are prone to constriction. Consequently, my friend looked terrified when they wheeled her into surgery. She spent her hospital visit heavily drugged, and was transported back to the hotel—not in an ambulance, but in a very painful cab ride. Yet now, I'd been informed by the hotel receptionist that the nurses weren't coming for their daily visit at all.

While there were plenty of staff to cater to the guests, I was the one queer person in the hotel not wrapped in bandages, so I left my window seat to check in on the girls I'd met in the lobby on our first day. Conversations ensued; fears confessed; dreams related; chocolate sought; Mai Tai's snuck in; bandages checked; and all manner of identities manifested, as no two patients had the same conceptualization of womanhood.

I met a New York bartender with breast implants she massaged by pressing herself against a wall. She'd managed to pay her way through facial feminization surgery by packing her bags with hormones and selling them at cut rates to trans girls and trans boys ignored by their insurance agencies. She told me a woman had to be resourceful, quick witted, and compassionate.

In another room I met a French part-time prostitute who'd come to Thailand for a facelift and gold jewelry, both of which were far more affordable than in Europe. She was a self-defined she-male, as she worked as a man by day in some business agency, only to transform between the hours of five and seven to the delight of a few loyal clients. Her sex work had bought her a second house in Arles. She told me she had no desire to have a sex change, as there were already plenty of women in the world, and she was a novelty.

A little further down the corridor was the youngest patient, checked in across the hall from the eldest. I was impressed with both of them—an eighteen year old from the Midwest who'd started taking antiandrogens when she was in high school, and a sixty-five year old from the West Coast who'd found herself when she was fifty. To my knowledge they never spoke to each other, being respectively bed bound, yet their hopeful anticipation was akin, as each had waited a lifetime for this.

A floor down I tried to console an angry young woman torn up inside herself. Gender dysphoria can, at times, be accompanied by body dysmorphia; her aspirations didn't align with her skeletal structure, and there was no way to change that. With tears streaming down a swollen face after having the brow of her skull shaved down, she wept, unable to see herself in the mirror. Impatient and restless, she had spent years chasing some far-fetched perfectionist ideal of womanhood utterly estranged from self-acceptance. She told me to go away.

I spoke the most with a lady from New Zealand, whom some of the more effeminate girls had taken umbrage with as she was a tomboy in a man's body. She'd served a stint in the military, had become a police officer, and preferred functional trousers to pretty skirts. She told me how, when people saw pictures of her prior to her transition, she fibbed about having a deceased brother whom she loved a great deal but had to let go.

Some of the girls relied on graceful, catty, or motherly archetypes emulative of their own great heroines, while others merely actualized themselves. Yet for all their differences they had one thing in common: they didn't want to be women, they *were* women, beautifully and undeniably so.

For years I'd questioned and daydreamed about transition, fantasizing about collagen, electrolysis, and antiandrogens. Born a bioboy, I desired to be a woman with the same curious passion I desired to be a man. Why? Because in the end I was neither. To identify as one was to disavow the other. Yet while each woman in the Baan Siri Rama Hotel—curious about the destruction outside as much as the creation between their legs—entered into their own true self, I felt as miasmic as the smoke above the city. For what was I?

In one hotel room I was a trans sister. After all, why else would I be checked in to the Baan Siri Rama Hotel? Having lived as an off-and-on girl throughout my life, I could relate in many respects. Just a few short steps across the hall, checking in on a Californian father-turned-mother of two, I became a handsome mister. As a divorcee, seeing me only as a man, she wanted validation from the opposite sex. And so I played the flirtatious part, sneaking up drinks from the bar downstairs to heal the esteem recently cut by a scalpel. Were there interactions with her meds? Of course, but the lady needed a Blue Hawaiian.

A few doors down I became a sassy gay boy of femme disposition for a former Floridian drag queen who realized, after so many years, that her makeup was more than just drag. Needing to fence wit against bitchy wit to distract herself from the protests outside, she demanded we play cards. With Bangkok in political upheaval, and her legs hitched up to let her labia heal, now was not the time to take things seriously. Like so many of the women checked in to the hotel, she had come by herself, facing the hardest change in her life entirely alone. At first I thought she didn't like me, but I quickly found that teasing each other was the only way for her to survive the tears.

Perhaps all my shifts from room to room were just social camouflage, but that wouldn't convey the magic of catharsis. Every bed-bound woman saw in me what they needed most, mistaking a single part for a multifaceted whole. Of course for me that resulted in terrible frustration mottled with a wonderful joy. For who on Earth can shape-shift through such dramatic social roles if not the genderqueer? Everyone in the transgender revolution knows how it feels to be mistaken, their pronouns casualties of misassumption. And while I wish I could attest to some resolution, to be genderqueer is to be in the thick of it. I avoided the title for a long time because I hoped the awkward social juxtapositions would end, though deep down I doubted they ever would.

Taking the elevator, I crept back to our room, where I found my old friend passed out on morphine. She had struggled through the worst of it, yet my desire to help her was met by her desire to be rescued, which only exacerbated things more. When she was alone, she could grit her teeth and grip her sheets and wait for her itching, burning stitches to heal. Yet when her eyes caught mine she began to tear up. She told me she was *fine*, a word used by the exhausted to hide their desperation.

When I was in our hotel room, I became someone else too. Perhaps someone more whole. Returning to the window, I watched Bangkok's bizarre skyline of modern towers, rundown housing, and ancient temples. I had been so many things for so many people in my short, bizarre life, and those who loved me knew all about my morphing balance. There were times I was lost in it, and times I raged against duality. Yet in our hotel room I could allow myself to be everything that I was, as I was something of everything.

I felt tired and well traveled. I had a proverbial passport like no other, allowing me to go where so few could. And I went there not merely for the catharsis of others—I am not so altruistic as that—but for my own sake, because in one room I was a sister, in another a handsome mister, and in another a sassy gay girlfriend. It is so rare and wonderful to find social situations acquiescent to hybrid genders and poly-identities, for there is as much comfort in fluidity as there is instability, granting as much reason to smile as to sigh.

Rejecting corruption, Thailand elected a new prime minister.

My friend and I returned to America. The courts changed the sex on her passport. I am still patted down by security guards. Of course, that's probably less about my gender and more about my steel-toed boots.

CHAPTER TWO

Deconstructing My Self

LEVI S. GOVONI

A NAME CAN CONJURE up societal presuppositions, and mine is no exception. I was born Alanna Marie Govoni to an Italian-American family in December of 1969. In Italian, all nouns, not just names, assume a gender. Generally speaking, nouns ending in the letter *o* are considered masculine, while those ending in an *a* are feminine. *Alanna*, therefore, with its myriad *a*'s strung beautifully together, is the melodic equivalent of a set of ovaries.

I hated my name. As a child, I attributed this animosity to the fact my name was relatively unusual. I was relatively unusual—the little girl who rode her bicycle through the streets topless and filthy, like one of the boys. Why couldn't I be named Chris like every other kid in school? Several times a day, someone would yell my name across the neighborhood, "*Aaaaalaaaannaaaa!*" Unfamiliar adults in the near vicinity would turn their heads toward my sun-tanned chest, my seven-year-old nipples exposed to the world, and debate whether a call to child protective services was in order. No responsible, self-respecting parent would let their beloved *daughter* leave the house that way; and there was no questioning, with a name like Alanna, that I was a little girl.

Fortunately for me, my mother was not concerned with such things until the actual formation of breasts occurred several years later.

The great Bard proclaimed, "What's in a name? That which we call a rose by any other name would smell as sweet." Far be it from me to argue semantics with Shakespeare, but I wonder if he would have sung a different tune if he was named, say, Martha instead of Will. I understand Shakespeare's point: a name, like any word, is merely a symbol, its intrinsic value derived from that which it represents. But a name is not trivial either. If Shakespeare meant to imply such, Juliet would not be left pondering its significance. Romeo's name might have smelled as sweet, but ultimately it cost the young lovers their lives. If the great tragedy has taught us anything, it is this: names are loaded.

Truth be told, I despise the name Stanley, but if so named, it would resonate more than Alanna, which I actually find quite beautiful. Stanley connotes masculinity. Anyone who hears the name expects to be in the presence of either a man or a boy who will one day be a man. They'd expect broad shoulders and flat chests. An image is concocted out of a name like a painting on a canvas. For better or worse, words induce stereotypes, and like Johnny Cash's poor boy named Sue, I, too, have found myself running from the shadow of a name.

While I like to believe I am above such black-and-white thinking, the sad truth is, I am not immune to its implications, particularly with regard to gender. When I was a child, I wanted to play outside without a shirt and to pee standing up. As a teenager, I wanted to talk baseball and girls while working on my car, to wear a tux to my prom and never, ever catch sight of anything resembling a used tampon. Stanley could have done these things. Alanna had to hide behind the mask of a tomboy, date boys, and succumb to her large boobs and monthly period. My body betrayed me, and my name was its little toady.

I married a man; I donned the dresses and played the role of bridesmaid in family and friends' weddings. I pierced my ears and tried to teach myself how to walk like a woman, to *be* a woman in a culture that forced me to choose. I felt like I was on the outside looking in, but what exactly I was looking in on, I was unsure of. I subjected my entire being to binary oppositions. I lost myself.

Even when I eventually divorced and came out as gay, I was still stuck in the binary trap. I was labeled a lesbian even though I recoiled from the term more than I hated my name. I am and always have been sexually attracted to women, but somehow, *lesbian* didn't speak to my identity. A lesbian, by definition, is a homosexual woman, but what was I if I didn't identify as a woman, exactly? Could I, must I, still be a lesbian, or was I a man by shear default? If I was not a woman, did I need the beard and Adam's apple to prove it? If I was not a woman, and I was not a man, what was I?

In 1967, two years before I was born, Jacques Derrida introduced the world to the concept of Deconstructionism. The world, according to Derrida, was not black and white, and infinite shades of gray started to rally behind him. Queer theory emerged, gay and lesbian studies started to think beyond mere sexuality, and the concept of gender started to wiggle free from the confines of biology. I have been struggling to wiggle free my entire life, but it wasn't until well into adulthood that I realized I was never really trapped in the first place. If an object is not green, it doesn't mean it is yellow; it can be blue or red or purple or grey, or a vast range of colors in between. I am not trapped because gender is no more binary than the color wheel, and green has never been either black or white.

I have always been the type of person who prefers ties to dresses, Esquire to Redbook. As I creep into my mid-forties, however, I see that much of my battle with femininity has been the result of having it forced on me by virtue of anatomy. As I grow older, I embrace my masculinity more fully, not as an abandonment of femininity, but as a complement to it. Even if I were born with a penis, I would prefer yoga to football, small cafes to strip clubs, and a great novel to the daily sports page. These, of course, are stereotypical attributes that merely braise the surface of gender identity, but as a whole they can add up. If gender were a spectrum rather than a set of poles, I would, however, undoubtedly lean toward the masculine. In my youth, I interpreted this as a desire to be a "boy," and as I grew older, I sought to conform and fit in by being a "girl."

I may have a uterus, but I was never a woman, and I have long forgone the need to pee standing up in order to feel like a man. I am comfortable with my masculine attributes, but no longer feel the need to eradicate the feminine aspects of my character.

I now go by the name Levi, a Hebrew name I chose for its meaning, "joined in harmony." I don't need to pick a side. I do not know the exact catalyst for these realizations other than viewing my identity through the eyes of maturity and having the fortitude not to look away, a fortitude many possess at a much earlier age. Like an abstract guitar painted by Picasso, I once only had the ability to make out fragments of my identity without any discernible trace of its whole; but, the guitar is still a guitar regardless of the order or placement of its various components.

The contemporary umbrella term "genderqueer" (GQ) has become the catchall nonbinary label seeking to put a name to all of us nameless. Like the drawer in everyone's kitchen that houses everything from a pair of pliers to birthday candles, GQ gives gender misfits a place to call home. I am not a male, and I am not a female. Therefore, I am not gay and I am not lesbian. I am not a homosexual or a heterosexual.

Heraclitus once said, "No man ever steps in the same river twice, for it's not the same river and he's not the same man." I used to believe my identity, having revealed itself in layers over time, was anything but static, but I was mistaken. While it is true that who I am today looks a lot different than who I was yesterday, the river has indeed changed too. My identity, however, has not. Like an unwavering beacon in the dark, it is the light that has always called me home.

"*Aaaaalaaaannaaaa.*"

Yes, the name may change, but the voice is always the same. I am Alanna. I am Levi. I am Me.

CHAPTER THREE

Coatlicue

FÉI HERNANDEZ

FÉI | COATLICUE

I stand naked before mami as she dries me with a towel after a cold shower. It's right after a wet sunrise, the only time I get to see mami smile with her tired eyes. I'm standing on the bed so I am eye to eye with her, shivering. I am ready to take her morning words of honey: mi vida, mi mundo, mi amor, the ones I have to preserve for days to come. The rush of the morning drips from my skin while my school pants are inserted around my stubby legs. Then the white button up that's too tight for my round body. But regardless of the echoing tick of the clock and the pressure to be in class on time, I stand still and wait to hold the damp rough towel in my hand: the long strands of hair I want to let flow from my head.

I love wrapping towels around my head like mami does after the shower. I love wrapping them like la Virgen de Guadalupe does. Holy. Priestess-like. In my mind this long brown towel is also the long hair Mulan shears clear before heading to war. It is long and beautiful, perfect for *trenzas* or ponytails like my cousins wear it. It is the hair that lifts with the colors of the wind like Pocahontas's. It is magic. It is my whole heart. It is my *tatarabuela*'s hair that sweeps the floor.

My mushroom haircut lifts as I run around in front of the garage we sleep in. I have good peripherals. I've learned to be satisfied with seeing my hair from the side, watch it take off from my head like a baby pigeon from its nest. I wish it was more like a crow that strikes upward into the sky and caws to scare everyone around, but I'm okay with it being a lazy pigeon for now, as long as it still flies.

Mami says, *Tu eres mi mundo*. She stared at me the same way she did every morning. In amazement? Or maybe just a lot of love. She weaves the sign of the cross on my forehead, uniformed, backpack in hand before I leave to school. She tells me I'm her world again. To say something like that, I wonder.

Jesse always says I wasn't supposed to be born. He says it every time he reads the lines in my palm, or talks to my deceased grandpa on my dad's side. He does it every time he sees me, as if to seek an update from above. Mami always makes me see Jesse when abuelita's *limpia de huevo* doesn't work on me. She worries when I can't sleep at night or when I tell her about the ghost people I see. There's too many eyes on him, *tiene mal de ojo*, Mami tells Jesse and thanks him compassionately again for coming from so far. Her tears always stop when he's around.

Maybe I wasn't supposed to be born, like Jesse says. Maybe the gods and goddesses, spirits and saints made a fast decision and gave me the wrong body? That has to be it.

Jesse says he will die soon and will pass on his knowledge to me. But for now he tells me to feel. *Her*, he says under his breath. He says he has Archangels protecting me, I don't know who they are, but apparently they're here to protect me from bad people, the ones here and *del otro lado* who crave my light. He says I have a mission, a big one that involves healing people like he does, with his hands. I'll be a type of teacher? But I don't know about that. He says I'll have accomplished everything by age thirty-three. Everything?! He tells me about the ancestors living in my eye sockets and gives names to the ones living in our apartment walls.

Jesse is here to dispel the bad energy clinging to my skin. He prays in a language that sounds like all languages put together! I only know Spanish and English, I exclaim, I won't be able to pray like you. He says my hands are enough. Just place your hands like this, he says and places them at my heart center. I start feeling lighter and a deep dark cloud slips out of my exhale when he presses my head back with his thumb, holds my small neck with his other hand.

Mami hands him a folded $50 bill. My peripheries let me see everything even when I'm far away. She smiles, Jesse hugs her, pats me on the head on his way out, and says he'll see me next time. He vanishes for months before he shows up at our doorsteps again, wallet grumbling, his hands ready to dispel the bad spirits.

The Aztec goddess Coatlicue (co-at-lil-cu-eh) was regarded as the Earth's mother, the patron of giving life and taking it: childbirth, and warfare; she is the reason for existence on Earth as we know it. Myth states that she found a bundle of heavenly feathers while she swept atop the legendary mountain: Snake Mountain, Coatepetl. Entranced with the bundle of feathers, like any abuela would after seeing an unattended $100 bill, she tucked them into her snake dress and was instantly impregnated with war. Some call it her son, the god of war: Huitzilopochtli. I call it karma.

The woman in me cannot be researched. She does not exist on the Internet or in the Ancient History Encyclopedia. She is the history I'm engraving in the hard minds of the world. Féi is very similar to Coatlicue, but is drastically different, a hybrid form of warrior goddess, shape-shifter, and animal. Anima incarnate. She is very comfortable being referred to as La Malinche, the war-starter, or La Llorona, the howling woman searching for her deceased children; she sees herself as Coatlicue, but has the eyes of the god Quetzalcoatl, the feathered serpent; at times she feels more Nagual, shapeshifter; sometimes she turns into a crow, sometimes the body I was born in.

When I first saw Féi, her black wings had fallen feather by feather, her beak had grown long like an ingrown nail that gently pierced the soft of her throat like a knife. She was a woman unattended, ignored, abandoned. She was threatened by her own fray. Naked and hungry, she stood before me as I dressed her. I opened her body rolls like an accordion and let the noise fill the temple. I whistled the snake call and they slithered back to join her thighs and form her skirt. Her childless womb filled her stomach. Her claw held a pistol. I didn't need to hold her in my arms like Mary did Jesus after he was brought down from the cross. She stood valiantly. *Papel picado* sprouted from the walls and the dust cleared. The gold of the temple shone bright. She whipped

her arms and feathers shot out. A beautiful goddess harpy stood rejuvenated before me. Before she took flight I held her claw and said, *Tu
eres mi mundo, eres mi vida.*

Eres mi otro yo.

Sea horses are my favorite sea animal, Mami, look, I say one Sunday
night. Do you know your father has real horses in México? Mami says.
Of all tones of brown and ages. She looks up and through the south
wall to see her desert valley. She wipes her face to dust the sand off and
returns her gaze to me. Yeah, yeah, I roll my eyes. You've told me he's
a cowboy, but the horses I like are in the sea! I argue. She laughs and
holds the seahorse book I picked up from the library on Friday and
skims through the pages. She gets sucked into the blue, Why do you
like them, *mi vida?* she says as she turns the pages. The boy seahorses
can carry the babies, look! I turn to the middle of the book where I
left my bookmark, to the chapter titled "Family," and point to a photo
of a male seahorse spewing tiny seahorses from his womb. *¿Verdad?*
she exclaims, then stares at my face and sees the ocean water that makes
me. It is then she knows the desert no longer holds me like it does her.
The seahorse peeks out and shoots water at her face to pull her back to
me. She laughs and says, *¡Que magia, de verdad!* and rubs my wing
bumps on my arms. *Te amo, mi vida. Te amo, te amo.*

The moon grew ten inches and inundated us in light that night.

I would give anything to have my stomach swell with kicks and
punches from a child sleepwalking inside of me. It's much harder to
accept those kicks and punches when they're from your demented goddess self, angered and unsatisfied, at war with the man's body that's
stripped her from her power. How do I tell mom about . . . Féi?

At that time neither of us knew what to call this. How could I explain
that my boy body was only a doorframe, a portal for the woman in me
to walk through? How could I explain that my stomach had the tenacity of a womb to carry new life in it, but not the moon cycle, or hips to
support that aspiration? How could I explain that the woman in me
doesn't need me to perform gender for anyone, that she's more than
fulfilled to reside in this body just as it is? She says it's her temple—she
doesn't need a knife to alter me. If we had the science to build a womb,
that's what she'd want. But truthfully, all she wants me to do is speak
her name: *Féi.* She is validated when I let her take flight from the tip of
my teeth. She loves it when I let her slide into my arms like long velvet
gloves to control my gestures.

It's not fair to put words to magic.

Tears rolled from her eyes like a wild river. I'm not crying because of what you said, she clarified, I'm just so proud of you, Féi. You are my baby. You are so, so brave. This is right, she continued as she held my hand, this is who I've known you always were.

A week after I came out to my mom (this was the second time, the first was as gay), Jesse, old and not yet dead, called her one moonless evening. Sorry for the late call, he said, but I'd like to see you and Féi.

Her cell phone slipped from her fingers.

We sat alone in my living room in silence for a long while before Jesse decided to stand up and give me a giant vampire-slaying cross. A necklace, for you, he said. I felt a coronation ceremony was underway without me knowing it. My palms and feet tingled and I felt all my descendant masters join me. Before I could speak I realized I didn't need to. Jesse had always known about the woman in me, all he needed me to do was see her. You're ready, he said and placed his hand on my claw. I'm so proud of you, Féi, he said before he closed the door behind him and vanished.

FÉI | MX. HERNANDEZ

H-e-r-n-a-n-d-e-z

Mami pronounces each letter in Spanish for me, slow lightning. She follows the storming, tumbling letters across my homework heading. Wild horses. I collect the wild letters of my name the same way I've done everything else: with tenacity, determination, and assurance.

Why does my last name feel like nine wild horses running across a *llano*, mami? I say. No matter what I do, I can't hold my last name down with my pencil's tip. I sigh. I lose a horse every time I write my father's last name. Or one horse tips the others over as I write them down across the homework heading: an upside down "e" or backward "z." It's a name that never wants to stay still. At the end of the *llano* the letters shrink into the distance and every horse takes off in different directions. Sometimes I feel abandoned by my last name.

My homework is always turned in mostly incomplete because neither mami nor I understand the language. *We no spik ingles*, my mom tells my third grade teacher with her factory hands. Toilet bowl hands. Napkin hands that wipe her tears after work. But these hands, although tired, are also the only lasso that were able to tame my wild name and make it stay when my father couldn't.

The truth hurts.

No. I understand he's my father, Ma, but why did you get with him if he was married!

Oh, you didn't know? Okay, but how did you allow him to register me with his last name then?! I exclaimed on the phone, 2,609 miles away.

Love has no culprits, I would later learn.

You knew he was going to choose his wife and kids and not us, Ma. I'm carrying around my father's dead horse of a last name, I said, restless. I leave a trail of its blood wherever I go. C'mon!, my claws start to curl inward and my palms sprout blood. I can't even hold the phone still.

Why couldn't I have your last name: Lorenzana—there's so much strength in it. I can see abuelo's eyes in it. I can see the coffee he picked, teaching himself how to read and write. I can see him protesting outside his company. I can see the legacy of me in that last name. But my dad? He's a sorry excuse for a man.

I speak in English purposely because she won't understand what I say. I retell the story she knows, blame him for making me queer, blame him for us still just getting by, for us being undocumented and struggling every day. For everything. I fluster and let my anger speak faster and faster and faster, all in English.

I hang up before she can reply.

His name should have stayed across the border after he left us here. His name should have stayed in the desert. It should have stayed unburied under the sun.

I storm out of my dorm building. I storm out of my last name.

M-X-H-E-R-N-A-N-D-E-Z, I realign the words on my tongue. I'm nervous so they gallop out of order across the desert and it's hard to keep them still.

I stand stoic in front of my largest class of sixth graders, their big bulgy eyes pushing out of their sockets from how tight their uniforms are. Beautiful brown and black eyes looking at my colors, my earrings, my rings, my wild hair and red-framed glasses. I remember sitting in those same chairs when I was a middle schooler, fidgeting, biting my nails. Their young hearts have far more compassion than adults. I take a deep breath and begin my introduction the same way I rehearsed it:

Who here knows what gender neutral is? Jorgie. Good! Yes. That's a great example: dresses are always for girls, jeans however are for everyone. We've all known teachers to be referred to as "Mr." or "Ms./Mrs./Miss" correct? I write the honorifics on the board and mark a mighty X over the "r," "s," "rs," and "iss." Well not anymore. I explain that teachers across the nation are implementing this. I obviously omit the adjective: queer. I assure them I'm not special or doing this to "sound cool." I explain that being a teacher is an instrument regardless of gender. I teach them the power of "X" in neutralizing gender. They nod in agreement, but a student asks, What's the simplest way to explain this?

"Mx" is the gender-neutral way of saying teacher, I say and smile. The wild letters cooperated today.

A student raises their hand and asks, How do you say it? I respond instantly, There's various pronunciations, but my personal favorite is just saying the letters "M" and "X." Much like Malcolm *X*, or Professor *X*; do any of y'all know who these amazing individuals are? No, okay, I chuckle, well that's a conversation for next class. As for my name, please, just call me "M" "X" Hernandez. Is this clear? Good.

I saw myself painting in a large studio with white walls and open wall-set windows after graduation. I saw myself writing hunched over a typewriter in a tenth-story apartment overlooking New York City. But here I am back in Inglewood teaching in a charter school forty-five seconds from my shared apartment. No studio. No desk for my typewriter. Just 150 students ready to soak my teachings in. Sometimes the mission is far greater than our own personal wish.

I clarify, revert to the whiteboard, point, ask questions, ask for comprehension. I smile at the way my mouth moves when I talk. The way my long earrings sway poetically with my movement, my hands serve as a second mouth. My outfits are always poppin'. "Poppin'," "Gucci," and "you good?" become their next favorite words. I feel like a high priestess walking to her throne when I walk into my classroom. Why do I feel like I'm flying above my kingdom right now?

Hands raise. I open ten floating books across the classroom and we jump in and out of them like flying fish. It's a wild alchemy, what we do in my class. Our questions about race, politics, identity, and art are always an adventure. Even the Goddess ruling her temple has questions sometimes and can use the help of Google. We tap gently into colonization, into police brutality, into *día de los muertos*, into dancing and the latest Sia song, into "How are ya'll feeling, you Gucci?," into the power of representation, and finally into art as if it were a dance. Nirvana walks into our classroom and stays many times a week—the students are at ease, learning, taking notes, observing. We are each other's mirror—coming to class feels like coming home.

Do you ever feel like it might be too much for them? a fellow coworker interrogates. They're all so young. Don't you feel like you're imposing your beliefs on the students?

To be a teacher is to prepare the students for survival. Identity politics is not an imposition. Intersectionality and positionality are not impositions. Meditation is not an imposition. Teaching youth of color, especially queer youth of color, about themselves is the biggest tool we can give them. We don't want to disenfranchise them.

But all I say is no, and chuckle. They love my class! Haven't you heard?

I know I've been closed off for some time, I tell the teachers, staff, and administration during a retreat icebreaker. I have trouble "opening up," so I want you all to address me as "*Féi*" from now on. It's my second year teaching and I'm still fearful of exposing the trans, queer, spiritual gold available at my core. To protect myself I've hardened a giant wall between myself and others. But that's no way to live, when there's already so many physical ones keeping me out. It's hard to be critical of people and places you love. But love is determined by said critique. More specifically, teachers that taught you, a school that held you during your upbringing. But my name was not granted to me to be a bridge, to resolve the mystery of bigotry, or to change anyone's mind. It exists to change through its sheer sound. I deserve to exist unapologetically and let that be enough.

Being the only openly queer teacher at school comes with answering a lot of questions. Some are learning experiences, appropriate. Some are not. Then there's a lot of silence at times. In said silence, I hear religious, homophobic, sexist jargon sprinkled around the hallways by students, staff, teachers alike. But what school in the United States, the world, doesn't suffer from the virus of ignorance? There might be a few pockets of safe space, but I love my school, and my students, and my coworkers, no matter how flawed, and can't picture myself working anywhere else.

So I've decided to stay. For the time being, no matter how hard it is sometimes. If I'm simply a placebo or band-aid then so be it. But I stay for the time being and mend what I can, save what lives I can. I don't think I can do it all. I can't save everyone. I can't. But I'll stay and make whatever change I can make. I was made strong like a horse. An invincible individual that has lost their name and found it one too many times. I storm across any desert, hooves behind me, kicking what was to the past, but always looking toward the sunset. I stay because my last name, my heaven-granted name, and my title have taught me forgiveness. Have taught me what it means to love.

Mx. Hernandez, we need to talk to you.

Six queer students shuffle into my classroom. My gender-neutral title, my bastard last name, Féi's Holy Ghost are transcendental safe havens. I'm glad I trusted the pain. Tears well in my eyes and I know my endurance thus far has breached silences and has created refuge.

They grip their backpack straps. Look away. Look back. The leader of the group stands forward mustering the courage to go on. Before they can ask for my help to start a safe space, an LGBTQ club or "healing circle," I say, Yes.

Yes.

Yes.

Yes.

FÉI | BELOVED

Anthony, the gay one. Don't let him hang out with us. He gives me the creeps. And why does he always have a rose? I lead the group around the blacktop away from him. I know he's trying to steal you guys from me. Or make me gay. Ugh, he's so gay. I don't want to be seen with him. I tuck my hands into my black hoodie under the strongest sun in summer.

But I look back at him. My peripheries remain strong. He sits on the bench alone looking through the fence to far-off places like France, Florida—anywhere but Inglewood—smelling his rose. I hate that he crosses his leg. I hate that he has a soft voice. I hate that I can't be there, on the bench with him. Why does my heart swell when I think about him? Who is that rose for?

Deep down I want his coral-blue eyes to look into mine. I want the red rose to be a gift—for me! I want him to teach me how to exist in the pit of middle school with wrists unhinged, speech and beautiful eyes like a girl's without fear. Teach me.

Senior year in high school I wrote him a letter with a rose taped across the envelope:

I'm so sorry, it said. PS: let's go to prom together?

I danced with everyone except Anthony that night, but he blessed me with his smile when I went over to talk to him. His edges softened like a desert rose after a storm. My heart lost its hard crystallized edges too. With his forgiveness, I gave myself a second chance at loving myself. I wasn't going to mess it up this time. Not when I was the one that needed it the most.

CHAPTER FOUR

Namesake

MICHAL "MJ" JONES

IT STARTED with a name—my name—Michal.

Used as a proper noun: *Michal* is a tomboy. *Michal* is not interested in the things she's supposed to be interested in. *Michal* smells like outside and scrapes up her knees too much. *Michal* is odd. *Queer*.

Mama liked the name. I didn't, for a long time. Part of me thinks she knew when she named me that I'd be queer as day, that I'd be different, but she'd just say that she liked the name. My namesake is from the Bible, which I don't know much about—mama didn't church us. But she didn't say it the Hebrew way, she said it like the "boy's" name. Which confused the hell outta everyone, including me.

Michal. "My gull," mama would call me. She wanted me to be proud of my name, but I don't know how I could be when the kids at school were having a fuckin' field day.

"*Michal*? ain't that a *boy's* name?"

"Well, she *do* look like a boy!"

"What is it? maybe it's a *it*!"

The thing is, I didn't realize I was an *it* until defined that way in their eyes.

Once you become undesirable you become an it—with your legs-spread-open, shoulders-slouched-in, scraped-up-knees nature. You are beautiful, but not to them.

To them, an "it" wasn't a person—maybe that's what made it easier for them to do the shit they did and talk the shit they talked. Easier to tear apart an "it" than look inside at their own wounds. I knew I had become an *it* one morning in sixth grade—that period of fuckin hell. A boy running full speed down the hallway collided into me, knocking me flat on my ass. He paused for a fraction of a second, evaluating my humanity before deciding I was something entirely too different to care about. Onlookers simply looked on. I pushed myself up and choked back hot tears.

Who had made him into a monster? Who had made me into an it?

I was taught to believe the best in people, so I didn't know what these kids were talkin' about when they called me queer, a faggot, a boygirl. (But I was clear on what "nigger" meant.) I didn't know what most of it meant, but it didn't really matter—they said it with hate and laughter in their throats so I got the message. And I was always soft and tender spirited—wouldn't even defend myself after a certain point.

Shit got so bad that I'd fake sick just to keep from going to school. Mama knew, I'm sure, but I made her tired in a serious way. Some days she'd drag me by my hair and up out the bed and holler till I finally slumped my way over to the bus stop. Other days she just had no fight in her and with a sigh, called the school.

I was black and light skint and now an "it" to boot so there was pretty much no day I wasn't picked on by someone.

I was eight, and my spirit was tired. Papa had left and moved two states away. Ma was there but not there. My spirit was tired.

How do you tire a spirit? Call it names, tell it what to wear, how to act, how to walk, how to sit, how to carry its books, what to say, when to speak, when not to speak. I wasn't interested in any of that shit, but I was gonna have to at least fake interest if I was gonna get out alive.

So it was around age ten that I finally started to get that everyone was doing a big circus act, a performance. Ain't nothin to gettin' by but pretending. So, I practiced:

I pranced up and down the hallway at home with an extra sway in my hips (I called it my "attitude" walk), painted my face up like a doll, did a sloppy polish job on my nails. I demanded the latest fashion in knee-high boots from my ma, who looked at me like I'd grown a second head. Even she knew the look didn't suit me. "You got some boot *money?*"

I lost on the boots, but I thought the rest of my act was on point.

But it didn't win me an award. The monsters at my school saw right through the thick makeup and pushed at me anyway. I still "looked raggedy, would never be pretty, would always stay an ugly oreo my whole life."

My tired spirit trembled, didn't understand. I had clothed it, called it "she," made all attempts to conceal it beneath lip gloss. Still they laughed. And still they pushed me, knocked me over. I pulled even further into myself and away from everyone else, feeling like an imposter. Feeling extinguished.

I continued this sad, quiet performance for as long as it took me to realize that God don't like ugly, but God don't like fake, either.

I stayed in this awkward pretense—which I would now define as drag—from sixth grade to ninth.

I tried the boyfriend thing for a while, but he told me flat to my face that I was gonna "end up like my mom." He meant that I'd grow up gay. It pissed me off at the time—just because I don't want to fuck *your* ugly ass don't mean I'm gay.

When I was thirteen and we got to exploring, I thought that I was turned on by him, but looking back I think actually I wanted to feel his hardness as he felt it. And I thought that's how everyone felt.

He'd be pressed against my body, kissing me terribly while I was someplace else, someone else.

One heavy humid summer I told him (and the one or two friends I was able to make—all of whom are out of the closet now) that we would be moving clear across the country to California.

My mother and her lesbian lover would be moving in together, uprooting me from all I'd known up until then. It hurt me, but I had tortured the woman for many unstable years, and I wanted her to be happy.

We moved to Berkeley and nothing was as I expected—no sunny, warm weather here. Just cold ass summer. The transition was rocky for me, thirteen and vulnerable, but that was the start of me shedding the it-ness that had stuck to me for so long already.

My mom seemed to be shedding her own skin, adding more color to her traditionally all-black wardrobe. To live in authenticity does something to a person.

The worlds of feminism were revealed to me with CodePink. I played on Telegraph Avenue for days, learning of the Free Speech Movement— all subjects that interested me from a young age but that I couldn't explore in my stuffy Midwest childhood surroundings.

It seemed that a lot of people in my new high school were bisexuals, queers, or other its. Still, that didn't make them friendly. I was new and awkward, so friends were hard to come by, but the handful who picked me up seemed to have liberated spirits—not silenced or tired like my own.

My spirit's head slowly peeked from behind the door like Boo Radley, seeking permission.

I slowly grew comfortable again in my baggy clothes and swapped sloppy kisses with girl friends who wanted to "practice for boys." *The L Word* became my own private sanctuary and I finally tried on the term "gay" at fifteen. I had a string of Internet-found white "girlfriends" too well intentioned to know or care that they were racist, and me too desperate to know I was being consumed and not cared for.

I explored their bodies but did not want them to explore mine. That's the way it was and that's the way it stayed for a while.

By the time I neared college, I had grown comfortably in my gayness, but it wasn't until I stepped on campus that I met dozens of trans kids and self-proclaimed gender freaks that my spirit began to breathe.

Being a fly in a glass of milk wasn't exactly easy, but at the same time, my college classes were the first place I was introduced to Audre Lorde, Bayard Rustin, Angela Davis, and so many others who showed me that I was not alone in my it-ness.

My it-ness continued to shed its skin. Tears came into my eyes when I read this opening to *Zami*, one of Audre's texts that was most influential to me: "*I have always wanted to be both man and woman, to incorporate the strongest and richest parts of my mother and father within/ into me—to share valleys and mountains upon my body the way the earth does in hills and peaks.*"

Never had a person—dead or alive—reflected the thoughts and feelings in the echo chambers of my mind and heart.

———

Today, I have come to terms with my sexual and gender journeys being just that—a journey, a process without a clearly defined endpoint.

Today, I straddle the borders of being not comfortable in women's spaces, yet not being fully seen as trans, with growing patience and acceptance for my own truth.

Today, my rejuvenated spirit has learned to breathe under pressure.

Today, I live in a liminality that is on neither side of the binary but all encompassing and surpassing it. "Both man and woman," I am all and none of these things. I've always lived in this space, and am grateful that language is slowly emerging for folks who feel this way.

Occupying this space is a constant coming-out process—a creative one where I come up with new names for myself and explain away the confused looks on strangers' faces. Where I used to be apologetic for my own personhood ("it's they/them—I'm sorry, I know it's confusing"), my only sorry now is to my younger self.

Today, I am weeks away from stepping into an entirely new realm of life—parenthood.

When we first embarked upon the journey of exploring family formation, I struggled to accept that I would not be the one to plant the seed—that the limitations of my body would not allow it.

But as the seed grew from a raspberry, to a peach, to an eggplant, my initial worry began to melt away. The baby was hearing my voice, kicking beneath my hands, and turning at my singing. When insecurity and resentment creeps in, I am reminded that nothing about being queer is easy, but it is always creative and reinventing.

I wondered what new language we could create that would really fit me. Not a mother, not a father—"what about baba?" I asked my partner excitedly, one hand on her swollen belly.

We both grinned ear to ear at the warm, blanketing term of endearment.

Today, my spirit breathes, and embraces the name I was given, and new names that I create every day.

CHAPTER FIVE

My Genderqueer Backpack

MELISSA L. WELTER

MY GENDER journey began before birth: the doctors said I was a boy, but my dad was sure I was a girl. Neither would ultimately turn out to be true.

Growing up on the rural outskirts of a small town in northern California, most people would peg my childhood presentation as that of a tomboy. My cousins, sister, and I spent our afternoons outside, climbing trees, sneaking up on one another through grass as tall as we were, and jumping off various structures we probably shouldn't have been on in the first place. Sturdy clothing and attitudes were required.

In sharp contrast, my school days involved trying to fit in. Other girls' interest in clothes, celebrities, and boys often left me off balance. Friendship in junior high meant doing girl things together. I gathered that I needed to develop opinions about actors and boy bands. I let my best friend talk me into more popular clothes and I started shaving my legs and trying out makeup. No one explicitly told me that it was required, but no one had to. I learned how to fake it.

In my later teens and into my young adulthood, I met women who widened my conceptions of beauty and attraction. Dykes, fairies, witches, butches, and hippies became part of my landscape. I decided I must be one of them. I became a free spirit, openly queer in jeans and a buzz cut or flowing skirts and fairy wings. I eschewed bras and shaving and I settled for a more radical sort of womanhood.

I was twenty-one the first time I heard the word "genderqueer." It fell into my heart like the seed of a redwood tree on moist soil. It felt deeply private. At first, I told myself that it was a small thing. Maybe I was only a *little* genderqueer? You know, enough that it affected me in the bedroom, but not in my daily life. I told anyone I dated about it. Surely that was enough. But steadily, my genderqueerness grew, taking up more space in my life. It eventually permeated everything I did and every relationship I had.

I experimented, picking up some gender behaviors and discarding others. As I unpacked what made up gender for me, it allowed me to repack exactly what I want to include moving forward. Much of what I've packed is from (and for) being a woman. I spent the most time identifying as a woman, so this section is full. Next, there are a few select pieces from manhood, things I've shopped for rather carefully. Sometimes, I still miss the mark. Finally, there are some specialty pieces I've obtained from being genderqueer. Here's a look at what I carry in my very own Genderqueer Backpack.

STUFF LEFT OVER FROM BEING RAISED AND SOCIALIZED AS A GIRL/WOMAN

A permeable space bubble. My openness allows me to use affectionate touch to communicate support, comfort, and happiness. It lets me do things like hug and cuddle friends and small children without feeling like I'm overstepping. When I came out as genderqueer, a friend looked thoughtfully from me to her three-year-old son, who was playing nearby. "Do you still want him to call you Auntie, or something else?" I can still drop my hand to casually ruffle his hair, patch up a scraped knee, and receive a shy hug before he goes to bed. The place where their acceptance meets my gendered space is precious to me. I'm definitely keeping it.

A mixtape of all the songs I learned how to move my hips to. When I first learned to dance, I was afraid of moving my body. I was scared I would seem too big, too obvious, too sexual—too much. It took time to grow into my curves. I flailed and blushed my way through middle school. At fourteen, I went to a pagan ritual and watched women leap, stomp, twirl, and undulate, all while making bold eye contact or laughing joyfully. I fell in love with those women, with their power and sexuality. I learned to dance. Now, I feel electric when I move, the rhythm of the music pulsing right through me. I love how my hips move and swing when I dance. I own my body in those moments.

One small hole punched in the side of the bag from that time I wore heels. I managed a pair of three-inch platform heels at my eighth-grade graduation dance—an unexpectedly elegant and feminine presentation from an unpopular girl. I was quickly dumped by my long-time crush. When I started meeting other types of girls and women that summer, I decided that heels were not for me. Let the amazing femmes in my life have their heels. My lovely, cursed heels moldered in the back of my closet for years before I finally got rid of them.

A slightly smudged hand mirror. Back when my presentation was more feminine, I used my mirror to put on blush and lipstick. That mirror was how I scrutinized my femininity, evaluating whether or not I looked like a woman. It has taken me a while to learn to look in a mirror and just see myself as I am, raw and beautiful and vulnerable. I still practice every day, which is why I've kept that mirror.

Fear, anger, and mace. I can't turn off the part of my brain that goes on alert the second I step outside late at night. The truth is that my height often gets me read as a woman, and it is not safe for women to travel in certain ways, times, and places. The ice at the back of my neck as I walk past a group of drunk guys talking too loudly, the tightness in my throat when someone catcalls, and the curl of my hands into clenched fists are here to stay. That I can't leave these at home or throw them out altogether just makes my anger hotter. Perhaps someday the world will be safe enough to allow people like me to go without, but not in my generation, and not in the next.

One very short skirt. It took a long time to believe in my sexuality, and longer to be confident in being sexual and genderqueer at the same time. When I wear this skirt, I defy everyone that tells me to play it safe. Fuck that. My body is mine to do what I want with. If there are wolf whistles, I answer them with a wolf's growl, a threat and a warning that I am dangerous, too. I display my sexiness because it pleases me to do so and I will take no judgments for it. My skirt is not an invitation to decide what I am. It makes me neither a slut nor a woman. My skirt means sex but it also means I am on fire, ready to stomp anyone who comes at me.

Sensuality. No one ever taught me that enjoying life's pleasures was weak or wrong. Potato chips taste like companionship and the long girls-only gossip sessions that often got deep into what we had experienced, what we wanted, and how to get it. Chocolate tastes like hot baths alone by candlelight. Satin and velvet feel like being stroked by a lover's hands. These things are mine and I get to keep them.

An old, stained magazine crumpled at the bottom. It features quizzes about my love life and tips on applying makeup and picking the perfect autumn sweater, and a debate on shaving versus waxing. The date can faintly be made out as September 2003, which is the last time I cared about any of that. I really should throw it out.

A FEW THINGS I'VE ACQUIRED GETTING SOCIALIZATION AS A MAN

One tie, rolled neatly and tucked carefully into its own pocket to keep it from being crumpled. It reminds me of the lovely rainbow of ties waiting for me at home. My first tie came from my English teacher, Mr. Vanderbilt, my senior year of high school. He offered a wide selection to the class when an uncle left them to Mr. Vanderbilt in his will. I took one, pleased to be a little different from the girls without quite understanding how important that difference would become. When I wear a tie, I straighten my shoulders and tilt my chin. Ties are a reminder that I am allowed to mimic the body language of the men around me and claim it as my own. Ties center my expression of masculinity. Whenever I remember that, I find myself running a pleased hand over the tie I'm wearing

A legs-sprawled posture and a direct stare that tells that creeper on the bus to find somewhere else to sit. I've learned to tell people to stay away with my body as clearly as I've learned to invite people to come closer.

A solid pair of work boots. These boots take up space, but they are important for getting the job done. My boots keep me grounded. The thin, slippery shoes women are encouraged to wear remind me of my feet sliding out from under me on a wet day and of being afraid, unsure I can run in the dark. When I wear my boots, I brace wide and take long strides.

A toy action figure of a knight. When I identified as a woman, my boldness used to feel defensive and transgressive. Claiming my maleness unlocked a deeper sense of certainty within me. All the women warriors in my life light up my heart, but I am not one of them. Instead, it is the knight of the countless fantasy novels I read as a teen that I model myself on. I am courtly without being condescending, offering my arm and my ear as needed. I am ready to be called on for aid. I am strong in my body as I run, jump, and tumble, unafraid of getting dirty or bruised. For all these ideals that I take seriously, it is a toy that stays tucked close. It is a reminder that I am still playing, learning, and exploring, that my honor and way of seeing the world are not set in stone.

SPECIALTY GENDERQUEER ITEMS

An enigmatic smile when a child asks whether I'm a boy or a girl. Without the alarm that adults often experience when they can't pin down my gender, it becomes simply a question. Children key into my deliberately mixed signals and ask for clarification. Children often see me more clearly than adults do.

A very particular fashion sense. I know that the short skirt and the tie actually go together, thanks, as do the tight dress with the men's work boots. Once, in a hot tub, a friend blinked at my board shorts and bikini top and drawled out a delighted, "Melissa! Are you in drag?" I grinned and shot back, "All clothes are drag." I hold the memory of my friend's laughter close when people stare and I meet their eyes unflinchingly.

A soft packer, for special occasions. The intimate curl of something that is both extra and a part of me pressed close between my legs is precious. It is a gift, that I can have this and be safe. There is no terrifying reveal coming, no accidental outing, no mocking laughter or awkward silence or threat of violence. The way my lover cups her hand over me—intrigued, protective, tender, understanding—is permission to be who I am. I don't need her approval, but I *want* it.

A hard packer, for even *more* special occasions. A cock extending in perfect replica of what is there-but-not-there allows me to touch my lovers in all new ways.

A notebook, for keeping track of my journey. At ten, I was a girl. At twenty, I was a woman. By twenty-five, I knew there was something more; I had heard the word "genderqueer" and tentatively recognized myself in it. By now, I see there is a path, extending both behind and in front of me. I remember being sixteen and sobbing hysterically at the thought of being forced into a skirt for a formal occasion, yet not knowing for almost a decade that this was a manifestation of my gender dysphoria. What I know in the present needs recording, to help me trace the complex web that my gender sometimes is.

Playfulness. As heavy as gender can be, as much as it can fill me with rage or grief, my genderqueerness is also the stage for guerilla theater. It is a place to try unusual combinations, to let laughter open up possibilities, to roll boldness and sexuality and self into a big ball and see what happens.

Lots of pockets, with zippers and Velcro and ties, because I am picking up new things all the time. I always want there to be space for everything I want to be.

CHAPTER SIX

Scrimshaw

RAE THEODORE

I SEE YOU looking at me with your mouth wide open and your eyes scrunched up like you've just swallowed a pint of sour milk.

A few years ago, I would have turned around to see what it was that you were looking at with such disdain. I would have expected to see an old woman with the face of a crow or maybe a middle-age man wearing stripes and plaid—contrary patterns battling each other for supremacy.

Today, when I am getting ready to leave the big box store with my cart overflowing with Kotex and Kleenex and Kraft macaroni and cheese, I know that I am the object of your stare, your glare, your visual inspection and split-second condemnation. I see you taking me in: the short hair, the oversized glasses, the lumps built into my chest and the squared-off sideburns that I wish were longer, darker, and thicker, like those of a Civil War general.

I don't even turn my head a fraction of an inch to glance over my shoulder. I've already wasted decades looking back and around, past and through. These days, I'm focused on looking straight ahead.

My eyes meet yours for a second, maybe two. You turn your head but look back again. And again. And again. Apparently, you don't have the stomach for things that make you question everything you thought you did such as nursery rhymes about snails and puppy dog tails and your high school textbook with the shiny red cover that confidently states "Human Sexuality" in big block letters.

You are just a child, even though you look grown up with your long blonde hair, pink painted nails, and upturned nose that seems to be floating in midair. Someday soon, you will start looking down at the ground or far away into the distance so that no one knows exactly what it is you're looking at. You will learn to disguise not only your gaze but your thoughts and feelings, too.

Your mother would tell you that it's rude to stare, that she didn't raise you that way, but I don't mind. I know that you are trying to figure it out, figure *me* out. I am a contradiction—soft and hard, rough and smooth—and you are working to solve the riddle printed on my spine as if it were a giant wooden Popsicle stick.

I used to stand in your shoes when I looked in the mirror, so I know what the view is like from over there. But here's the thing: we don't see things as they are, we see them as *we* are. In my mind's eye, my frame is more sinewy and my chest is flatter. I stand straight and tall and walk with the swagger of a rock star. These are not lies that I tell myself, but how I give life to those parts of me that pulse electric blue beneath the surface of my skin.

I know that I stand out like a red kite in an azure sky. Whether I am seen as male or female, boy or girl, there is always something that people can't quite put their finger on. If I listen real hard, I can hear the wheels in their heads whirring like tiny fans mounted behind the whites of their eyes. If I think too hard, I get lost in that middle place, that center space between male/female, boy/girl. If I'm not careful, I slide too far down the slash separating those absolutes and get wedged into that tight space where everything begins and ends.

I wonder what it is you see in me. Maybe you see a part of yourself and that is why you wrinkle up your face like a used paper bag. Perhaps you are sending a message to that spot deep inside you—the place in your chest that holds the rolled-up plans and diagrams that show who you will grow up to be.

If I knew you'd stop and listen, I'd tell you what I've learned. But you are already walking with purposeful steps through the mechanical doors of the store and into the freedom of the summer day.

I would have told you that you can't rewrite what has been written. It has been carved into your bone like scrimshaw: fancy engravings on bright-white bone. You can still admire the delicate lines and the intricate design and pay homage to an ancient mariner with a steady hand who etched mermaids—backs arched, tails curved, hair flowing behind like soft green ribbon—on a single side of a whale's tooth.

I would have pointed out the obvious, the couplets of fine and beautiful mixed with coarse and brutish, but your eye is already drawn to such juxtapositions like a bright red stop sign.

PART TWO

Visibility
Standing Up and Standing Out

CHAPTER SEVEN

Being Genderqueer Before It Was a Thing

GENNY BEEMYN

WHEN I TELL PEOPLE that I have identified as genderqueer since the term first began circulating on the Internet in the mid-1990s, I often add that, now in my fifties, I am the oldest assigned male at birth (AMAB) genderqueer person found in captivity. I say this jokingly, but it is not far from the truth. In my personal life and in my experience as a researcher on the lives of trans people, I have met few AMAB individuals who identify as genderqueer, and even fewer genderqueer individuals who are beyond their mid-twenties. Genderqueer people who both were assigned male at birth and are over the age of forty are as rare as an endangered species. In fact, I do not personally know anyone else like myself.

I certainly understand why relatively few male-assigned individuals claim a nonbinary identity. Acting or presenting in any way that deviates from the narrow parameters of what is considered appropriate "male" behavior can be dangerous, inviting physical assault or even murder. At the very least, the person faces the likelihood of harassment, discrimination, and ostracization from their peers, particularly from boys and men. Trans women who cannot or choose not to be stealth have a similar experience. The difference for nonbinary AMAB individuals is that many of us do not want to be seen by others as female (or as male), so we will always stand out and be potential targets. For many male-assigned individuals who do not feel themselves to be men, this cost seems too great, especially coming from a place of male privilege and, for some, also white privilege.

Because of the lack of media representations of nonbinary trans individuals and the widespread ignorance about nonbinary people, even in LGBT communities, it was a gradual process for me to claim a nonbinary identity for myself and longer still to come out to others. When I was growing up, I had no idea that there were options other than male and female, so I thought my inability to relate to other male-assigned individuals simply meant that I was a different kind of guy. Even when I learned about "trans" in college, it was only about individuals then referred to as "transsexuals," who were described as being "trapped in the wrong body." While I increasingly felt that I was not male, I did not identify as female either and did not reject my body to the extent of hating or feeling disconnected from it. The first trans people I met while working on the 1993 March on Washington for "Lesbian, Gay, and Bi Equal Rights and Liberation" only reinforced my sense that that was not me, as they were hyperfeminine trans women with big heels, big hair, and big breasts. While I strongly agreed with them politically on the importance of trans inclusion in the march's title (which was voted down, unfortunately), I felt that I had little in common with them personally.

My revelatory moment came through reading Leslie Feinberg's *Stone Butch Blues* when it was published in 1993. The book's gender-nonconforming narrator is harassed and assaulted for not being readily identifiable as female or male, and they ultimately take testosterone to be stealth and survive physically and financially during the economic recession in Buffalo in the 1970s. Although I too had grown up in Buffalo, I was born about twenty years later than the narrator, in a working-class/lower-middle-class suburb, and others rarely had difficulty determining my sex assignment. But I was able to relate to the narrator's discomfort with being neither female nor male, and the novel empowered me by enabling me to see that identifying outside of a gender binary was a possibility. However, I continued to feel alone, because even though *Stone Butch Blues* was based on Feinberg's experiences, the protagonist was a fictional character; I still did not personally know anyone else who identified as nonbinary.

In some respects, my experience is no different from the experiences of many nonbinary youth today. More than twenty years after I was figuring out my gender identity, there is still not much visibility for nonbinary trans individuals. When I give talks at colleges, I sometimes ask the audience members to name a person in popular culture who identifies their gender in nonbinary ways; invariably, they cannot think of anyone.

But while there continues to be a lack of well-known nonbinary trans people, there are many nonbinary individuals on social media, particularly Tumblr. As a result, young nonbinary individuals growing up in the late 2010s who are trying to understand their gender have online resources that did not exist in the 1990s and early 2000s. They can quickly find out the meaning of terms, read about other people's experiences and relate their own, and directly communicate with other nonbinary youth. These options were not available to me. While I did discover the term "genderqueer" online, that was the extent of information I could find in the mid-1990s. I did not have the opportunity to learn about or talk with others who shared my identity; I had to figure it out on my own, which meant that I made more than my share of missteps.

As a first step in coming out publicly as genderqueer, I decided to adopt a new, feminine first name—"Genny," after my grandmother Genevieve—because my given name, which was somewhat nongendered when I was growing up, had become a decidedly male name. But because I wanted to be seen as nonbinary and not as a trans woman, I chose to combine "Genny" with my birth name. Over time, though, I found that this part "male"/part "female" name did not work. People would still call me by my birth name only, seeing "Genny" as optional, or would think "Genny" was my last name. I eventually decided to be just "Genny" and let the dissonance between a "female" name and a largely "male" appearance serve to indicate my nonbinary identity, along with adopting nonbinary pronouns for myself (at first, I went by "ze/hir" and now use "they/them").

Determining how I wanted to present as nonbinary was also a gradual process. Since beginning college in the mid-1980s, I have had very long hair and have dressed fairly androgynously in shirts and jeans. When the word "genderqueer" was coined in the mid-1990s, and I began to use that term to describe myself, I initially thought that I would not do anything more to appear as nonbinary. But I became increasingly uncomfortable with having facial stubble, so I began rounds of laser hair removal and electrolysis. I had no interest in having my body look traditionally female, so had no desire to take an estrogen-type drug. However, I did consider going on a testosterone blocker to prevent my body from continuing to virilize, which made the benefits of facial hair removal short-lived. But my endocrinologist was unsupportive, saying it would lead to osteoporosis. Not able to find anything online from people who were just taking a blocker, I did not pursue the idea further.

I ultimately decided that I did not have to look extremely androgynous in order to be myself and that I should not have to do so to be treated as how I identify. If others did not see and respect me as nonbinary, this was their problem, not mine. This is not to say that being misgendered does not feel invalidating and hurtful, but I try to recognize it as an indication of their ignorance about gender diversity and, in some cases, as a misguided attempt to be polite (such as customer service people referring to me as "sir").

Even before I began to identify as nonbinary, I was an activist for trans rights. In 1995, when I was a grad student at the University of Iowa, I worked with other activists to have "gender identity" added to the nondiscrimination ordinance of Iowa City in response to discrimination experienced by a trans person in a local business. After this success, I and a University of Iowa faculty member, Mickey Eliason, decided to advocate for "gender identity" to be included as well in the university's nondiscrimination statement. As a result, in 1996, the University of Iowa became the first college in the country to have a trans-inclusive nondiscrimination policy, and probably the first college to have *any* formal trans-inclusive policy.

At the time, I was completing a PhD in African American studies at Iowa, focusing my research on the intersections of race, gender, and sexuality. As a white person, I had gone into African American studies as an undergraduate to begin to address my own ignorance about race and racism, and I continued in the field with the aim of teaching other white people, as I did not (and do not) believe it was the responsibility of people of color to educate whites about the ways that we engage in oppressive behavior. But after coming out as a nonbinary trans person, I decided that I could make more of a difference in the lives of trans students. I felt that if they knew someone like themselves but older, they would hopefully have an easier time understanding and accepting their gender identity than I did. Only three years after earning my doctorate, I went back to being a student to earn a master's degree in higher education administration from the University of Rochester so that I would be more capable of advocating for trans and other LGBTQIA+ students.

After graduating once again in 2001, I was hired to be the LGBT office coordinator at Ohio State University. At the time, trans students were beginning to come out there and at many other colleges across the country and asking for institutions to address their needs; however, they typically found that staff, faculty, and cis students were largely unknowledgeable and unsupportive. As a result, the fact that I was an out trans person was an asset to me on the job market—the opposite situation to what I often encountered, understandably, as a white person in African American studies. When so many trans people face employment discrimination and are passed over for jobs because of their gender identity, it felt strange for my nonbinary gender identity to be seen as a positive, or at least not as a liability, in obtaining professional work.

I recognize that I have a tremendous amount of privilege to be in a position where I can be out as trans and, because everyone expects an LGBTQIA+ center director to be queer, not have to worry about workplace discrimination to the same degree as someone in another area of higher education. In the early 2000s, when I was one of the few trans academics who had the opportunity to be out, I used this privileged status to write individually and in collaboration with colleagues some of the first articles that addressed the experiences and needs of trans college students. I also joined the board of the Transgender Law and Policy Institute (TLPI) to be their college point person, which involved consulting with institutions on trans inclusion and tracking trans-inclusive campus policies (a role I assumed for Campus Pride in 2012, after TLPI became inactive). While there are thankfully relatively more out trans scholars today than fifteen years ago, colleges still largely ignore or marginalize trans students, especially nonbinary trans students, so I continue to focus my writing and public speaking, as well as much of my LGBTQIA+ student services work, on educating about and advocating for trans inclusion.

Even though I work in environments where I typically do not encounter outright discrimination as a nonbinary trans person, I regularly experience microaggressions in the form of misgendering. Soon after I began at Ohio State, I added "Genny" to my name and asked many of my colleagues, friends, and members of the local LGBTQ community to refer to me by "ze/hir." But even after an adjustment period, I discovered that few people remembered my pronouns in the moment, and I quickly tired of continually correcting others and having to explain how to use and spell "ze" and "hir."

Ironically, some of the most frequent misgendering I initially experienced—and the most painful—came from other trans people. The trans people I knew at the time were mostly trans women who were ten to twenty years older than I. When they began to self-identify, being trans meant that you were either transsexual or a cross-dresser, so they had no lens with which to understand me as someone who felt more female than male, but who was not intending to present as female or medically transition. As a result, they looked at me as a cisgender ally and would refer to me as "he" and "him" in meetings. I found myself in a surreal situation where my gender identity was more often disrespected by other trans people than by some cis colleagues who had much less understanding of trans issues but wanted to be supportive of me. Eventually, many of these trans people did see me as one of them, after I legally changed my name and began electrolysis (there is nothing like shared pain as a bonding experience). But it was especially disappointing that the people whom I expected would be the most affirming were at first among the least.

In 2006, when I took my current position as the director of the LGBTQIA+ center at UMass Amherst, I decided to switch to using "they/them," hoping that I would have less difficulty in getting people to remember and respect these pronouns because they would not have to learn a new vocabulary. I am misgendered less frequently now, whether for this reason, because I am in a relatively more progressive area of the country, or because people have become more educated about pronouns in recent years. I think it has also helped that I legally changed my name to "Genny" and that I regularly present on and advocate for trans students at my university and at campuses across the country, so that others are constantly reminded of my nonbinary identity. If I was not so visible as a trans policy wonk, I believe that I would be misgendered much more often.

Being seen as a nonbinary trans person is very important to me, as both a personal reflection of my identity and a political challenge to the dominant gender system. But I struggle at times with how to be recognizable and thus recognized as trans, when being transgender is often equated with being a binary trans person who has transitioned or is transitioning. Moreover, to the extent that nonbinary trans people are perceived by the larger society, it is because our gender "stands out"—i.e., because we are not readily able to be placed within a gender binary or our appearance sends "mixed gender signals." The result is that only individuals who present androgynously or whose gender expression clearly violates societal expectations get to be seen as nonbinary. For me, this means that my gender identity is often invisible, especially as I age and look more male because of the long-term effects of testosterone. I am left wondering how to enact my gender in the absence of visible signs of gender nonconformity, as well as the absence of cultural images of older nonbinary people. Society may never "get" me in my lifetime, but I can only be myself.

As I stated at the outset of this essay, I do not personally know any other male-assigned nonbinary individuals who are over twenty-five years old. But nonbinary female-assigned individuals and binary trans people also remain scarce in higher education. At my institution, which has thousands of staff and faculty, I am one of the few out trans people who are not a student. I am regularly reminded of this fact at campus committee meetings, many of which begin with the attendees sharing their pronouns (at my request), along with their names and offices. Invariably, I am the only person who uses pronouns other than "he/him" and "she/her." I greatly appreciate that the chairs of these committees ask pronouns, so that I can indicate mine and hopefully not be misgendered by other group members. But, at the same time, I am disheartened to always be the only one and to have to call attention to myself as *the* out nonbinary trans person.

I know that this situation will change in time, as the many nonbinary trans students on college campuses today graduate and take positions in higher education and elsewhere in the workforce. While I may not personally benefit from the growing number of out nonbinary students, I hope that they will benefit from me. Through my visibility and efforts to educate others, both at my college and at campuses nationwide, I hope that I am helping to create a more welcoming environment for the next generation of nonbinary trans people.

CHAPTER EIGHT

Token Act

SAND C. CHANG

TOKEN: TO·KEN /ˈTŌKƏN/

1. A piece resembling a coin issued for use or as money

To be nonbinary is to be used as currency. As a nonbinary, queer person of color and clinician, my value and utility are quite high—or so I am led to believe.

2. An outward sign or expression

Nonbinary is a label that doesn't tell you anything substantial about what a person's gender is, only what it is not. I have reluctantly adopted this term to describe myself (I started as genderqueer, and that surely dates me) because it's the easiest shorthand to let others know that their systems, this world, creates multiple challenges and barriers for people like me (or not like me) every day.

We who identify as nonbinary spend so much time saying who we are *not* that we never get time to focus on ourselves, to celebrate and honor who we *are*. Nonbinary is only in relation to the colonizer, to

White culture, to Western, mutually exclusive ideals of masculine and feminine. It still centers their experiences as normal, typical, the true measure of gender.

3. A symbol, emblem

My identity is conveniently used as a symbol, especially for employers and organizations that want to show how welcoming they are of DIVERSITY! I hate the word "diversity," almost if not more than I hate the word "multicultural."

Sometimes I think it would save me time and emotional labor if I just sent an automatic email response: "Thank you for contacting me. For all inquiries about my capacity to serve on your diversity committee, recruit research participants, provide trans 101, or add color to your otherwise drab organization, free of charge for the time, energy, effort, and knowledge I bring, please refer to your own process of self-reflection about your power and privilege."

4. A small part representing the whole

The job of being a token comes with the responsibility of representing entire groups of people who are completely different from you.

As a nonbinary person, I am expected to be a spokesperson for *all the transgender and gender nonconforming people across the land*!!! This is a responsibility that I do not want, and it's a position of power that I should not be given. I cannot speak for those of us who seek medical interventions and face barriers every step of the way simply for wanting to feel more comfortable in their bodies and lives. I cannot and should not speak for trans women of color who are at the greatest risk of violence and discrimination. I cannot even speak for all nonbinary people whose ways of describing and experiencing their genders (or lack thereof) are different from my own.

Similarly, as a Chinese American person, I am expected to speak for all Chinese Americans, all Asian people, and all people of color, which is ludicrous. To be used as a token in this way is harmful to me as an Asian American, and it often pits me against other people of color, particularly Black and Latino folks. In a system of White supremacy that fuels itself on anti-Black racism, Asian Americans are used as model minority tokens to keep other people of color down while allowing the system of power to fulfill their quotas.

A DAY IN THE LIFE OF A NONBINARY GENDER THERAPIST

6:45 AM

For fifteen years, strangers on the street have asked me if Theo Chang, my pug, is a boy or a girl. I find this question amusing and irritating at the same time. Zelda Sesame, my smaller pug, wears bowties most days. People call her handsome. When they realize she is female, they apologize profusely. As if she cares! I usually say, "Yes, she is very handsome."

7:30 AM

Nothing seems right as I'm picking out my clothes in the morning.

The dress code of "business casual" is highly gendered, and I have to decide which "drag" to wear to work. I veer toward the masculine: slacks, button-up shirts, and the occasional bowtie when I want to feel especially dapper. It's not that I don't want to wear my femme clothes to work; it's that I know as soon as I do, my entire nonbinary identity will be disregarded. I won't be seen as "trans enough"—my clothes will give people permission to treat me like a woman or feel entitled to use the wrong pronouns. Even people who claim to be accepting of nonbinary gender still expect that our expression must deviate from the norms associated with our sex assigned at birth.

The only work environment in which I ever felt totally comfortable in my body and gender was at the Gender Identity Project in New York, where the director said to me, "Wear whatever you want here. A sequin dress, shorts, nothing at all . . . whatever makes you feel comfortable. That's what we want for our clients, so we need to practice that ourselves." It was a relief to feel that I could get away from the heteronormative (and classist and racist) assumptions embedded in the concept of "professionalism." I haven't felt quite as comfortable at any job since.

I wish I could say that as a psychotherapist and educator working in trans health, I feel safe in my own gender. My clients usually don't know how much I resonate with their struggles to be seen and validated in this binary world.

Some self-proclaimed trans allies can barely tolerate a move from one binary option to the other. They learn to use a new name and pronouns and treat you like a man or a woman, as long as you are just a man or a woman. Gender fluidity confuses them, makes them visibly uncomfortable, and this often incites rage ("just pick one!"). They don't want to do the work to truly challenge their conceptions of gender. Even *I* have to work to unlearn the gender binary I've so deeply internalized, or at least I try not to let it dictate my actions.

8:25 AM

As I walk into the lobby of the large high-rise building I work in, the security guard greets me, "Good morning, ma'am." I've learned that it's not worth my energy to correct people, especially strangers. Yet at the sound of the word "ma'am" my body clenches regardless; "miss" and "young lady" elicit the same physical reaction.

I am irritated by the wasted energy that others put into sizing someone up and choosing a salutation based on not only gender but also age; I'm more annoyed that it even gets to me. To correct the security guard, I would have to put on my emotional armor: monitor my feelings of hurt or anger, try to package my request in an "appropriate" way, deal with the fear in anticipation of how the other person might respond, and be prepared to self-soothe in case the other person gets defensive or hostile. On the other hand, it also takes a hell of a lot of that same emotional labor to put up with being referred to as "ma'am" every day.

Sometimes I wish I had thicker skin. It took a long time to give myself permission to feel the disappointment of getting misgendered. There's nothing wrong in feeling hurt. My sensitivity is a gift that helps me notice and care when shit is fucked up. It fuels the work I do to liberate myself and others from the gender binary.

9:15 AM

I sift through emails and brace myself for the inevitable. My pronouns are "they/them/theirs" yet people (who know my pronouns) refer to me as "she" or "her." There's something more painful about seeing pronouns in print, because, as opposed to the spoken word, writing involves intentional reflecting and editing.

10:30 AM

I'm distracted as I remember the job interview I had the previous day. I applied to be a therapist at a large tech company, thinking that maybe I need a change and that perhaps working in a more general (i.e., non-trans-specific) environment as a mental health provider might give me a break from thinking about gender *all the time*.

The manager who interviewed me asked for my pronouns and my gender identity, then proceeded to tell me about the trans clients she has been working with. I could tell that she was trying to demonstrate being "in-the-know" and "down" with people "like me." At the end of the interview, she asked, "How do you react when people make mistakes about your gender?" I spouted off some line about being used to people misgendering me and not having energy to educate everyone about my gender (which is true). But since the interview, I've been kicking myself, wishing I had asked, "What are you and this organization going to do to support me when that happens?"

So here I am the next day, still mulling over whether to give the manager feedback about her question. It just didn't feel appropriate. It's like saying to someone, "How do you react when you are being sexually harassed?" or "We know our system is racist. What are you going to do when well-meaning people tell a racist joke?" The question really felt like, "How big of a problem are you going to be for us? How uncomfortable are you going to make us feel?"

Sometimes I notice my hesitance to speak out and risk being labeled as an angry trans person, an angry person of color, or, god forbid, an activist. Activists and advocates aren't well regarded in health care; not only are we seen as the enemies of science and intellectualism, but once we start talking about social justice we are no longer seen as professionals. We are written off as being biased and wanting to advance our own agenda.

(I did get an offer, by the way. Though the pay and salary made it hard to turn down, ultimately I had to choose self-preservation. This highlights the choices that many of us are forced to make between career advancement, financial stability, and true respect.)

11:15 AM

I need to use the restroom. So, I am faced with the decision of quickly using one of the gendered restrooms on my floor, or taking the elevator down sixteen floors to use the gender-neutral restroom that was essentially installed just for me at my request. My employer likely expected me to be grateful or impressed, but I can't say that I'm excited about this option.

Workplaces tend to be reactive when it comes to accommodating trans and nonbinary folks. They wait until a trans or nonbinary person gets hired, then they scramble to figure out how to make the environment safe and accessible. In my ideal world, workplaces would do the work before a trans person gets hired or even before they are interviewed. They would figure out their HR policies, restroom facilities, and documentation (e.g., name badges, email addresses, electronic records, computer user accounts) ahead of time. There is always the chance of having employees who do not disclose their trans status or identity, so waiting for the first "out" or vocal trans person to report problems is not really an equitable approach.

I end up avoiding going to the bathroom altogether until I grab lunch at a sandwich shop nearby that I know has a single-stall all-gender restroom. On other days it's easier to just go home.

12:45 PM

I glance at social media, which is a crapshoot. I see posts about trans women of color being murdered followed by posts of celebration for trans youth who are being supported followed by posts about trans youth taking their lives. I notice how quick liberals are to support a binary transition yet scoff at any mention of how racism and poverty influence the transphobia that is killing so many. "But it's getting better!" they say. Not for everyone.

Trans women of color and people whose genders are unintelligible won't have their photo on the cover of *Vanity Fair* or *National Geographic* or *Men's Health*. So many in our community are uninsured or cannot afford copays or even transportation to get the general health services they need, let alone access to medical transition. Then there are those just fighting to live each day and walk down the street without being violently threatened or arrested.

I feel at a loss when trying to convince health care providers that the everyday experiences of trans and nonbinary folks should be just as much our concern as whether they can get surgery.

3:30 PM

My inbox dings with a new email. It's from a listserv of therapists who work with trans and gender-nonconforming youth. In this group, I don't feel like the only one advocating for supporting youth, affirming their right to explore and live in a gender that feels true. I'm also not the only one who is nonbinary or trans. But I am the only person of color (that I know of). It feels lonely to be the one who has to repeatedly remind everyone, "Ahem, what about race? And class?" We cannot pretend that a young trans person of color struggling with poverty has the same experiences or opportunities as a White, middle-class trans youth living in a liberal suburban enclave.

Cookie-cutter approaches to providing medical or mental health care are inherently biased toward the dominant culture, and it takes intention and effort to make sure that these care systems are truly inclusive. I feel exhausted at being the only one who notices, or at least the only one who feels compelled to vocalize it. As a token, I want more from my allies.

I also feel like a broken record player in the repeated conversations about how trans youth are "redefining gender" or starting a "gender revolution." Today's youth didn't invent deviations from the binary gender system. I have to remind people that "nonbinary" predates "binary" in many respects; those of us who don't fit the expectations for what is "masculine" or "feminine" have existed across almost every continent, going back centuries. But one of the impacts of colonization is that histories are forgotten, and not by accident, violently muffled until they don't make a sound.

Being a token can be misleading at first. It can make you feel wanted, admired, and special. Who doesn't want to feel that way, especially after a lifetime of not feeling seen or validated? You hear the message "We really value your unique perspective," which really means "You have something we want from you!" I have to admit that I've been lured in by this message, along with my own savior complex and sense of over-responsibility. When you become a token, it's hard not feel owned by a system that continually pats itself on the back for being so open-minded and progressive for hiring you while simultaneously putting you in your place. Good intentions say nothing about a system's capacity to change. For me, even monetary compensation is no longer the main motivator for being cast as the token because I know there are many hidden, unacknowledged costs, and I choose self-love and self-respect.

5:20 PM

I'm sitting in my private practice office waiting for a therapy client to arrive. I feel immense gratitude for the freedom and comfort that running my own business provides. I can be myself. Overall I feel a sense of purpose and love for the work and the people I get to serve. However, being a trans/nonbinary therapist comes with its challenges. Trans communities are small and interconnected; I often have overlapping social circles with my clients, and I need to be very intentional about protecting my clients' privacy as well as my own.

The work I love the most is healing work; it is the work that I feel I am hired by my clients to do. This is different from making sure that my clients have jumped through all the hoops required by the WPATH *Standards of Care*, including endorsing a Gender Dysphoria diagnosis (whether or not the diagnosis fits). Historically, trans people have needed a mental health provider to "sign off" on their requests for gender-affirming medical care or assistance with a legal gender marker change (this practice continues even today). I resent the history of exploitation and manipulation of trans people and their truths because it stands in the way of clients feeling that they can be honest and get the help they need. They are too busy toeing the line between "too sick" and "too healthy" to let their guards down.

I want my clients to know that they don't need to regurgitate the same medicalized trans narrative in order to be taken seriously. But in this role I am seen as gatekeeper; I am part of the establishment. And rather than try to convince my clients that I am a "good therapist" it is instead my job to make amends for the harm that mental health providers have done to my trans ancestors. I don't get the privilege of a clean slate.

It is an honor to be in the position of helping people heal from the toxic effects of transphobia and cissexism. There is so much beauty in seeing people come alive, shed negative beliefs about themselves, and move forward with their lives.

7:55 PM

I listen to a voicemail message from my mom:

"Hi Sand! This is Mom! Sand . . . Sandy . . . Sand! This is Mommy. How are you? You very busy with work?"

Her messages are hilarious, and I have many of them saved on my phone. She gets my name right 50 percent of the time; the rest of the time she gets a pass. My family is important to me, and if my seventy-five-year-old Chinese immigrant mother doesn't get it right, I still know that she *knows* me. She will never know me in ways that I wish she could, and I grieve that, but she also knows me in a way that no one else ever will.

"I talked to Nancy . . . he said you are writing a book? I hope I can read it! Your dad, she is very busy cleaning out the garage. Let me know when you are free. I want to see you! Say hi to your little pugs from Grandma!"

In her long messages, my mom invariably flips the English pronouns he/him/his and she/her/hers. In spoken Mandarin, there is one pronoun ("tā") used regardless of gender. All my life, my parents, both born in China, have had difficulty with English pronouns. I used to get angry and correct them, which I now recognize as a product of my own internalized racism, that inevitable pressure to assimilate as a child of immigrants. But now I find it amusing! Gendered pronouns are fairly arbitrary in many contexts, and I don't see anything that needs correcting.

9:00 PM

At the end of the day, I feel relief at hiding out at home, at not having to be out in the world, to be perceived or referred to or gawked at. It's easier to feel comfortable in my body and in my gender with no one else around. I don't have to second-guess myself. I don't want my gender to be special or different. I just want it to be what it is.

I'm hanging out on the couch watching bad TV with Theo Chang and Zelda Sesame, and they couldn't care less if I am a boy or a girl.

CHAPTER NINE

Hypervisible

HAVEN WILVICH

MOST DAYS I wish I could be invisible. It's not that I don't want to be seen and heard—I am a very extroverted and opinionated person. In fact I *long* to be seen, not only for who I am, or on the deep soul-searching level of intimate partnership and friendship, but in the most basic human interactions. But there's a difference between being understood and living life under a metaphorical microscope. On some level I get it: people aren't used to seeing a beard and a dress together on one body, except as a joke. And even in a city like Seattle where we have a large queer and trans community representing a broad range of gender expressions, my brand of androgyny still isn't commonplace. The world doesn't give me a middle ground between invisibility and hypervisibility.

Now that I have had a taste of what it is like to finally get to be myself at home, at work, and around my family, I can't go back in the closet. I can't live my life pretending to be a man, wearing clothes that distort my self-image and performing a masculinity I have no draw to achieve. Yet I don't have access to the full range of femininity either. Androgyny is tied up in complicated ways with whiteness and masculinity, where slender-but-muscular genderless bodies are neutral, and any sign of femininity is erased. But for me, these are unattainable standards. When I look in the mirror all I can see is my six-foot-two-inch towering height, my broad muscular shoulders, my huge hands, and my masculine chin, which I've been hiding under a beard for ten years.

I often dream about what life would have been like if I had been born a girl. Some days I desperately wish I could snap my fingers and have a conventionally beautiful, cisgender woman's body. I know being a woman is no cakewalk, though fighting against oppressive gender roles and for basic human rights is in my blood. *That* I can handle. What tears me down is being constantly on watch for the unpredictable things that can trigger my gender dysphoria. I can go into a dressing room and try on dozens of outfits that just don't work for me and be fine. But every once in a while, I encounter one that gives rise to an intense desire to tear it off as fast as I can because it feels so horribly wrong. Suddenly, I don't recognize the face staring back at me. It is like looking through a window at someone else, as my heart tries to avoid admitting it is my own body in the mirror.

For me it is far less about genital configuration and much more about the freedom to be feminine without being questioned for it. Even if I could scrape together the thousands of dollars for vaginoplasty, facial feminization, hair removal, tracheal shaves, and hormone replacement therapy, I would still stand out. It would be frustrating to be closer to the expression I want yet be unable to "pass"—unable to choose invisibility when I want it. Hypervisibility seems to be my fate no matter what route I take.

That is the choice I face every day: Do I hide myself and put on my cloak of invisibility while being tortured internally, or do I show up as myself in a hostile world that rejects my identity? If I wear a dress or capris, I can count on at least half the people around me gawking openly, and the other half trying to do it out of the side of their eyes. But if I wear loose pants and a T-shirt, I will feel intensely uncomfortable all day. And with a beard, I am likely to be misgendered by strangers with "he" and "sir" either way; I have yet to experience a spontaneous public interaction where I am correctly gendered as "they." I blend performance and authenticity because eyes are on me everywhere I go, and because I just want to be me.

There are some days when my gender fatigue is so great that I wish I could step outside the whole system and exist without a gender. Those days I want to give up and not devote a single neuron more to defending my identity. I want the freedom to be myself without having to prove to people on a daily basis who I am. I wish I could throw on whatever I feel like and go to the store without having to delicately balance my dysphoria with my ability to tolerate stares. But my daily reality is one where I can be pinned as trans or "deviant" from across the block. If I'm wearing tight pants and a neutral top people may not notice me until they are closer. Frequently I encounter people who see my shoes, my painted fingernails, or my jewelry, and invariably do a double take. On the good days, the stares from strangers are accompanied by a friendly smile or even a compliment. I know these comments are meant in kindness, but they are also a reminder of how inescapably visible I am. I hear kids say as I pass, "Mommy, why do some guys dress like women?" I wish I knew what answers they were getting from their parents.

In so many ways, I'm one of the lucky ones. I have supportive partners and friends who truly see the many complexities of my identity and gender, both inside and out. I have a job where I can be out at work and a boss who consistently uses my pronouns and helps teach others. I have a family who loves me and genuinely wants to spend time with me, even if they don't understand me. And since I am white, well educated, mostly able bodied, and earn a livable wage, I don't have to face the multitude of other barriers and threats to my physical and mental safety that many of my siblings in the trans community experience.

Even with those privileges, my life is not safe. Just last week, I was walking to my mailbox when I was jarred back into reality by my neighbor across the street as he started yelling transphobic and homophobic slurs and approached me threateningly. I've had my fair share of street harassment before, but something about it happening in my own neighborhood, on my quiet suburban street, really shook me. I'm still scared of walking down my own driveway.

Hypervisibility means that there are few public places I can go where it doesn't take mental alertness to just exist. But there are moments when the hypervisibility of my life is worth it—when gender euphoria overrides the dysphoria, when I feel good in my body loving the things that make me *me*, when I'm finally, *finally* able to look in the mirror and like what I see. Changes that may seem insignificant have often led to those moments: getting earrings or fun purple glasses; trying on a particularly flattering dress that emphasizes my hips and the little natural fat I have in my prehormonal breasts; or reading an official performance review and realizing my manager used the correct "they" pronouns the whole way through. Because of those little steps, I am starting to feel sexier as well. I realized my leg and chest hair was causing a lot of my distress when I looked in the mirror; it was limiting my decision for what clothes I felt I could wear. So, with the help of some very generous friends and supportive allies, I've started laser hair removal (a painful and expensive treatment, but well worth it). Already my legs are easier to keep hairless, which has made me feel a billion times better. I've also been able to engage with my sexuality more fully, shedding the constant shame over my penis as I find more ways to be intimate that are outside of heteronormative ideas about sex. I am now able to get out of my head and just enjoy the moment.

Right now I'm still in a phase of intense exploration of my gender, although parts of it are starting to solidify. Most days I feel a strong sense of a tangible gender that is squarely in the middle—made up of femininity and masculinity, and also containing aspects of neither. Genderqueer is such a broad category, a subset of nonbinary transgender identities that often emphasizes the rejection of social norms and gender roles. It's meant to subvert and not conform. It means living in the gray area between the binary genders and asking a lot of questions. That's part of why I keep my full beard. Even though it does add to my hypervisibility, it is a way of claiming my identity visibly and showing the world I have no interest in trying to "pass" as a woman through my own construction of androgyny.

I long for a world where my actions weren't gendered and I could just interact as a human, where people, trans and cisgender alike, didn't have to carry around the constant pressure of gender roles thrust upon them. Gender is about so much more than just what a person wears. It is tied up in how you talk while gesturing with your hands, or how you walk with a sway of your hips, or how you are highly empathetic and listen without jumping to give advice. But the brain without the body to match doesn't help me fit in anywhere. It doesn't matter how feminine my actions, thoughts, and ways of being are—with a beard and a dress I'm usually not welcome. Men are taught to treat femininity as weakness, and I embody everything men fear. So I've spent my whole life primarily around women, whether that was being the only "boy" in a class or the only "man" in an office. At the same time, there has always been a barrier shutting me out of women's spaces and conversations.

What is the way out of this hypervisibility trap? I wish I knew. I suspect it will get better with generational change. Already we are seeing more varied expressions of gender fluidity and acceptance of nonbinary identities in our young people. When I was first coming out two years ago, I had a hard time finding examples of bearded nonbinary people online, so I decided to start a gender blog and post photos of myself, along with some of my thoughts and struggles. I hope my online visibility is making a difference in changing the way we are allowed to live our gender, although I still don't know whether my daily public presence has changed strangers' preconceptions. Acceptance by some people doesn't make all the hostility of our inflexible systems and norms go away. And since nonbinary people are invisible in most data collection, it is hard for our voices to be heard. The irony of this hypervisibility is that while my body and identity may be open to public comment, my thoughts and needs don't seem to matter. I might as well be an alien (at least I'm a sexy one!).

Until recently, not a day went by that I didn't think about my gender: my presence, the way I was talking, the things I was wearing, or the genderedness of the roles I was either fitting into or subverting. Now, I devote a little less brain space to that consciousness of gender, and it is amazing how much energy I have reclaimed. Feeling seen and heard without the pressure of gender roles and expectations has been liberating. Spaces that are heavy on the BTQ part of the LGBTQ+ acronym don't have as much baggage around the cultural norms and roles, so I have the latitude to let loose among my queer community. But it can happen elsewhere too, even in the most mundane interactions—like when my coworkers treat me more like one of "the girls." Those are the times that I live for.

CHAPTER TEN

Making Waves in an Unforgiving Maze

KAMERON ACKERMAN

BY 8:30 PM I was roaming the halls of a suburban high school, working my usual shift. I slowed down with my cart full of cleaning sup-
plies and sauntered by a full-length mirror in one of the hallways. I saw
myself wearing the same thing: button-down navy blue work shirt, yellow school crest embroidered above the left breast pocket, grey military style cap with the brim pulled low, cargo pants, hiking boots. The
mirror-moment was a big part of my night, every night; I was trying
to see if I could recognize myself. I couldn't. I just looked like a small,
lost person, hiding in a solitary job.

The job felt transitory, and so did I. I flew under the radar; no one
was quite keeping track of me. There were no punch cards or human
relationships grounding me to this place. I just showed up. I was always
where I was supposed to be, but no one would have noticed if I wasn't.
I would say hi to coworkers curtly, but nothing more.

This wasn't just *any* suburban high school—it was *my former* suburban high school, laden with latent feelings and memories. I was a
ghost floating through my oldest haunts: if I saw a former teacher
or the parent of a classmate, I'd lower my head and keep going,

acknowledging their presence in as small a way as I could get away with. I would feel my face flush as shame washed over me. I had been a top student, involved in lots of extracurriculars, and look how far that got me.

Twenty years ago, I walked these same halls feeling full-blown terror. I never made eye contact; I learned to identify people by the shoes they were wearing: a quick glance up at their face to verify, yep, still them, same shoes. The hectic times between periods were the worst: *Just go with the flow. Stop getting into personal-space standoffs with people walking the other direction! Run around these slow moving masses— you're never going to make it to class on time!* And, of course, plenty of internal berating about my appearance was heavily sprinkled in, just to keep me in check: *You gotta make compromises between what you want to look like and how you should look. You are perverse for wanting to wear sneakers and these jeans, wind-pants and puffy vest, cargo pants and hiking boots. There is no chance to fit in.*

What I did fit into was the tomboy trope. By middle school, I was getting plenty of hints I should be growing out of it, but I couldn't. I had short hair and wore boys' clothes, was close with no one, and tried to fade into the background to avoid being bullied. Although I must have stood out, I dissociated to such a degree that it actually felt like I wasn't there at all. I started to self-injure: digging and dragging my jackknife's blade through my skin in an attempt to remind myself I was for real. I also tried really hard at things: I was on the cross-country team, played trumpet in band, and obsessively did my homework on the bus so that I could watch TV when I got home. By high school, I stopped shaving my legs and armpits. I tried growing my hair long, but that was short lived. I tried buying clothes from the mall, but that felt soul crushing. I was in a bunch of AP classes, and I worked at McDonalds and the Goodwill. I was supposed to be figuring out my next move with college and a future, but stress progressed, piling layers and layers of heavy scrap metal on top of the pins and needles of anxiety at the edge of a giant endless pit known as depression.

Things began to fall apart slowly, gradually, and then super fast. One day in November of my senior year, I made it to school—that was all I could manage. I went to my homeroom in a dazed haze, walked out with everyone as the bell rang, then just kept walking, around and around the hallways. Security saw me, but he didn't say anything. I briefly wandered into my friend's art class and told her, in so many words, that I was over the edge. Back in the hall, I ran into my brother, getting a drink, I think. The nurse's office seemed like a potential sanctuary. I had never been to the nurse before, nor had I ever skipped a class. In fact, I had a drawer full of awards for perfect attendance. The nurse let me lay on a cot for one period, but then said I had to get back to class since I wasn't sick. I wandered into to the library, the *real* sanctuary, went to a cubby area, lay my head on my arms, and stayed that way for the rest of the day. The pieces of the world around me had become fractured and splintered, and my sense of self had slipped through those cracks.

When I got home, I convinced my mom I had to go to the hospital. I was there for nineteen days, grasping at anything I could, trying to communicate my experience for the first time ever: gender, sexuality, despair, worthlessness, hopelessness, and, above all, invisibility.

I had suffered from a psychotic break, and was coming back slowly, only to be met with an even wider, gaping pit of depression. Medication wasn't helping; I spent my late teens and early twenties on a lot of different medications (antidepressants, mood stabilizers, antipsychotics) trying to find some balance. None of these worked for me; some even made matters worse. Eventually, I gave up and went off all medications; I just tried to live with my mental illness. Therapy was helping, gradually, but it was a bizarre experience for someone who did not yet know how to speak up.

At eighteen, after a therapy session, I wrote in my journal, "I told Dr. Slankster about the movie, *Boys Don't Cry*. It's the true story about a woman who feels she is a boy, and as a result is beaten, raped, and ultimately killed. Dr. Slankster wanted to know if I ever feel like I'm in the wrong body. She then asked, 'Do you feel comfortable with a chest?' I sidestepped that question. I wouldn't want to be a man though. My personality wouldn't permit it."

At twenty, I attended a presentation held at my college about transgender rights. The girl I had a crush on sat right next to me, and my on-campus counselor sat right behind us both. It was the first time I considered that the term might apply to me. That night, I wrote in my journal, "Apparently, 'transgender' is much broader than I thought. I guess . . . I am transgender? I like the idea of 'boy' but not of 'man.' 'Man' is intimidating and evil and perverse and repulsive and disturbing and . . . *where did these thoughts come from?*" After that, I started experimenting even more with my gender presentation, wearing tight boy's undershirts instead of bras, and boy's briefs exclusively. I regularly cut (or, rather, hacked away at) my own hair, sculpting a rough mohawk or something thereabouts. On one occasion, I shaved it down to my scalp and wore a ski cap that whole spring.

At twenty-four, I pursued a friendship with a drag king. She showed me that by shopping in the women's sections at thrift stores, you could find the most fabulous costume elements, perfect for over-the-top strutting and flaunting. This flamboyant take on masculinity didn't go over so well with audiences, but we were having a blast. We infiltrated the pride parade a few years in a row, wearing outrageous costumes, carrying a boom box playing new wave jams. We were affiliated with no one, just a rogue pair, dancing among the floats and interacting with the crowd.

On Sunday mornings, I would go to a gender identity support group, my stand-in for church. We would convene, sit in a circle, and engage in a very specific, ritualistic dance. The two mediators would welcome us and invite everyone to open up. We all had predictable roles that had been established early on. Here was Kara, who was transitioning on the job as a prison guard; she was the star member of our congregation. She was always well composed and ticking off her journey one bullet point at a time. We would hear her update and then congratulate her on her newest accomplishment. Then Brian would speak up. He hadn't started his transition yet, but he too was commanding and confident. Then with some coaxing, either Kristin or Wesley or Casey would talk, and the struggle would suddenly get real, much more raw and vulnerable. Commonalities would surface: family rejection, job discrimination, trouble making ends meet, substance abuse, even homelessness. I'd sit in the same seat week after week and play the closed-off compassionate empath, the one who always had cautious advice and reassuring words, but maintained distance.

Even here, I was an outsider: the only one who wasn't transitioning. I felt a mixture of envy and admiration, as others in the group worked through real hardships and began their journey with full forward momentum. I had yet to pin down where I was going, stuck in my own self-created anguish, as if I were the sole member of an exclusive club. I *wanted* it that way. I was too out there—a subgenre within a genre of the T within the LGBT, still struggling with the paradox of wanting to stand out and remain invisible.

––––––––––––

By my late twenties, gender had stopped being a fun motif to play around with. I was supposed to have settled into it by now. Anyone I'd known who had identified as genderqueer had made a shift and started transitioning. I came to believe that I too needed to face that decision: to transition, or not. Since that was too heavy to sort out, I stuffed my gender-related feelings out of the way, trying to sink them down into that bottomless pit that was still shadowing me.

Every night, year after year, I continued to stand in my oversized work uniform—button-down navy blue shirt, grey cap, cargo pants, hiking boots—looking at that lost person in the full-length mirror. Outside of work, I volunteered for a lot of different things, but I struggled to actually engage. Even in a group of like-minded people, I couldn't find my voice. I spent a lot of time at home, carving out spaces that felt comfortable, but it was hard when my housemates were always around. I was in a solid relationship by then and surrounded by a group of supportive people for the first time ever, but I didn't know who I was in relation to them. I couldn't be present at parties and potlucks. Or at the gay bar where I did drag. Or meeting a friend for coffee. Or during sex. The only times I *did* feel at peace were when I went swimming or dancing. So I started to go out dancing by myself on a regular basis. I also started going on long solo walks around the neighborhood. I mapped out which streets I had already walked down and kept expanding my circumference.

It seemed to be helping. I felt like I was doing an okay job at juggling the things that needed juggling and squelching the rest. However, things came to a head one summer day. My partner (now spouse), Caitlin, was joining me on one of these walks, and something suddenly bubbled up too close to the surface. Pertinent to nothing, I blurted out: "I'm attracted to masculinity." Then I started crying. Caitlin reacted well, not giving into the fraught situation. They casually said, "one of the many perils of being in a queer relationship . . ." They sensed the seriousness of what I was saying but didn't push it. They let me go at my own pace.

That pace was a snail's crawl. I had a false start with a therapist. Because he was an out gay man, I hoped he might have some answers.

Was I supposed to transition from female to male? Was I actually a gay man, in a long-term relationship with a genderqueer femme? Could this therapist be the person to illustrate what being a gay man was all about?

Our sessions were underwhelming and disappointing. We sat there in silence for the most part. He had a laptop in front of him and would type notes while we talked. He'd look at me quizzically. We didn't even graze the topics I was there to discuss: gender and sexuality. The missed connection was blatant—every appointment was like a date without the chemistry, all awkward silences and visceral tension. We were just not a good match. I gave up after a few sessions.

Another year and a half passed, and I was at another impasse. It occurred to me that I could look up my old therapist, the one who had helped me in the wake of that period of psychosis as a teenager and the debilitating depressions that followed. I had liked her! Was she still around? Yes she was and yes she was excited to see me again and yes she looked exactly the same, and she said the same about me. She was not a gender therapist, but that didn't matter—the connection was instant and gratifying and I felt like I was very quickly making leaps and bounds.

I didn't focus on transition at first. Instead, we addressed some other tricky stuff: self-injury, sex and sexuality, anxiety, isolation, depression. Very early on, she commented that I seemed to be doing an excellent job at minimizing stress in my life. She said, "What if I told you you could ease up on all your self-imposed regulations?" I replied immediately, "No I don't think so." If it appeared to her that my stress levels were low, it sure didn't feel like it!

When we did get around to talking about gender, I made it clear I was searching for a new finality. Previously, I had come to the conclusion that, no, I wasn't going to move forward because if I were, I would have done so by now. And I hadn't, so I never would. I had convinced myself that I must be lacking some internal drive, so medical transition must not be for me. I had settled on feeling neither male nor female, with no need to take any further steps. And I was satisfied with that.

Or so I thought. Once I started to get into it, a bunch of options seemed within reach.

I found myself thinking nonstop about trying testosterone, but it seemed testosterone would take me further than I wanted to go. I didn't want a beard; I didn't want broad shoulders or a deep voice. I didn't want to be read as a man by those around me. I had watched, very closely in some cases, the changes my trans friends had gone through with hormones, and it was hard to think that path could be for me. And as far as I knew, even on a low dose, masculinizing changes would still occur; they would just occur at a slower rate. I could find no information anywhere that told me otherwise.

Was it possible to settle into a perfect dose? One that was low enough so the physical changes would be negligible, yet high enough to make a difference, at least in my internal landscape.

Intuitive reasoning and gut feelings continued to gnaw at my psyche, telling me that hormones react differently with every person. I took comfort in the idea that I could discontinue at any point; testosterone is slow moving and forgiving in that way. I'd have time. There would be leeway. I glommed on to any resources that validated other options and that said there was space in the middle. I attended a national trans health conference annually. As I walked into a workshop titled "Nonbinary Physical Transition," I scrutinized the presenter as an ambassador for what might be possible for me. Were they more masculine than I wanted to present as? Yes they were. Did that mean my goal was not obtainable? I would have to find that out myself. I *needed* to try testosterone.

I chose a topical gel so I could micromanage the dosing on a daily basis. Still, this was uncharted territory. The first time I lathered the gel onto my thighs, I thought about how I had no idea what I was in for. For two days, nothing felt different. Then on the third day, I started to feel something . . . it was a distinctive warm and fuzzy feeling, brand new to me. I felt as if I were immersed in a pile of soft blankets and pillows and stuffed animals. I was walking on fluffy clouds. My clothes were suddenly all made of chenille and satin. These sensations went on for days, weeks, months; they gradually morphed into my new normal.

The first few months on testosterone were an exercise in managing a hyperawareness of my body, thoughts, and feelings. I noticed my upper lip fuzz growing more pronounced. My voice dropping ever so slightly. My clitoris growing. I felt I was nearing my limit in terms of visible physical changes. Freak-out mode struck my consciousness: What if these changes snowballed and I crossed the point of no return? But my inner self was screaming, "Don't stop it!" I didn't.

As I've become more capable of listening to my body, I've been able to effortlessly answer the questions about my sexuality that I'd brought to therapy years before: I'm attracted to my spouse and also I'm attracted to men. Gay-male sexuality is a huge turn-on, but you know what's even better than that? Finally finding ways to interact sexually with my spouse that celebrate how I relate to my body. I don't know what that all adds up to; I just call it "queer." The nature of attraction feels a *little* less cerebral, and a *little* more physiological than before. I like that. My spouse and I talk about all of it. None of it is threatening to them. None of it feels worrisome to me. It's all just puzzle pieces that, although not straightforward or easily translatable, create a complete picture that I'd never been able to see before.

My relationship to pain has also changed significantly. I've stopped self-injuring. My body and the world around me used to feel all jagged, straight-edged, numb, and rigid, but I didn't have *this* to compare it to. I had no idea I was walking around totally detached and watching everything happen from far away, easily getting overwhelmed and dissociating even further. Everyone around me probably saw me as aloof and distant. Some of this anxiety was based in body dysphoria, but the vast majority was just plain old general anxiety, a direct chemical imbalance in my brain.

I had been living in an unforgiving maze I had designed myself, where there were too many rules at every corner—which way to go, when to go, how far to travel. I never ventured beyond the same pathways that would lead to predictable outcomes. Now, walls crumble down around me. I see the sun shining. I feel the path under my feet. Except it's not a path anymore, it's wide-open space; I have the freedom to go any which way I want.

In no way has testosterone been a cure-all. It gave me a solid base of new sensations; I now understand what it's like to inhabit a physical body. But I've tripped up many more times since, including two more hospitalizations in the recent past. Both times, I again became psychotic and manic, with delusions rooted in facets of identity, including gender. I got swept up in wild ideas about my role in the "Transgender Tipping Point," and how I was going to change the world. I thought I was being case-studied. I was on a voyage with a fleet of dazzle ships. Crashing waves lifted me higher than I've ever been.

I'm back down to Earth now; thank you for having me back. I'm medicated again, after years of trying to make do without. For the first time, a psychotropic drug actually feels like a good fit. I have a psychiatrist that I like. But I walk a very thin tightrope with testosterone and my other meds. I'm still customizing exactly how I want to appear, still working out how real I can feel. The idea that a low dose will bring all the changes, just at a slower pace, turned out to be a myth. I observed the slightest masculinization of my physique plateauing and smoothing out, and for years I barely saw any changes at all, which was right where I wanted to be.

Other things do change though. I am now attempting to tip the balance a little further toward "masculine." I got on a regular dose of testosterone injections to see where that might take me. I'm along for the ride, and so far, I like it. I doubt I'll always be comfortable in this spot; most likely I'll be on and off testosterone, at varying doses, for the rest of my life. I also recently got top surgery, after years of deliberating. I continue to be amazed on a daily basis with how incredible it feels to wear clothing that fits my body. Days of feeling frumpy are long gone.

I go to work now, every weeknight wearing a fitted navy blue uniform T-shirt, slim jeans, and hi-top throwback Reebok Pumps. I don't hide behind the hat anymore. The Monday after Caitlin and I got married, I took the hat off and never put it back on. My curly mullet mohawk flies free. I stand much taller, deeply knowing that I own this body. I look at people, I make eye contact. I even chitchat a little bit, change the tones in my voice, make facial expressions. I laugh. I have no idea what shoes you're wearing.

My name is Kameron and my pronouns are he/him/his. Yes, even here at work. The nameplate on the custodial door says, "Mx. Ackerman." There are no mirrors in these halls—I work at a different school now—but there are still mirrors everywhere, in the bathrooms, over sinks in classrooms. I spray and wipe them clean. Whenever I catch a glimpse of myself, I'm no longer searching.

CHAPTER ELEVEN

Life Threats

JEFFREY MARSH

HE TOLD ME where he'd shoot me. Not where in the world, but where on me—where on my body. He told me much more than that, but his message started with where the bullet would go in and where it would come out. He was thorough and detailed. He weaved the story of my murder, and it was the first time anyone had threatened me directly with death. It wasn't the last.

I never thought threats would be part of getting famous. At first, I never even thought about getting famous. Well, I thought constantly about getting famous, but I never thought about getting famous *like this*. I was going to be a Hollywood movie star or a TV star, and for a while I even dreamed of being a Weimar-ish New York City cabaret star. But a Vine star? A six-second video star? You've got to be kidding me.

I remember my friend Jonathan telling me about Vine. "It's weird. You make little looping videos." The app had just come out. Jonathan worked for a high-powered LA talent agency and he heard a rumor that the agency was looking to represent creators from Vine. "You should do it," he said. "You could be a star, a capital-V capital-S Vine Star." My first thought was, *no freakin' way. I am an* artiste. *I have so much to offer. I can't be reduced to a short clip. Six seconds is far too brief for all I have to say.*

I was full of myself. But the circumstances helped me get over that mentality. A possible doorway into a reputable talent agency, the chance to have a career, the ability to spread goodness, not to mention the ability to pay off student loan debt . . . it was all too tantalizing. In the end, only one of these things would happen because of Vine, but it was the most important one: I would spread a ton of goodness. But in the beginning, of course, I wanted money and fame, and because of that I at least had to try this new Vine app.

On that first day, I had to sing a song.

You can hear my partner's voice in that first Vine. My partner is a private person and has never appeared in my social media except for that one word—the word that started my whole messy beautiful starry-eyed scary viral fame: "go." You can hear my partner speaking from behind the iPhone camera urging me to begin. When I look back, it seems silly to spend the first two seconds of a six-second video being told to start, but there it is, the word "go" from the get-go. Then I sang. I sang my heart out for four seconds.

Part of the charm of Vine was that the videos were so brief. A little attention is all it took to hook into a joyful work of art. But this was always secretly sad to me as well. A six-second video is a metaphor for life. We all have so much to say and we all feel like the clock is running down fast on our time to say it. The song I sang in that first Vine was tiny, over almost as soon as it had begun:

Out with the new
In with the Olden Times

Being popular online often means hitting a sweet spot between being hated and being loved. It's hard to create something that haters *and* lovers will share. My first superpopular viral Vine was a dancing one. This Vine was for the Fourth of July. I wanted to celebrate with pride: pride in being genderfluid, pride in my city, pride in my happiness. So I borrowed an all-sequin Statue of Liberty costume from a friend (who always seemed to have stuff like that lying around) and I danced. I kicked up my very high heels with the real NYC skyline as a backdrop. I had a crown, a torch, a book, and a toga all made of bright glittering green shimmer. I was on the roof of my apartment building and I high-kicked and twirled with my iPhone on a minitripod to take a minute or so of video footage. This minute would be culled and honed and pared down to Vine's six-second time limit, creating a pure lean burst of joyful, unabashed glitzy comfortable-in-my-own-skin entertainment. I added Miley's "Party in the USA" as a soundtrack, hit publish, and within a half-hour the video reached fifty thousand views. The video would gain over a million views and beyond.

I have to say, I loved going viral. At the time, I hoped I was creating art. I was happy that the message was getting out far and wide; people were discovering my little corner of love and positivity on the Internet. It wasn't until years later that a friend pointed out some bigots and haters probably shared that video too. Hateful people probably found it so shocking, so queer, so . . . odd that they wanted to share it ironically and simply make fun and be mean. People do that on the Internet sometimes.

People also threaten to kill you on the Internet sometimes. When your profile starts to grow and you become well known and you have some modicum of attention, all kinds of responses pour in. All kinds of people with all kinds of motivations have all kinds of opinions about you. And my first death threat, that description of being shot, was a true turning point for me. It was just after the viral Vine, and I remember reading the threat and thinking *Is this what I want? Is this worth it?*

But there is another side to going viral. My inbox was all of a sudden stuffed with hate, it's true, but it was also instantly filled with kind messages pleading with me to keep making videos. I was getting messages every single day about how my Vines were helping people deal with unhappy lives and desperate times—people were using my videos to get over all the gunk of being human. I heard from fans how they'd been told that who they were didn't matter, that who they were was wrong and bad, and how my videos helped them see those beliefs in a broader context. People would say time and again, "You saved my life. I was thinking about suicide and then I saw your video and I want to stick around. If you can live without shame, maybe I can, too."

Some messages were good, some messages were bad, some were both all at once. That yin and yang of good and bad meant I had some decisions to make. Would being me, and representing the often misunderstood and ridiculed and hated nonbinary community, be worth it? Would the constant and evil and uncontrollable hate that are Internet comments be worth facing? Would the death threats be worth it?

If people were helped, if a life could be saved, would it be worth the negatives of fame? Would it be worth being the target of hate?

Being nonbinary can feel like being a wisp around the edge of heteronormativity. We are ghosts. Sure, we're being recognized more and more—we're even on TV! But, we're still on the edge; enbies[1] are seen as fringe and outside the mainstream. This is a blessing and a curse.

From the outer edges we can live free from the system. I knew that the system of gender was bogus since elementary school, so I never even thought to strive to "be the perfect man." To this day interviewers ask me, "When did you know you were different?" I use that question to make a broader point: I never felt that I was different. Deep down, all of us want the same things—we are all so very much alike. We want acceptance and freedom and recognition and happiness. So I never felt different in the context of whether or not I was a part of humanity. I never realized I was different because I could plainly see that I wasn't. What I did realize (and what I couldn't comprehend or articulate as a kid) is that people *treated* me differently. I knew that I was just like everyone else, but the way I am and the way I express myself seemed to be a huge problem for everyone else. People could never let me be, and it was incredibly mysterious.

I grew up being constantly policed. It's hard for me to remember anybody—another kid, a teacher, or a pastor—who didn't try to butch me up. I knew who I was. I knew what I liked. I knew that Bea Arthur and Wonder Woman were my heroes, not Tom Cruise or Joey from Friends. And the feminine facts, those ways of being, were never a source of internal conflict. I never struggled with wanting to be different than how I am and I can't remember ever wishing I could change. But I always wished that the world would change. I wished people would leave me alone and let me play with Barbies. I wanted the Easy Bake Oven and the hikes in the woods and a sparkly fairy skirt—not

---

1. From Tumblr: enbies = NBs = "nonbinaries" or nonbinary people

just on Halloween but every day. Every. Damn. Day. I didn't get why I was such a burden and an annoyance for adults. And I couldn't understand why it was so violently difficult for everyone else.

My fortitude and surety of character was constantly met with harsh reactions, side-eyes, and ridicule. If people couldn't trick me into "fixing myself" or force me to stay in line through physical violence, they used laughter. Femininity in all forms is still a joke in many places around the world. And, in my case, to be what the world thinks of as a "man" who is feminine is one of the worst sins.

Most people are taught the following sequence and believe it without question for their entire lives:

1. There are (only) two genders.
2. These genders are different and distinct and separate.
3. These genders are unequal.

I have a bone to pick with all three of these ideas, the last being the unfortunate consequence of the first two. An average person never realizes that when it comes to gender, "separate" is the foundation for "separate and unequal." This is why I'm a nonbinary feminist. This is why the nonbinary movement and the feminist movement are so linked. This is why the two movements have so much to offer each other. When I was a kid it was astonishing that people viewed me as a Man when I was so clearly a Disney Princess. But, I never really thought of myself as a Woman. When I was a kid I had a genderless view of myself. And this ungendered view is the essence of gender equality; it is the essence of *people* equality.

Perhaps we should pause here for a moment and clarify something that I'm often asked about and that seems to be a point of grave misunderstanding. I don't want to take away *your* gender. I don't want to abolish gender roles, or even gender rules. I do want to abolish gender assumptions, and therein lies the most exciting part of my identity: I am a metaphor. I am not a metaphor for how "you too can be genderfluid." If you aren't inherently fluid, I would never suggest that you try to be or you pretend to be. I'm a metaphor for being free, for a grander ideal. I am a walking, breathing representation of the fruits of self-acceptance.

I represent one idea and one idea only: how to be you. Over the years I have become an emblem and example of how we can all embrace and accept who we are. I am genderfluid and I accept that. If you are a Man and you love that word, if it feels comfortable, I want you to enjoy that about yourself. I want you to be you.

In fact, I literally wrote the book on this idea. When Penguin Random House decided to publish *How To Be You*, I became the first author with a major publisher to openly identify as genderfluid. I was the first author at Penguin Random House to use they/them pronouns. The book is a love letter to the reader, in which I do my darndest to use snippets of my own life as a vehicle for the transformation of the reader; my self-acceptance is a metaphor for your own. The book tells you that you can love yourself too. I embrace the fact that I'm genderfluid; I never hide it or even downplay it. But I strive to make everything I do less about the labels and more about the process. Everything I do is about how similar we are and how we all deserve to feel free. Whether you are Man or Woman or a Grey-Sexual Demi-Boi, you can express yourself without shame.

I never bargained for being a spokesperson. I still get the heebee-jeebees when I think about "representing the genderfluid community." I do like the attention and the chance to help kids feel better about who they are. But I am also acutely aware of the darkness that comes with the light. I am aware of the straw(hu)man murders that occur online. They don't hate me; they hate the idea of me. But it is still a lot of hate coming my way. I represent a freedom around gender, an idea of freeform identity, and people hate me with enthusiasm. This has true lasting psychological effects.

The hate is unbearable some days. It's reminiscent of the sixth grade, when I tried to end my life. I once made a post about how "everyone wants to commit suicide at some point" in their life. I wanted to help people who were suffering to not feel freakish or alone. The Trevor Project, a major organization that works with LGBTQ suicide prevention, pointed out to me that "everybody does it" is the worst message to send, and that people try suicide or they don't, but no one "commits" suicide. Suicide is not a crime. I had screwed up royally and I had been guided toward a new understanding. I knew that day—in that painful learning experience—that my learning curve was a heightened road, it was completely public, and it had real lasting consequences. I was a role model and what I did and said mattered, whether I wanted it to or not. I represent and affect real nonbinary lives.

To this day the press does still call and email and tweet of course—there are so few of us publicly nonbinary folks. They quote me in magazines and interview me on TV. And I'm not complaining! It's not that I don't want to think of myself as a star. Oh, I do! But I get queasy when the way I represent us means life or death to people like me. I get uneasy when I ponder how a quote I give for a podcast or a phrase I use in an interview could "represent all genderfluid people." What happens if the parents of a genderfluid kid see me on TV, and I blow it? What if I make those parents think of genderfluid people negatively because of a word or an expression I use? What if, because of me, a kid gets kicked out or rejected? I know, I know—perhaps I'm not all that important. But I often think about the real lives I represent, and the real consequences of the work I do.

I feel an immense pressure to get it right—to get our movement right. Of course, a movement is not a thing you "get right" and that's okay. Just having me in magazines and on TV does so much good that it outweighs the harm that may be done to myself personally or to others because of my visibility. At least that's my hope. We're in a very important and unique time of misunderstanding and assumptive approaches to nonbinary identities. While I strive not to say anything that would fuel more hate or write something that would undergird more wrong-headed beliefs about us, I will make mistakes. And when I do, I can manage.

This pressure I feel isn't actually a bad thing: in fact, it creates crossroads and opportunity to make choices that would be unavailable without visibility. Is it worth it to be scrutinized and constantly to blame and/or to praise for The Movement, if I can also convince people that genderfluidity is a natural part of the human experience? Is it worth it to be put on the spot and to give up privacy and anonymity, if the movement moves forward? In all of these questions lies an inherent truth. I only feel the pressure and have grave earnest concern, because I care. I care about our future and our movement.

The reason I know in my heart that fame—and the public scrutiny that comes with it—is worth it is because I live it. Yet even if I worked in an office, I could be the target of these same negative experiences. I would likely feel pressure to represent others and have people make assumptions about me in any setting, even in a more private, less spotlighty life. In fact, humans seem born to deride and judge other humans. You will be judged and blamed no matter what you do, so you might as well do what makes you happy. And being nonbinary famous makes me happy. Being a symbol for something greater—giving a voice to those who are often left out of the conversation—makes me very happy. I didn't exactly make my genderfluid viral internet-fame bed, but I'm happy to lie in it.

Last week, someone asked if I wanted to "increase my profile." I started laughing. I said "I want LGBTQ kids to feel like they are not alone in this world. I want people to feel less desperate."

Whatever happens to my "profile," I want you to feel less desperate.

———————

That death threat was specific. You might even say it was obsessive. Over a series of comments I got all the details including the kind of gun he would shoot me with, how it would feel for me to be shot, how joyful he would feel about shooting me, and even how he would find out where I live in New York City. The threat was real and vivid. The threat was fulsome. It was abundant.

And today, with all I've seen and all of the choices I've made, it is nothing. The threat that affected me so deeply and hit me like a ton of hateful bricks back then is nothing to me today. There are bigger problems to solve than threats. There are bigger reasons to keep going.

CHAPTER TWELVE

Just Genderqueer, Not a Threat

JACE VALCORE

A NINETEEN-YEAR-OLD COLLEGE SOPHOMORE is walking down a sidewalk in the middle of a Midwestern university campus, headed back to their dorm room for the night. It is late in the evening and chilly, so they are walking quickly and with their head down past the rugby field where they compete, past an empty parking lot, and toward the lights of their dormitory. They are wearing sweatpants, a hoodie, and a ball cap, typical attire for any student-athlete. Ahead of them on the sidewalk is a female student headed in the same direction. She catches sight of the athlete walking quickly behind her and begins to visibly panic. She quickens her pace toward the door and unlocks it while staring at the person approaching her. She begins to yell up the empty stairwell that she is "here" and coming to join whoever is inside—a common strategy taught to young women to ward off attackers. The athlete makes no attempt to stop her from shutting the door, because they live in that dorm building, too, and have their own key. They say nothing, but feel anxious and embarrassed to have been viewed as a danger and a threat to another human being.

That was certainly not the first time that I'd been perceived as male, but it was the first time that attribution included the fear that I was a potential criminal threat to another human being. The latter has, sadly, since become commonplace. Fourteen years ago, I didn't have the vocabulary or ability to describe my gender as nonbinary; I was just a rugby player and a "tomboy" struggling with my sexual orientation. Over the next several years my identity would develop and I would find the courage and awareness I needed to come out—first as a butch lesbian, and then more accurately as genderqueer. I have learned that it is not only my masculine presentation, the clothes I wear or the way I walk, that distinguishes me from the women around me; it is my daily lived experience that separates me from them.

None of the public debates or discussions about gender and crime or about access to public facilities includes me or others like me. Transgender men and women who visibly conform to the gender binary have been at the center, with more and more policies allowing them to use facilities that match their gender identity. But this still leaves genderqueer individuals without much assurance of safety or protection. To ensure that I can exist in public space without risk to my physical or emotional well-being, we need to promote gender-neutral or nongendered spaces.

My personal experiences are evidence of the confusion and contradictions caused by society's failure to recognize nonbinary genders. For instance, though I have received the same messages about violence and victimization that women do in American society, I do not live with the same daily concerns that many other female-bodied individuals have about walking alone at night or being harassed at the bar. Women in the United States have been made to believe that they must fear any unknown male, that they must be constantly vigilant and take preventative measures, such as carrying pepper spray, avoiding unlit streets, and walking in pairs or groups. My masculine presentation, however, allows me to move through many spaces with much less care. I do not fear walking alone at night. I do not carry mace or pepper spray. I am perceived by most to be a white heterosexual male and I recognize that my gender and racial attribution provide me with a sense of freedom and safety on the street that people in other demographic categories may not have. But it is severely limited, because as soon as I need to use a restroom, everything changes: I become both a potential victim and a perceived offender.

As any trans or nonbinary person can attest, "gender is a project which has cultural survival as its end, [and] the term 'strategy' better suggests the situation of duress under which gender performance always and variously occurs. Hence, as a strategy of survival, gender is a performance with clearly punitive consequences."[1] Every time I approach a public restroom I steel myself for the confused looks, the fingers pointing to the sign on the door, the questions, and the less common instances of harassment or assault.

One of the most upsetting encounters I've had happened in a restaurant in downtown Houston. I was having dinner with some friends before going to see a show, when, as often happens to human beings, I had to use the restroom. I was anxious when I pushed open the door, but unprepared for someone on the other side attempting to block my entrance while stating, "This is the women's room." She was peering at me from just behind the door, all I could see was her face. Anxiety rushed through me and I stated flatly, "Yeah, I am one." An utterly false statement; I'm genderqueer, I'm not a woman, but I did not want to argue my identity with someone who was controlling my access to the toilet. The woman opened the door and allowed me to enter the small restroom. I stood against the wall behind the door, holding it open frequently to allow people to get through the crowded space without hitting me. She stood next to me, so close that our shoulders were touching, and began to nudge me little by little until I was trapped in the corner. I was standing in my usual protective position when forced to stand in line in a women's restroom: head down, eyes staring at the floor, arms crossed across my chest. I make a point of being as small and as nonthreatening as possible, hoping to avoid confrontation. But on this night, an intoxicated woman thought it was funny to bully me, regardless. She laughed loudly as her friend feebly attempted to apologize and excuse the drunken behavior, but made no attempt to intervene.

That entire encounter is representative of pervasive myths and stereotypes about gender, and their relationship with criminal offending. Gender is a master social status; it determines how one is treated,

---

1. Judith Butler, "Performative Acts and Gender Constitution: An Essay in Phenomenology and Feminist Theory," *Theatre Journal* 40, no. 4 (1988): 519–31.

viewed, and described by others. A very limited understanding of gender as being directly linked to biological sex has dominated American social institutions (e.g., marriage and family), social interactions (e.g., defaulting to sir or ma'am), and the organization of our social spaces (e.g., men's room and men's sports teams always separate from women). The concept of gender developed legally, socially, and academically as a means of acknowledging and addressing the existence of women in contrast to that of men. When we see the word "gender" in the title of an article or book the immediate thought is not "Oh, great! I bet this piece is going to discuss the construct of gender, various gender identities, and how those identities are expressed." No, we recognize the word "gender" to mean "Oh, so it's time to talk about women." And not all women, just cisgender heterosexual women. Lesbian and bisexual women, queer women, trans women, and nonbinary females are discussed separately, in a different article or specific chapter. Similarly, when we hear and see the term "gender identity," we know the topic is focused on trans and nonbinary persons. It is in this way that society ignores and even denigrates the gendered experiences of millions of individuals and views their lives as a different issue or someone else's problem, rather than recognizing that we all have and perform gender based upon our internal sense of identity.

As Judith Butler and many other feminist theorists have long contended, biological sex does not dictate or necessitate anyone's experience. My life is evidence of that. But the overwhelmingly common binary view of gender assumes that being male or female is a universal experience, that all males identify and present as men and therefore experience the world in comparable ways, and that all females identify and present as women and therefore can be assumed to share certain unique experiences. So when an individual, like me, who fails to meet gendered expectations about appearance enters a space designated solely for one sex, they are frequently met with fear, alarm, and even anger. It is immediately assumed that they do not belong to that group, and are therefore assumed to be a threat to it.

As Simone de Beauvoir so eloquently wrote, "One is not born, but, rather, becomes a woman." That process of becoming is both an individual and a social process, involving the development of an internal identity that is shared and negotiated with the world through expression and presentation. It is a constant, ongoing transaction that varies across generations, cultures, locales, religions, races, classes, and the like. For me, the negotiation of my gender is a daily constant. A cashier asks, "Can I help you, sir?" and when I respond, they switch and apologize, "Sorry, ma'am." They think they're being respectful, but it actually makes me feel embarrassed, anxious, unseen. There is nothing feminine about my outward appearance, yet the waiter refers to me and my lunch companion as "ladies"—yet I choose not to correct him because it seems more difficult to do so than to endure being misgendered for the next hour. And when I enter a public restroom, I often must prove two things simultaneously: that I'm not a threat, and that I do have the requisite biological characteristics for utilizing that space.

As a professor of criminal justice at a public university, I regularly teach a course on sex crimes in which students learn that over 90 percent of rapes and sexual assaults are committed by males and that roughly 80 percent of victims are female.[2] Out of context, most readers initially picture the student-athlete in the opening story as a male, perhaps even a black male—after all, cultural stereotypes dictate that an individual wearing sweats and a ball cap is likely to be male. Readers might further assume that since the female student is expressing fear, the athlete *has* to be male, because women have no cause to be afraid of each other—and the idea that a person might be neither male nor female doesn't even occur to them. They make these assumptions because that is the common understanding of gender and crime that they have been given their entire lives: men are perpetrators and women are victims.

In class we discuss the pervasiveness of rape myths based upon faulty and even dangerous gender stereotypes. My students shake their heads when I bring up current cases in which female victims are blamed because of what they were wearing or how much they drank, and judged because they had dared to flirt or have previous sexual partners. They sit in stunned silence when we go over the various studies and statistics that indicate approximately 20 percent of women in the United States will experience rape or sexual assault in their lifetimes, but less than 10 percent of their rapists will ever see a jail cell.[3]

2. M. G. F. Worthen, *Sexual Deviance and Society: A Sociological Examination* (New York: Routledge, 2016).

3. Worthen; RAINN, *The Criminal Justice System: Statistics* (Washington, DC: RAINN, 2017), www.rainn.org/statistics/criminal-justice-system.

Yet the social narrative that males are offenders and all females are potential victims contradicts my lived experience, and that of many others—whether female or male, trans or cis. I was assigned female at birth, but my victimization has been primarily at the hands of women, not men. I am not male, yet I have been treated as a potential sex offender countless times because of the perception that I am a man. Existing surveys and studies about rape and sexual assault do not even ask the kinds of questions that would need to be asked in order to get at these issues; the assumption is that women are the victims of heterosexual males and would never have cause to fear the presence of another female. Hence, the essentialist arguments about keeping "male bodies" out of bathrooms and locker rooms designated for women, even though it is not genitalia that is responsible for rape or assault, perpetuate the misogyny, sexism, hegemonic masculinity, and extremely faulty notions of the performance of manhood that are at the core of this behavior. There is no logical basis to fear being sexually victimized by a stranger in a public restroom, regardless of their biological sex. It is a myth that strangers commit a large portion of violent and sexual offenses:[4] approximately 88 percent of sexual assaults and rapes are committed by known persons, i.e., friends, spouses, family members, and acquaintances.[5] Limited, invalid, binary understandings of gender, masculinity, and crime hurt us all.

Due to advances in both the physical and the social sciences, we can now say with certainty that sex and gender are not binary categories, but exist on a spectrum similar to sexuality. Many scholars and philosophers now recognize that gender can be broken down into three distinct components: physical sex characteristics (i.e., body hair, tone of voice, genitalia), gender identity (one's internal sense of self), and gender expression/presentation (i.e., clothing, hairstyle, mannerisms). Each of those components exists on a spectrum and includes an almost infinite variety of combinations of traits, attitudes, thoughts, and behaviors. However, our laws and social institutions continue to detrimentally focus solely on biological and physical sex characteristics, rather than the expression and presentation of gender identity as masculine,

---

4. C. Mancini, *Sex Crime, Offenders, and Society: A Critical Look at Sexual Offending and Policy* (Durham: Carolina Academic Press, 2014).

5. Worthen, *Sexual Deviance and Society*.

feminine, androgynous, or otherwise, which actually dictate our daily lives.

What is sorely missing from our public policy and social discourse is the process of gender attribution that occurs in each and every human interaction. We rely on audio and visual cues presented in the form of clothing, hairstyle, mannerisms, facial hair, tone of voice, etc. in order to determine whether the person in front of us should be addressed as sir, ma'am, or otherwise. For the most part these cues are implicit and culturally recognized proxies of otherwise invisible physical sex characteristics. It is in that usually subconscious task of attribution, and its consequences, that the impetus for criminal offending and the risk factors for victimization can often be found, especially for genderqueer and nonbinary persons.

The surprised, confused, or angry women that I encounter in public facilities respond as they do because, to them, my short haircut and nonfeminine clothing style are external indicators of a male physical form, implying strength that can overpower them and genitalia that can be used as a weapon against them. It is my masculine presentation and the attribution of male/man made by others, not my biology or even my identity, that protect me against unwanted attention from straight males, attract confused gay males, and trigger fear or anger in many cisgender women. It is the attempt to categorize my gender into one of two invalid options, made by those I come into contact with and share space with, that determines my experiences and necessitates a survival strategy for going to the restroom.

Genderqueer, agender, pangender, gender fluid, bigender, androgyne, etc.—those are all nonbinary gender identities that need recognition; but the words alone reveal nothing about how an individual presents to and interacts with those around them. When we discuss gender and develop laws and policies concerning it, we must take into account not only physical sex, but individual identity, expression, and the social process of attribution.

PART THREE

Community

Creating a Place for the Rest of Us

CHAPTER THIRTEEN

What Am I?

CK COMBS

BOY, TOMBOY, LESBO, LESBIAN, BUTCH

At seven, I knew that I was a boy who had the misfortune of not having a penis. Even though I prayed every night that I'd wake up with one, God wouldn't admit the mistake he'd made. Waking up day after day to find that no change had been made, I started to question the concept of god as all knowing and all powerful.

Adding insult to injury, my mom insisted on trying to turn me into a "little lady."

Against those authority figures, I honored my truth as best I could, wearing boy clothes whenever I was allowed. Little by little, my mom—with the help of the church, my peers, and society at large—wore me down until I gave in and accepted their truth. My mom explained to me that I was a "tomboy," just as she had been when she was younger. She assured me that it was perfectly fine to be a tomboy, and would I please sit up straight and not walk like a football player. I saw this as a compromise: I would have to be a girl, but I could be one that was kind of boyish and liked to do boy things. It wasn't the best solution, but I didn't know any alternatives at that time.

I was born in 1964 and hit puberty thirteen years later. The terms "transgender" and "transsexual" existed then, but were not used widely until the 1990s, which is when I became aware of them. I didn't have the vocabulary to describe myself as a person whose sense of gender didn't match my body when I was seven, or thirteen, or twenty, or thirty . . . I spent decades bouncing from identity to identity, looking for something that aligned with the real me. It's almost impossible to form a sense of identity without the words to describe yourself.

I was still calling myself a tomboy into junior high. My classmates picked up on my otherness; shortly after entering eighth grade, some girls started a rumor that I was a "lesbo." I vehemently denied their accusations, though I really didn't know what "lesbo" meant— I just knew it was bad and as close to being a leper as you can get in junior high. For three quarters of the school year, I was on my own, an outcast no one would claim as a friend. I was harassed and bullied by both girls and boys, all of whom seemed downright gleeful to have someone to pick on. My time in the negative spotlight ended that spring when the bullies found new victims.

In high school, I did my best to fit in. I tried wearing makeup and shaving my legs. I went to a couple of dances with boys. I had mostly forgotten about the eighth-grade rumor when I was approached by an underclassman who told me she had a crush on me and that she'd heard from one of my classmates that I was a lesbian. I'm sure I blushed to the roots of my hair from shock and fear. I stammered something about it being just a rumor, yet I couldn't escape the growing feeling of recognition. Later that night, I had to admit that I liked the attention from her. I liked the idea of a girl having a crush on me. Did that mean I was a lesbian, after all?

By the time I graduated from high school, I'd had a girlfriend for a year and a half and spent a lot of time hanging out with a small group of other lesbians. One of my friends told me that I was "butch," which meant I was a masculine lesbian. I liked that word; it made me feel tough and rebellious. Being a lesbian in high school in 1982 was a radical act and taking on the label of "butch" helped me feel tough enough to shrug off the homophobic taunts that were the norm.

By my eighteenth birthday, I'd tried on five gender/sexual identities and thought I'd finally arrived at the one that would stick.

STONED HIPPY ROCKER, POLITICALLY ACTIVE QUEER DYKE

In my twenties, I settled into young adulthood and tried to figure out where I fit in with the lesbian community—both locally and in the larger sense. In the early 1980s, the lesbian community was heavily flavored with separatism: men were the oppressor and anything masculine was the enemy, including butch lesbians and penetrative sex. Nonrepresentational dildos were the rage (and you didn't admit you liked the other kind unless you wanted to invite scorn or shunning). Butch/femme dynamics were seen as anachronistic at best and patriarchal at worst. I suppressed my butchness and grew my hair out.

For about a decade I was distracted by rock and roll, marijuana, and the circle of gay men my girlfriend and I hung out with. We didn't spend a lot of time with other lesbians; I followed the lead of my gay brothers by adopting some of their mannerisms and tastes in clothing and music. I didn't go so far as to admit my growing attraction to masculinity. Pot dulled the edge and made it easier for me to ride along with what everyone else was doing, quieting voices and desires that I feared would lead to rejection.

In my late twenties and early thirties, I stopped smoking pot and stepped out of the haze, feeling the first stirrings of political activism. The early 1990s brought the end of the Reagan/Bush era and the dawn of the Clinton era. Political conservatives, energized by religious-right evangelicals and the AIDS epidemic, were pushing for anti-LGBTQ laws, Don't Ask, Don't Tell, and DOMA. Queers began to push back with ACT UP, Queer Nation, and other local and national movements. Pride events were expanding out from the larger cities to smaller cities and towns. I'd made the June Pride pilgrimage to Seattle for their pride celebration for several years, before marching in Olympia in 1992—only the second time Olympia had held a march. Walking from the state capitol steps down to Sylvester Park with about a hundred or so others, while curious and sometimes hostile bystanders stared and called out to us, was a very different experience than the anonymity of a big city pride event. It was a huge step to be so visibly queer in a place where there was the possibility of being seen by coworkers or people who knew my parents.

By the end of that day, I was hooked. I started describing myself as queer and a dyke. Older lesbians in the community often visibly cringed at those words, but I liked how in your face those words sounded. I liked that dykes were not soft and accommodating; they were a slap in the face of assimilation.

I've had a long-term, love-hate relationship with assimilation. On the one hand, belonging to a group and feeling the warmth of that kinship and understanding is appealing. On the other, none of the groups ever fit me exactly. I would try for some period of time to blend in, eventually realizing that there was too much of me that didn't fit, as if I'd tried to stuff myself into a box that was too small. The search for identity became like a journey through a series of rooms. I'd enter at one end and mingle, happy for the companionship. Eventually, I'd find myself at the other end of the room trying to find an exit, but not knowing where to look. Even if I saw the exit, I'd sometimes linger, unsure what was on the other side, knowing I didn't really belong where I was, but with no assurances the next space would fit me any better.

The early 1990s brought people out of their closets and into activism with increased visibility. The gains came slowly, but more and more people were taking that risk and pushing back against political and social oppression. Though most of the organizations serving our community were dominated by lesbians, bisexuals, and gay men—with goals that reflected their priorities and concerns—transsexual people were beginning to make noise, too, stepping in from the fringes of the movement. Trans people were not welcomed with open arms by the LGB movement at large, even though they had taken a pivotal role in initiating the movement.

The reaction of lesbians to butches who chose to transition was harsh; trans men were seen as traitors and woman-haters looking for a way to cash in on patriarchal power. I remember feeling abandoned by them, as though their choice to embrace masculinity and male identity was a repudiation of me as a masculine woman. Fast-forwarding to the present, it's hard for me to understand why I would take it personally. I remember hearing about Sam, an acquaintance I saw regularly at the gay bar in town. I remember the rumor mill on fire with the news that *she* was going to be a *he*, and wasn't that awful? What was wrong with her that she thought being a man was the better option? Clearly that meant she was rejecting women and femaleness and choosing to be a man as an easy way out rather than staying in the feminist, queer trenches with the rest of us. What a shame.

There's bile in my throat as I recall how I nodded in agreement and repeated those condemnations. Yes, the butches who transitioned left the lesbian and queer community, and maybe some of them left voluntarily, but certainly many weren't given a choice. The community rejected them, as well as their partners and girlfriends. Twenty years later, when I finally opened my heart to the possibility of my own transition, those words of condemnation came back to me in the voices of others. There are still lesbian feminists who angrily denounce transitioning butches as traitors and victims of the patriarchy, and who declare with utter certainty that anyone taking that path cannot call themselves a feminist or an ally to women. It's a bitter pill to swallow, when those words are aimed at me, knowing I'd once said the same things.

At the time, I didn't identify as trans and my memories of being a boy were clouded by the reframing that happened during my adolescence. I do remember feeling a frisson of recognition, an identity spidey-sense trying to get my attention. I pushed it down, choosing the community I was familiar with over an alternative that would lead to my exile.

As the 1990s turned into the 2000s, I returned to and finished college, bought a house and started a family with my partner. Being queer and a dyke was close enough to the truth that I could put identity questions aside for a while and concentrate on the challenges of being a parent and a homeowner and embracing the middle-class dream of upward mobility.

REAWAKENING, RECLAIMING, RETURNING

As I entered my forties, much of my life had become routine. My partner and I were in a good place: we'd bought our second home and were trying to add to our family. I had time to think about deeper things, like who was I and what was I meant to do with this life? As I dug deeper into those questions, I began to reclaim elements of myself that had been shelved since my youth.

Reuniting with my first girlfriend, whom I hadn't seen since I left high school, helped me reconnect with my butchness. Rediscovering my butchness brought back a connection with masculinity that had been lost for decades. And that in turn brought back memories of the time when I was a boy. These revelations didn't come easily; I questioned everything I thought I remembered before eventually accepting the truth. I *had* been a boy once, and had abandoned him to fit into the world my parents, school, and church believed in. These realizations were part of what inspired me to begin writing about my exploration of gender and identity. I began to rebel against many of the constraints I'd previously allowed myself to be controlled by.

It was a time of rebirth. I accumulated the symbols of masculinity that my younger self loved and longed for and that my adult self had suppressed a desire for, small things that I never allowed myself in order to avoid uncomfortable questions—chunky watches, cutting my hair shorter than ever, shopping in the men's section, pocket knives, men's underwear and deodorant, and using a packing penis. For a couple of years, I reveled in my butchness and believed I'd finally found my identity space in the world.

That certainty was temporary. As my reading and exploration of gender continued, I found two new labels that seemed to fit me even better than "butch"—genderqueer and nonbinary. I discovered it was possible to be neither female nor male, to incorporate both, or neither. As I looked back on my history, I recognized times I had been adamantly male, and others I had been stridently female and queer, and other times when gender hadn't had much meaning for me. It had never occurred to me that I could occupy any or all of those spaces without restrictions based on binary gender.

Getting myself to the point where I accepted that there was an alternative to male or female took a couple of years; trying to explain it to other people has been an ongoing difficulty. I remember when I sat my wife down to talk to her about not being female, *exactly*, and also not being male, *exactly*. She asked me how I knew I wasn't female and why I couldn't be *female* in a way that matched how I felt. I responded with "Well, how do you know you're female? You just know, right?" I was defensive and frustrated that I didn't have any other way to explain myself. How do you convince someone of something they can't see with their own eyes or understand through their own experience?

At that time, I only knew about one kind of transition: it involved a predefined series of steps meant to bring a person from one side of the gender binary to the other. This didn't fit with my genderqueer identity. I hadn't realized there were other ways to transition until I went to a workshop at Gender Odyssey[1] on Genderqueer Transition. Micah, the session presenter and blogger behind *Genderqueer.me*, introduced us to the concept of transition as a series of options. We could see these options as a buffet, selecting the items we wanted and leaving the rest behind. We could choose to socially transition rather than medically transition, for example. This workshop was a pivotal moment for me; it's not hyperbole to say it blew my mind wide open.

With this new information to ponder, I came up with a plan for myself that would honor my identity as a masculine-leaning genderqueer. I decided to change my legal name and begin taking testosterone. I wasn't sure I'd take "T" forever, but I knew I wanted to try it. Coming up with my plan was the easy part. Once again, the hard part was telling my wife. I didn't tell her right away; instead, I kept working out what it all meant for me. I wanted to be sure of my choice before I talked to her. My delay had everything to do with my fear about how she would react; I had watched her reaction to close friends transitioning and it hadn't been easy for her to accept.

By the time I told her about my desire to start testosterone and change my name, I had been immersed in the process of figuring out my identity for a few years and seriously considering transition for almost a year. Having arrived at a decision, I wanted to start right away. My wife, on the other hand, was taken by surprise. She explained it to me this way: "You've had a couple of years to process what you're telling me, but you don't want to give me any time at all." I'm not proud to say that my first reaction was defensive. Later, I was able to acknowledge that I had put her at a disadvantage by holding out so long. We are still working through the ways my approach and her reactions have impacted our relationship. Among other things, she is struggling with her queerness being rendered invisible as I now pass as male among strangers. I also struggle with the erasure of my obvious queerness, and sometimes feel guilty for having chosen this path for both of us. Like her, I can no longer take for granted that other queers will see me and recognize me as one of their tribe. I don't know when, or if, the pain of this invisibility will ever ease.

---

1. Gender Odyssey is an annual summer conference in Seattle, Washington, for the trans community, their families, and their health providers.

Fortunately, my transition didn't damage the relationship with my parents, although telling my mom I was changing my name, and hoping for her blessing, was a difficult conversation. The name she gave me was something she made up herself, and I cherished the story behind it even as I wanted to christen myself anew. She had to take some time to work through her feelings, but reassured me she loved me and supported my decision.

Coming out to my employers was nerve-wracking. I spent several days considering how to approach it, rehearsing what I would say about my new name and upcoming physical changes due to testosterone. I was pleasantly surprised to receive no pushback from my manager, who asked me how I wanted to notify the rest of the company. I chose to send the email myself, clearly articulating what I wanted from all of them in terms of acknowledgment and respect for my pronouns. Most of my coworkers were male and amazingly supportive, to my happy surprise.

The easiest part of this coming out process was talking to my kids. My youngest, who was almost four when I started taking testosterone, has always referred to me using he/him pronouns and has called me both "mommy" and "dad." One of her terms for me was "he-mommy." Even now at eight, she doesn't see a problem in calling me "mommy" while using he/him pronouns. My eldest, who I gave birth to, was fourteen and had a lot of questions about the process and how I would change. We'd been having conversations about gender identity for a couple of years by then, and I'm sure that helped a lot. He had one demand for me: that he could keep calling me "mommy."

Dealing with strangers was both easier—less emotional investment in their response—and harder—they had less reason to be kind and less motivation to understand. Before I started medical transition, I was assumed male most of the time, with the remaining occasions becoming more and more jarring. Once I decided to transition, something in my energy must have shifted because I was seen as male more and more of the time, even before changes to my voice and face became apparent. And though I prepared myself for odd looks, hostile reactions, and questions, I found that people tended to react to the energy I was putting out. As my confidence in my masculine presentation grew, the assumption by strangers that I was male became increasingly the norm.

I used to rehearse what I'd say if someone questioned my gender in public. I always imagined it would be an adult and I'd pop off with

"No" or "Yes" or "All of the above." Turns out, adults don't typically ask those questions, but kids sometimes do. Children are wonderfully honest and direct; when adults can't figure out my gender without asking, they react with embarrassment, irritation, and, sometimes, anger. These reactions used to confuse me. Why embarrassment and anger? What had I done to them?

I finally realized that confusion and embarrassment are onramps for fear—fear that we don't know what's going on, fear that others will mock us for that ignorance, fear that we'll embarrass ourselves by incorrectly gendering someone and have to deal with their anger or the derision of our peers. My androgyny didn't threaten them physically, but the confusion it caused translated into an emotional threat. For people who cling to their worldviews like life rafts, having that worldview challenged is a threat. And I have found that people who cling to biology-based binary gender are *very* threatened by those of us who cross gender lines or don't believe in those lines at all.

Fear is a strong emotion and it does a great job of keeping us out of mortal danger. It also does a fine job of directing us to avoid discomfort, confusion, embarrassment, and a host of other nonfatal outcomes. I wonder where I would be now if my mother hadn't been fearful of my masculinity, or if I hadn't been fearful of rejection. Where would I be now if I'd responded to my desires rather than my fears?

It's easy to fall into second-guessing about what I would do if I could go back in time. I now have a vocabulary and understanding that were nonexistent when I was a child. Back then, I was marooned on an island of misfit gender with nowhere to turn for validation or support. Certainly, if I were experiencing my childhood now, in the age of trans activism, Gender Odyssey, and the Internet, things would be different. I do sometimes imagine what it would be like if I had taken hormone blockers to keep my breasts from growing and if my parents had called me "son" and used he/him pronouns. What would my body feel like if I had taken testosterone earlier, when it could influence my skeletal structure as well as my muscles? Where would I be mentally and emotionally if I wasn't still battling the demons who were born during the years when I had to masquerade as a girl in order to survive?

As appealing as that fantasy is, I can't rewrite my story at this point and I'm not sure I would—at fifty-three, I know I've benefited from the whole journey. I think about all I've experienced and learned by being a woman—lesbian culture (fraught as it was), learning about sex as something other than penis-in-vagina, experiencing sexism firsthand, pregnancy and childbirth, building an authentic understanding of misogyny and feminism, and the ability to step into male privilege with that knowledge.

Is my identity a destination waiting at the end of a long journey? Or is it more like a shopping trip where I try on different looks and styles until I find one that fits? Each time I made a new discovery about myself, I breathed a sigh of relief because it felt as though I was finally "there." Each time, without fail, I would get to a point where I was questioning my identity again.

When we are asked, "What are you?," the only true answer is "This is what I am right now." Everything I've been through and all the identities I've embraced have been true to me. Right now, I am at a unique intersection of identity that includes what I wear, whom I love, my current passions and fears, my deepest held secrets, hopes, and dreams. Right now, I am a writer who is polyamorous and a parent who is trans and nonbinary. Right now, I can simultaneously feel good about the work I've done to discover and honor my authentic self and also acknowledge that I'm not nearly finished with the job of answering the question "What am I?"

CHAPTER FOURTEEN

Questions of Faith

JAYE WARE

I'VE BEEN ASKED about my transition many times, and I never really know how to answer. I know how people expect me to answer. I could reel off a list of milestones that happened along the way: Coming out as a trans woman. Starting hormones. Passing as female. Changing my name. Coming out as genderqueer. Cutting my hair short. Changing my name (again). Getting a date for surgery. As major as those events might have been at the time, they aren't what my transition was actually about. No, my transition has been going on far longer, and encompasses much more. It is the story of how I became the person I am today—of which my gender identity and expression is only a part.

I undoubtedly knew I was different by the time I was a teenager. I didn't feel like a boy, but didn't feel like a girl either. However, that inner gender turmoil was always upstaged by my desire to be "normal" and fit in; being my true self meant nothing to me compared to belonging to something.

For a long time, my faith gave me the sense that I had a place in the world. I went to church, was part of a Christian youth group, read the Bible daily, and camped at Christian festivals. Christianity came first and foremost in how I identified; everything else, including my gender, was relegated to insignificance.

If you go by media depictions of Christianity, you might imagine that there are two warring tribes of Christians, with liberals rushing to embrace queers into the church, and conservatives fiercely opposed. That wasn't the Christian environment I grew up in. Some people held strong views either way, but generally everyone avoided talking about sexuality—or anything controversial—altogether. This silence was particularly resonant in my home church, which had split a decade earlier in two over the issue of homosexuality. Although I was part of the more liberal remnant, it never actually felt like it. Being queer may not have been condemned, but it wasn't spoken favorably of either.

I was left searching for answers alone. I didn't know what my weird gender feelings meant. I found plenty of Christian viewpoints online, ranging from "there is nothing unchristian about being queer" to "anything gender atypical is sinful"—all of which just added to my confusion. I went through periods of feeling intense guilt, thinking that my gender feelings would go away if I ignored them or just prayed hard enough. There were other times when I felt God might be able to love me just as I was. But throughout this time I always had doubts. How could I, a teenager, possibly be certain about what God thought?

Questions of right and wrong were central to how I felt about my queerness as a teenager. The confusion and guilt was also compounded by fear. I was terrified of being thought abnormal; I dreaded the mere possibility of being rejected by my friends, family, or faith community. My solution was to never confide my gender issues to anybody. I hoped that experimenting with my feminine side while alone at night would satisfy the gender conflict within me. It didn't. I only became *more* comfortable with my nonmale gender identity, which in turn made it harder to keep up a masculine façade in public.

By the time I reached university, I had drifted toward a more androgynous style. I was still committed to remaining silent about my gender, which meant acting like a gender-conforming man. That's why I didn't have any qualms with joining my university's Christian Union. Despite being known for its homophobic teachings, it was a vibrant, active campus group with plenty of opportunity for connection and belonging. I also joined a lively evangelical church that emphasized community volunteering. I wanted to be part of a faith that was about doing good as much as saying nice words on a Sunday. I surrounded myself by many people who would have judged me harshly for being queer. But that didn't matter to me: I had no intention of them ever finding out.

Around Christians I would put on my masculine act, but I'd embrace my androgyny the rest of the time. When I look back, it is as plain as day that I was heading for a fall. I thought I could balance my need to conform against my desire to be comfortable in my own skin.

The inevitable happened sooner rather than later. One day while walking to campus I bumped into somebody from my Bible study group. On that day, I happened to be wearing nail varnish and eyeliner. I hadn't thought I'd transgressed the rules of masculinity *that* far, but the look of disgust she gave me very quickly clarified that, indeed, I had. We both continued along our separate ways silently, but I knew I'd messed up big time. I attended one more Bible study session in the vain hope that all would be forgiven and forgotten. But it only took that one woman's contemptuous stares and snide comments to make me hate every moment. When word got out afterward, I was written off by the Christian Union as gay: I was no longer welcome, and none of them would speak to me.

This rejection didn't come as a surprise; I had known all along what their attitude toward queer people was. Still, it stung like hell. The silver lining was that it finally gave me the impetus to confide in others about my queerness. It was a Friday evening, and I'd already spent the week trying to find the courage to tell my friends, but had chickened out at every chance. Finally, out of desperation, I came up with a plan I couldn't back out of: I arranged to meet them at our local pub, and I'd go wearing one of my skirts.

Walking the mile or so to the pub on my own was nerve-wracking, and I still hadn't worked out what I was going to say. Every worst-case scenario played through my head, and many times I wanted to turn back and head home. When I did meet my friends, it was rather anti-climactic. Nobody seemed particularly surprised and the only reactions were compliments about my outfit. Over the course of the night and the following weeks I did my best to explain my gender and answer their questions. I called myself gender confused, gender questioning, a crossdresser, transgender, trans woman, neither woman nor man . . .

I could have come out in a less risky manner, or given more thought to what I was going to say. But opening up about my gender helped me make sense of how I felt and, more importantly, focused me on what

I wanted to do next. Continuing to live as a man didn't feel like an option anymore.

Transitioning to female seemed like the obvious alternative. After a couple more months I was calling myself a trans woman. I was worried people wouldn't take my transition seriously if I expressed any doubts, and I lacked the self-assurance to assert my gender as anything else. For the next three years my goal became to pass as a woman.

I came out to my parents and friends back home during the next university break. I come from a small village in England where everybody knows everybody else's business, so it didn't take long for news of my coming out to spread. I began hearing from friends and family what people thought of me. It wasn't all bleak, though I did lose friends because of it. There were people within the church I had grown up in who viewed my transitioning as immoral and wanted nothing to do with me. The Christian Union's rejection was one thing, but on top of that, folks from my home church not accepting me . . . it tore at my soul.

In the end, I don't know if my faith community rejected me or I rejected it—or both. I never went back to my home church, or any other church. I don't know how many people in the congregation would have been truly unwelcoming—possibly only a handful. But the possibility was enough to crush any hope that I could simply go back as if nothing had changed; a few hostile people were as bad as the whole church condemning me. It would have turned *me* into a divisive issue, and I didn't want to risk being responsible for any disagreements or falling-outs. My village church simply meant too much to me.

It would have been possible for me to continue along my Christian path. I could have joined a queer-friendly church, surrounded myself by Christians who couldn't care less what my gender was or wasn't. But these experiences left me feeling angry, hurt, and questioning whether Christianity was right for me. I couldn't get past the uncertainty instilled by knowing that pastors and bishops continued to debate the morality of my very being.

I began exploring other spiritual paths, from Wiccan to Buddhist to Unitarian traditions. Without a single religion to hold on to, I focused more on what felt right to me. My values were still centered on love, forgiveness, compassion, and charity, but other paths now fulfilled my spiritual yearning and enabled me to grow as a person.

I found Wicca's "live and let live" approach to morality liberating, freeing me from the paralyzing cycles of fear and guilt that I and my gender feelings were sinful. Wiccan ideas around gender shifted my perspective on being trans and helped me feel more at ease about it. Wiccans believe that the Divine comprises a goddess and god working in equal partnership. If the Divine has female and male aspects, then how can there be anything shameful about my having experienced life as a man and as a woman, or not identifying entirely as either gender?

I followed the path for several years, but I still read widely about other faiths and traditions. The ideas in Eastern religions resonated with me, particularly Buddhism and the mindfulness it espouses. By focusing my attention on the here and now, my moments of insecurity, worrying about the future, and obsessing over past mistakes became a bit more manageable. At a time when I was figuring out where I was heading in life, Buddhism offered a more structured way of thinking through what's right and wrong.

However, I found some of the Buddhist ideas to be uncomfortably at odds with my previous ways of thinking. Buddhism teaches that desire is unhelpful; it leads to suffering since it causes one either to fixate on what one doesn't have or to worry about losing what one does have. There is also the idea that there is no such thing as the self, and clinging to self-identities leads to suffering as it constrains us to being a particular way. These ideas made a lot of sense to me—until I tried reconciling it with how I felt about my transition. Wasn't I desiring to have a particular body? Wasn't I desiring to be perceived in a particular way? Wasn't I focused on fitting into a particular gender identity?

I had fallen into the habit of thinking about my transition in terms of wanting to fit some ideal image in my mind. In reality, that image had changed over time, and I still wasn't certain what I wanted my complete transition to look like. Gradually I shifted my focus from how I wished my body or society were different to what I could do to lessen my gender discomfort moment by moment, trying to let go of everything else that was outside my control.

For a long time I remained halfway between Wicca and Buddhism, following elements of both. Eventually I reached a point where I was turning to my Wiccan goddess and god less and less. I had begun identifying as genderqueer, and was finding it harder to connect with the many Wiccan ideas and rituals that focus on gender in terms of female and male. I celebrated one last Sabbat, and with a heavy heart let go of my Wiccan goddess and god.

Despite this, I don't feel that my spiritual self at its core has radically changed, and it is still as much a part of who I am. Christianity, Wicca, Buddhism—they all share similar messages about loving thy neighbor, not harming other beings, and being compassionate. At different times in my life they have all given me a belief structure that has helped me make sense of who I am and my place in the world.

Like with my spiritual meanderings, I had no idea where my transition would eventually lead. When I first came out, I dreaded the thought that being transgender might be the first thing people saw when they looked at me. Over time I got fewer stares and transphobic comments from strangers, yet passing as female was never completely possible. Too many people had known me before and during my initial transition. So when I graduated from university, I took it as an opportunity to make a completely fresh start.

I moved to Scotland, where nobody knew my past. For the next two years the only people I confided in about being trans were other trans people and a handful of queer friends. At first, passing as female was a massive relief. It alleviated the mild disorientation and confusion as my mind tried to process an image at odds with how I saw myself. Dysphoria was not something I constantly felt; there were days when it was particularly bad and other times when my mind was able to internally translate an incorrect pronoun before it agitated me.

The most significant part of my transition was social, yet there were still times when my body caused me intense discomfort. I didn't feel comfortable with the body that I had, but managed to ignore those feelings for the most part. When I came out as a trans woman, all those feelings came to the fore. My body was a constant reminder of being male assigned at birth.

Attending a gender clinic and starting hormones seemed like the obvious course to take. Estrogen helped with being seen as female. Knowing that I was doing something about my situation helped me feel more self-assured. I had my mind set on surgery as well, and was counting down the days until I could get a referral from the gender clinic.

Passing as female eased the dysphoria associated with being misgendered. But I also found passing as female stressful. It felt similar to when I was seen as male; I was still driven by a fear of not fitting in, scared of being different, always anxious that somebody would think of me as "less than a woman." Over time I began to experience moments of disorientation, the same unsettling I had experienced when I was misgendered as male. They were easy to ignore while they were infrequent, but gradually I began to have more and more doubts about my identity as a trans woman. I knew I wasn't a man, but I still couldn't quite work out what having a female gender identity should feel like.

When I started reading more about nonbinary genders, something clicked: this was describing my experiences perfectly. It took me a while longer to fully accept it. I still felt shame about being trans, and was terrified of the idea of being a nonbinary person in a binary-gendered society—the epitome of standing out. But it became a lot harder to ignore how I felt when I was perceived as female. I knew I had to come out . . . again.

Coming out to friends for the second time was just as nerve-wrecking. I was worried I wouldn't be taken seriously, especially since I was having to admit that my previous coming out was a mistake. In reality it went a lot more smoothly than the first time, eased perhaps because my friends either were in the queer community or had previously been supportive of my initial coming out.

This happened just before I entered graduate school, so it felt like the perfect opportunity for another new start. I cut my hair short, and presented my gender more ambiguously. I changed to a gender-neutral name and asked others to use neutral pronouns for me. My experiences at university were mostly positive, and as a whole people were accepting and respected my pronouns. This transition was made easier by joining student societies that sought to be safe spaces. I made friends with people who were already accepting and knowledgeable about nonbinary identities, where my gender was never a big deal.

Outside of these spaces I found it more challenging, not because of people's reactions but because I repeatedly needed to come out to everyone I met, ask them to use my pronouns, and correct them when they got my pronouns wrong. Sometimes it required explaining what nonbinary meant and answering the same questions over and over. I don't mind educating people, and I much prefer telling people my pronouns than being constantly misgendered. However, it took time getting used to doing it and figuring out how best to say it. At times it is exhausting and stressful. To this day I still don't feel comfortable asking or correcting people about my pronouns. There is always a fear at the back of my mind as to how people will react, and I worry about turning my pronouns into a divisive issue.

Coming to terms with being genderqueer brought me to question whether I wanted hormones and surgery at all. Weighing up the options felt an impossible task: How could I possibly know for certain whether I'd feel better having a lifetime of estrogen or testosterone, a penis or a vagina? Unable to figure it out, I opted for the status quo, continuing to take feminizing hormones. I put off any decisions about surgery, as ill health would have made that impossible for the foreseeable future anyway.

Five years later I was still struggling with the question of surgery. I found very little information about nonbinary people having bottom surgery, and worried about being unusual for even considering it. But I needed to do something to lessen the discomfort I felt about my body. That I'd previously been wrong about my gender identity left me with doubts about trusting my own judgment, and for the same reasons, I was reluctant to share these doubts with anyone else. I was scared that I'd continue to feel discomfort afterward, but this time for my body being too feminine rather than too masculine.

In the end, I chose to have surgery—a labiaplasty without a vaginoplasty. Having feminine external genitalia without a vagina felt like a middle ground between no surgery and the more typical surgeries for trans women. Although I struggled to imagine how I'd feel afterward, I trusted my gut instinct that it was the right decision.

In all my thinking about my gender over the years, I've found more questions than answers. If my transition and my faith have been a journey, then they are ones where I had no map, no compass, and no idea where my destination was. But if I'd waited until I'd figured out all the answers, I wouldn't have gotten anywhere. All my life experiences have made me the person I am today. I still don't feel any closer to really understanding my gender identity, but I do feel more comfortable in being me.

CHAPTER FIFTEEN

Coming Out as Your Nibling

What Happened When I Told Everyone I Know That I'm Genderqueer

SINCLAIR SEXSMITH

LATE IN 2013, I put a note up on my personal Facebook account and tagged as many of my cousins, aunts, uncles, high school friends, and former coworkers as I could find. I don't generally censor my Facebook account, so if they were friends with me there, they probably knew at least the basics of my gender identity.

But I'd never had a conversation with most of them.

I grew up and came of age in the Pacific Northwest, where the culture is stereotypically passive-aggressive, and my family has never been one to have direct confrontations. While I'd heard through the grapevine from my siblings that occasionally my aunt or cousin would ask them about my gender, they hadn't actually talked to *me*.

I feel completely and totally out in my day-to-day life, and anybody who doesn't know these kinds of things about my gender or sexuality probably just hasn't asked—I would tell them if they did. To some degree, my gender expression doesn't really allow me to be closeted: I've been wearing men's clothes exclusively, cutting my hair short, and even letting the hair on my chin grow into a goatee off and on for almost fifteen years, so there is clearly something not traditionally womanly or feminine about my appearance. But people draw their own conclusions about what that means. Some—like my feminist parents— think I've rejected femininity as a tool of the patriarchy, and support whatever I want to wear, though they are still a bit confused by the cufflinks and ties and dapper urban masculinity I sometimes dabble in. Some see it as a natural gender expression for someone who grew up in the woods and the rainforest. Some assume it's how "gay women" look.

And that may be all well and true, but maybe not. So I thought I'd delve a little bit into what it means to me to express this way, and to make my request about pronouns public and clear.

Here's the note I published:

Dear family & friends,

Especially friends from my childhood and high school years who have found me for whatever reasons on Facebook, and family with whom I'm not particularly close, and coworkers from previous jobs who I have perhaps never had this chat with:

I have something to tell you: I'm genderqueer. That means I live my day-to-day life somewhere between "man" and "woman," often facing all sorts of daily interactions where the general public doesn't "get" my gender, from kids in the grocery store asking, "are you a boy or a girl?" and their mom hushing them and turning away, to little old ladies in the women's room staring wide-eyed and backing out of the restroom slowly, only to then return with a confused and self-protective look on their face, to service industry folks saying, "Can I help you, sir? Uh, ma'am? Uh . . . ?"

That confusion, that in-between state, is precisely it. That's who I am. I'm neither, and both. I'm in-between.

You may already know this about me, just from following me on Facebook and doing whatever sleuthing you've done about my projects. You probably know I'm queer. But, if you want to know more, I'm going to explain a few things about my gender for a minute.

On Gender

I consider myself butch, I identify as masculine, and I consider genderqueer part of the "trans*" communities, using trans-asterisk as the umbrella term to encompass people who have transitioned from one gender to another in addition to anybody who feels in-between. I've been identifying as "butch" for a long time—perhaps you've heard me use this word, an identity I consider to mean a masculine-identified person who was assigned female at birth. I consider myself masculine, but as I delve further into gender politics and theory and communities, the boxes of "feminine" and "masculine" feel too constricting and limiting for me to occupy them comfortably.

I have for years thought that it was extremely important that people like me—masculine people with a fluid sense of gender and personality traits, who don't feel limited by gender roles or restricted by gender policing—should continue to identify as women as a political act, as a way to increase the possibilities of what "woman" can be. That's really important. And I still believe that is true, and heavily support that category.

The problem is, "woman" has never fit me. I had bottomless depression as a teenager (perhaps some of you remember I was sent to the Principal's office once for "wearing too much black"), plagued often by the idea of "woman" and adult womanhood. I could not understand who I would be in that context. And honestly, I still can't.

But—even though it is in some ways harder, living outside of the gender norms—this in-between makes so much sense to me.

On Pronouns (This Part Is Important.)

For a few years now, I've been stating, when asked, that I prefer the third-person pronouns they and them when referring to me. That means, if you're speaking of me in a sentence, you'd say, "They are about to walk the entire Pacific Crest Trail, it's true," or "Did you hear they just published another book?" or, "I really like spending time with them."

See? Easy.

Lately, when people ask what my preferred pronoun is, I have been saying, "I prefer they and them, but all of them are fine and I don't correct anybody." I don't mind the other pronouns. They don't irk me. But when someone "gets" it, and honors the they/them request, it makes me feel seen and understood.

There are other options for third-person pronouns which are gender neutral—or rather, not he or she. "They" is the one that I think, as a writer, is the easiest for me to integrate into sentences. I completely believe in calling people what they want to be called (that has always been one of my mom's great mom-isms), so I always do my best to respect pronouns, but I still struggle with the conjugations and the way those words fit in a sentence.

Some people—particularly those (ahem like me) who were English majors and for whom grammar rules are exciting—think the "singular they," as it's called, is grammatically incorrect. But it's not. It's actually been used in literature for hundreds of years. Read up,[1] if that intrigues you.

Why the Big Deal?

I haven't sat any of my family—immediate or extended—down and said, *Hi, I'd like you to use they/them pronouns for me.* I don't generally tell people unless they ask. I've been thinking a lot lately about why I haven't told you, what I'm afraid of, and what is keeping me from this conversation.

I'm not particularly afraid that you won't "get it" or that you won't honor it. If you don't, that's actually okay. I am part of some amazing trans and genderqueer and gender-forward communities full of activism, respect, advocacy, and understanding, and I'm very lucky to feel whole and respected in that work.

And really, I believe that the very vast majority of you actually really want to know, want to honor my choices. I think you are probably curious about this. But for whatever reason, my (and probably your) West Coast sensibilities are keeping us from having a direct conversation.

So, here ya go. It's not particularly personal, but it's the beginnings of something, and it's my offering to you to talk about this, if you want to.

---

1. Try these three articles, for starters: "Singular 'They' and the Many Reasons Why It's Correct," *Motivated Grammar*, https://motivatedgrammar.wordpress.com/2009/09/10/singular-they-and-the-many-reasons-why-its-correct/; Patricia T. O'Conner and Stewart Kellerman, "All Purpose Pronoun," *New York Times*, www.nytimes.com/2009/07/26/magazine/26FOB-onlanguage-t.html; "This Pronoun Is the Word of the Year for 2015," *Time*, http://time.com/4173992/word-of-the-year-2015-they/.

The thing is, by not having this conversation with you, by not giving you the opportunity to respect my gender and pronouns (even if you think it's weird-ass and strange and don't get it), I'm limiting our intimacy. I'm not giving you all the chance to really know me. And maybe . . . you want to. Maybe this will open up something new between us.

Or maybe you'll just go, "Huh. Okay. Whatever." That's fine too.

If you have questions, or want to talk about all this gender stuff, I am open to that. Ask away. (You don't always get a free pass to ask weird questions, so you might want to utilize this opportunity.) But before you do, you might want to check out *The Gender Book*[2] for some basic terminology, concepts, and ideas.

Sorry I haven't told you yet. I've been telling myself that it "isn't that important," but actually it's been a barrier between us, in some minor big ways.

Sincerely,
That kid who was in English class with you in high school,
Your former coworker,
Your cousin,
Your nibling (did you know that's the gender neutral term for niece or
    nephew??),
Your grandkid,
The older sibling of your childhood friend,
Your best friend from 6th grade,
That queer who was crushed on you before they knew they were queer,
Sinclair

PS: To any queers or gender-non-conforming folks reading, feel free to steal this idea for your own Facebook pages.

I *thought* it wasn't a big deal to publish.

I thought I was "out" to basically everyone.

But it has been a long time since I published anything that I was so goddamn nervous about.

---

2. See www.thegenderbook.com.

I kept going back to the note over and over, refreshing it. At first, nothing. *Who was going to read it?* I wondered. Who would "get" it? Who would dismiss it, or unfriend me, or ignore it?

The response, when it came, was lovely. So many comments made me tear up.

My cousin wrote: "Thank you for this! I am now pretty disappointed that Facebook made me choose 'male' or 'female' in identifying you as my cousin! Grr."

An old friend whom I sat next to in high school English wrote: "Thank you for opening your mind to those who may seem closed, your heart to the world that can be so judgmental and loving all at once, and your very self that you are clearly acknowledging, honoring, celebrating. Thank you for allowing all of us, for allowing me, to celebrate that self (and that heart! ah, that heart . . .) and join in your wellspring of intimacy."

My aunt wrote: "Thank you, my nibling—that is a very enlightening post and it felt very personal to me, as if you were writing just to me. I am now interested in the *Gender Book* and think I have more to learn."

I didn't get a lot of people taking me up on my "go ahead, ask me whatever you want" offer, but it made me feel good to put that out there, to make it clear that they were welcome to ask, should they have anything they were confused about. Sometimes, when awkward questions come, I answer explaining why they shouldn't ever ask that about genderqueer or trans folks, and then answer the question anyway.

Now, months later, the announcement still gets occasional comments and likes, and people still mention it to me. It's proved to me that these kinds of expressions of vulnerability are yearned for in the world. I do believe that there are lots and lots of folks out there who *want* to know about things like pronouns and gender identities, but they aren't in the same genderqueer circles we trans folks often run in, and they don't recognize the meanings of our expressions. They might be too polite or nervous or unsure to even ask about it all, opting instead for confusion rather than risking mistake.

When I really thought about it, there wasn't anybody in my life I could identify whom I had heard make homophobic or transphobic remarks. Am I not listening hard enough? Or do they censor themselves when they're around me? Or is that simply a reflection of me and the people with whom I surround myself? Maybe. Of course it makes sense that my closest friends are not only tolerant but celebratory. But what about my extended relatives? My former coworkers? My classmates from high school or college? There are many people in my life—and many of my Facebook friends—who were more the result of life circumstance than deliberate choice. Maybe I'm just really lucky.

I decided to test that out, to put myself out there, to make myself, my gender, and my truths visible and vulnerable to those immediately around me. I offered a place for everyone I knew to bring their knowledge or understanding or ignorance or confusion, and to have an open conversation. Don't get me wrong, my boundaries are spring-loaded and ready to go up at the first hint of hate or phobias. But I do have a lot of trust in my old friends, childhood teachers, extended family, and former coworkers. As much as I love going to gender groups and reading radical gender blogs and books and going to performances, these are the folks in my life who may in fact be the most hungry for education and explanations about gender. And this is the place where my knowledge can have the most impact: on those whose lives I've touched personally, on those who know me and have interacted with me, even if it was years ago or in certain limited contexts.

It was a calculated risk, one that came from the strength of willing vulnerability. Thank you, friends and family, for receiving it well. I feel even more seen, and even more like *me*. Which is uncharted, uncertain territory for me, as I'm so used to hiding. But I feel confident that you and I can navigate this together.

CHAPTER SIXTEEN

Purple Nail Polish

JAMIE PRICE

TODAY, I'm wearing purple nail polish, just because it makes me happy.

Once, in kindergarten, another kid asked me if I was a boy or a girl. I thought she was making fun of me. I tried to glare, mumbling while blushing with embarrassment. How awkward, to be seen as masculine and strange. Not "girl" enough. But now I realize she was just asking because she didn't know. Children can be very upfront about asking questions when they're not sure of something.

It didn't bother me to be seen as a girl during my childhood. In fact, I was even proud of being the first girl to join the rocketry club in my elementary school. Twelve boys and I got together each week to build and paint model rockets, and then light them and watch them fly. Until I joined the club, it had been a "boy thing." Motivated by my example, the following year two more girls became members.

Yet something changed after that. When I started puberty, I became decidedly uncomfortable with my body. Probably everyone does, to some extent, because going through changes quickly causes one's own body to become unfamiliar, but my discomfort was intense and long lasting. I thought about slicing up my chest, trying to cut off parts of it. I thought that if I did that, I'd go to the hospital and they'd fix me up, and I'd have a flat chest from then on. I thought it would be painful, but only a temporary setback.

When I was thirteen I told my psychiatrist I wanted to be a boy. He said I should wait to finish puberty before making any decisions about that.

When I was growing up, everyone I knew of was either male or female. And to my knowledge, either they were all fine with that or, if they were transgender, they ended up transitioning from one all the way to the other without stopping in the middle. It seemed like I had only two options for what my gender could be: cis female or trans male. And I wasn't really comfortable with either one. The problem wasn't that I wanted to be a boy; I just didn't want to be a girl.

If I had started transitioning at thirteen, I would have transitioned toward "male." I probably would have taken a full standard dose of testosterone, grown a beard and body hair, and tried hard to fit in as a masculine man. As I'm sure is true for many men, cis and trans alike, I might have ended up just as uncomfortable with some of my male characteristics as I had been with some of the female ones.

At sixteen I told my dad I didn't want to be a girl, and he asked for a logical explanation, some well thought-out reasons why being a boy would be better in general. I didn't have any, so I tried to make some up on the spot: for example, that boys have an easier time building muscle. He argued back that plenty of women are strong, and plenty of men are not. I didn't even care about building muscle, I just didn't know how to explain myself. So I stopped trying.

I got used to thinking of myself as "female with gender issues." I even started to enjoy wearing women's clothing in my twenties. I remember going to some effort to put together my outfits for work, coordinating colors, layering different shirts on top of one another, choosing necklaces to go with my outfits, and liking the way skirts accentuated my waist and hips. It was fun to style my long hair in different kinds of ponytails and braids. There were a few times in my life when I tried wearing makeup and was excited about it. These bursts of enthusiasm never lasted more than a few weeks, either because it felt uncomfortable on my skin or because I lacked the confidence to experiment and improve. But the ability to colorfully decorate myself always intrigued me, and I started to collect nail polish in bright and cheerful shades.

As I approached thirty, I started feeling anxious every time I was called by my name, or "she" or "miss." I can't explain where this feeling was suddenly coming from—the pronouns felt incorrect in a way I couldn't ignore anymore. But "he" didn't completely resonate with me either. At the time, I understood transitioning to mean both changing pronouns and using hormone therapy; social and medical transition went hand in hand, as if you couldn't have one without the other. The "male" physical traits I didn't want, and which were a big concern of mine, were tangled together with my feelings about my body, my identity, and the way I was seen by others, the words people used for me, and the clothes and accessories I wore.

At around this time, I was invited to a bachelorette party, the only one I've ever been to. Even though I had come to enjoy wearing casual summer dresses, I felt very strange getting dressed for this particular party. I wore a fancier dress than usual, one that was quite low cut. I added coordinating high-heeled shoes, and I styled my hair to be curly and pretty. My typical style of dress at that time, even though it was feminine, was much more casual and easy, low effort, something I didn't have to think about very hard. On the night of the party I remember feeling distinctly as if I was wearing drag, as if anyone who saw me would see how strange the outfit was on me and call me out as a fraud.

Of course nothing of the kind happened—my difference and my discomfort were invisible to everyone around me. I went to the party, and it was an overwhelmingly feminine event. Everyone there was a woman; the topics of conversation ranged from the kind I had no interest in, like weddings and dresses, to the kind that made me feel outright uncomfortable, like childbirth and breastfeeding. I remained awkwardly antisocial, only piping up when subjects like superheroes and computer programming came up.

Even among my friends, I started feeling like the odd one out. At one of our regular get-together sessions, we were playing the card game Magic: The Gathering. I was doing very well, having built up an army of minions with great attack and defense. My friend next to me said, "Wow, you've got some big dudes." Another guy piped up, "No, that's just a low cut shirt," playing off the joke that "boobs" sounds a lot like "dudes." There was a round of laughter as the game continued.

That experience magnified the discomfort and self-consciousness I had already been feeling. I was the only one there who was not a dude, so I felt excluded, the butt of a joke in a way none of the others would be. It's hard to say how much of what I was feeling was the typical discomfort one would feel about a sexist comment, but in that moment the dysphoria I felt around my chest became all encompassing. Eventually, the only way for me to feel at ease in public was by wearing a chest binder so that my chest would be flat even under women's clothing. This became my everyday uniform.

If it hadn't been for the Internet, I would have continued to think male and female were my only options. The stories of the trans people I met online were invaluable. One of my new friends identified as FtMtF (female-to-male-to-female): she was born and raised as female, then lived as male for about ten years before retransitioning to living as female again. She felt completely happy with that decision; her gender identity had shifted over time, and as it did, she had outwardly transitioned to match the way she felt. Talking to her made me realize that transition isn't necessarily permanent. It doesn't have to be a terrifying, life-or-death, all-or-nothing decision, partly because it doesn't have to be forever.

Years later I made another friend who identified as genderfluid. This person felt more masculine on some days, and more feminine on other days, and changed hairstyles and outfits to match. It's not just that gender identity doesn't have to be permanent, it also doesn't have to be consistent from day to day. I continued making more and more friends who existed outside the gender binary, and each one sparked a revelation.

But I needed more than a handful of examples. I began watching a lot of YouTube videos. In one video, a trans male femme wore a beard and sparkly eye makeup and fierce red lipstick. In another video someone who had no beard and no makeup avoided gendered characteristics altogether. These strangers' lack of adherence to either 100 percent maleness or 100 percent femaleness strongly resonated with me. I loved the idea of making my own rules, avoiding gendered pronouns, and being a feminine man or simply androgynous. It was so freeing to know that some people wear pink and sparkles, gesture emphatically, giggle, and blush, all while being perceived as men.

One of the most impactful videos I saw was by a trans man named Stephen Ira. He explained that since he is now consistently read as male, he can "do femme" without being read as female. He can wear makeup and jewelry, and otherwise present himself in ways that are considered feminine, and people still call him "he." He talked about how liberating that was for him. *Doing femme without being read as female*—I wanted to do that, too. That was the spark I needed to decide to transition.

At first, transitioning was frustrating and stressful. I changed my wardrobe from dresses and bright tops to polo shirts and argyle sweaters, and people still called me "she." I changed my haircut to an androgynous one, and then a masculine one, and still they called me "she." I started to avoid anything "feminine," including jewelry and hand-talking and giggling about puppies. I changed my name, deliberately choosing one that was gender neutral. I experimented with forcing myself to speak in a lower range and with a deeper resonance, which took way more effort than I was comfortable with. I let my brand new bottles of nail polish sit around unused. And still, people called me "she."

It was this frustration—my apparent inability to make people see me as anything other than female—that led me to consider hormone therapy. But I went back and forth about it for a long time.

My reflection in the mirror looked pretty much how I expected it to—neither particularly male nor female. It was just . . . neutral. The problem was other people. Strangers looked at me and saw a woman, and instantly started using female pronouns without checking with me first. I knew that with testosterone my face would become masculine, my voice deeper. But the reason I wanted to change it wasn't because I had any issues with my face as such, but because I had issues with other people's reactions to it. However, that seemed like too tangential an issue; I thought changing the way I was perceived by others wasn't a good enough reason to take hormones.

When I returned to those YouTube videos, I learned that different people take different doses of testosterone, that low doses have subtler effects, and that it's okay to start slow, or to try it for a while and then stop. It was those videos—seeing people with a diversity of genders feeling happy and comfortable with themselves—that ultimately changed my mind in favor of using hormone therapy. I started using the lowest possible dose so changes would happen more slowly and I'd feel more in control. My body's testosterone level now sits right in between the typical male and female ranges.

Though my voice has changed considerably, my face looks pretty much the same to me. I still recognize myself in the mirror. I still think of myself as neutral. But my appearance has clearly changed in some subtle yet significant way, because I get called "she" a lot less often now, and it's balanced out by all the people who call me "he." This gave me space to change the way I feel about pronouns: strangers who call me "she" aren't jerks, they're just regular people who have never thought that much about gender.

Because I'm no longer worried about being seen as female, I also feel freer to reembrace femininity. I've gone back to buying more colorful shirts, including pink and purple ones. I use the whole range of my speaking voice and my facial expressions. I talk more openly about musicals, fashion, and cute animals. Reintroducing femininity into my life has been an ongoing process, and these only feel like the very first steps.

Once again, I looked toward someone else for a model of who I could become. One of my heroes is an actor and a musician; he's talented, handsome, charming—the standard celebrity package. He self-identifies as a straight man, but he has fun with gender in ways society doesn't generally encourage straight men to do. He wears colorful nail polish, and sings songs about being a girl without changing the words. And I thought: if he can wear nail polish without being seen as a girl, maybe I can too.

Even though waiting until long after puberty wasn't what I had wanted when I was thirteen, waiting to the age of thirty-one gave me the opportunity to learn from people of all different genders, doing their transitions in all different ways. I know that my options are limitless.

For the first time in two years, I felt brave enough to wear purple nail polish. I had worried for so long that anyone who saw it would immediately consider me female, and it would cancel out all the transitioning I'd spent so long doing. But I wanted to wear it, and I was sick of limiting my self-expression for the sake of a binary worldview I don't believe in anymore. Anyway, my hero gets to wear it and no one thinks he's a girl.

After the nail polish finished drying, I went out to the farmers market. I saw people I knew, and people I didn't know, and not a single person called me "she." Later I giggled girlishly about it in my new, deep voice. (I might have done a little dance too.)

Today, I'm wearing purple nail polish, just because it makes me happy. Which has nothing— and everything—to do with my gender.

CHAPTER SEVENTEEN

Uncharted Path

Parenting My Agender Teen

ABIGAIL

OUR MIDDLE CHILD, Bailey, has the special ability to accept everyone as they are. Relatives and friends have always been drawn to them; as a toddler, Bailey was a head-turner with bright eyes and an easy smile. As they grew they exhibited the best of attributes: outgoing, steady, hugely intelligent, and good at sports. Despite an occasional temper flare-up due to a competitive spirit, they were upbeat and laughed easily.

But once Bailey started middle school, they became more withdrawn and solemn. Although the school was academically rigorous, Bailey didn't have a problem with even the toughest classes. What I witnessed was more a dampening of the spirit. With adolescence, Bailey's confidence was slipping away.

Bailey became distressed with their changing body; they were dismayed at having to wear a bra and extremely unhappy with the onset of menstruation. But I didn't dwell on these things—I assumed Bailey would grow out of this discomfort. Instead I focused on Bailey's complaints about their uncooperative hair, their newfound awareness of social hierarchies at school, and how they didn't feel pretty. I was bothered by our culture's misogynistic ability to put women in a box based on their looks. It was now affecting my child, who had up to this point effortlessly bucked the trends. Bailey's struggle with self-doubt stemmed from a distressing, teenage hyperawareness of how they were viewed by others.

From a very young age and with an amazing degree of confidence, Bailey had always challenged gender stereotypes to anyone who would listen. Over the years I had gotten a total kick out of their tomboy persona. After all, I had two other girly girls, and Bailey's nontraditional interests and personality were quite refreshing. We envisioned Bailey growing up to be a pioneering feminist who would one day change the world in a better way for all women. My husband and I couldn't have been prouder.

Bailey joined the Gay Straight Alliance and began writing reports on gay rights. Soon Bailey declared themselves to be asexual. I was somewhat perplexed; they'd learned so many terms I had never heard of. I questioned Bailey on this sexual orientation, not understanding how they could know at only fourteen. I figured they were most likely gay but hadn't come to terms with it yet.

The first years of middle school had taught Bailey a lot about both themselves and the complex world of social norms, but eighth grade proved to be unusually intense. Bailey's friend Julie was hospitalized for depression and suicidal thoughts. Bailey explained that Julie was now going by the name Jade and using the pronoun "they" instead of "she." Bailey was extremely concerned about their friend and checked in with Jade's mom regularly. Sometime after Jade came home from the hospital, I asked their mom if Jade was androgynous. (I did not have the terminology to ask the right question because I'd never heard of anything like this. Truthfully, the only image that came to my cisgender mind was the decades-old androgynous "It's Pat" character from *Saturday Night Live*.) Jade's mom told me that their child's gender identity was called nonbinary, and explained what that meant. I wasn't put off by the revelation—but I was confused.

Bailey's genderqueer friend Jade continued to have a very challenging time, with sporadic incidents of self-harm as well as an eating disorder. Bailey was, thankfully, wonderful about letting us know what was going on. My husband and I could also not let Jade struggle on their own. When Jade texted Bailey about hiding razors from their parents, I alerted Jade's mom. And over winter break, after Jade texted

Bailey from a party saying that they wanted to die, I called their mother once again. She assured us that she was at the party with Jade and that her child was safe. We discouraged Bailey from becoming Jade's personal therapist while cautiously allowing the two to continue their friendship, but we could clearly see how traumatizing Jade's agony was to Bailey.

One day after school I received a frantic call from my child. Bailey and a friend had followed Jade around the corner of the school, where Jade had picked up a piece of glass and threatened to cut themselves. Bailey and the girl managed to get Jade onto the bus home without harm. Afraid of what could happen if Jade was alone, Bailey, now crying, asked me to ensure Jade would be met by their mother at the bus stop. We were all traumatized by the event, but my husband and I—in a move I still question in retrospect—stopped short of demanding that the friendship end.

My husband and I were never under the illusion that Bailey's struggling friend had any choice in their identity or was in control of their suicidal ideations. We worried that if we cut off the friendship completely, Bailey would accuse us of rejecting Jade for those aspects of their life, and we emphatically did not want to send any negative messages about gender identity or mental illness to our child. In an attempt to shield our teen, we instead decided Bailey could talk to Jade on the phone or in person, but not have any more digital contact. While we felt for Jade, our primary focus was on protecting our own child's mental health.

A few weeks later we discovered Bailey and Jade had been texting each other against our wishes, and the conversation was wholly alarming.

"When I was at your house for your birthday, I noticed a razor missing from your pencil sharpener," wrote Jade. "Did you take it?"

"No, I didn't take it, you know I don't do that," replied Bailey. "Did you?"

"No," wrote Jade, "but if you ever feel that you want to hurt yourself, please tell me first."

This backhanded suggestion that Bailey harm themselves was the last straw, and we forbid any further interaction between the two. My husband and I met with the school, told them everything, and switched Bailey out of the classes they shared with Jade. Although the friendship had been tumultuous, Bailey felt the loss acutely. I would better understand why in a short time.

About six weeks later, when Bailey and I were alone in the house, Bailey told me that they were agender. My primary reaction to them coming out was a simple one: "They're still Bailey—that hasn't changed. And they're still here." I knew I had so many things in my life to be grateful for, including a great relationship with my fantastic kid. "I'm so glad you felt comfortable telling me," I immediately responded. I also asked how they knew. Bailey said they had always felt that something was wrong, but they hadn't had a name for it until they came across the term "nonbinary" in their GSA meetings. They explained that they didn't want to waste another minute of their life being someone they weren't. Bailey was so brave in this moment.

However, I couldn't help but wonder if it was Jade's influence on Bailey that encouraged them to identify this way as well. Jade was a very compelling, influential kid who had led their friends through the past year with dramatic episode after dramatic episode. What were the odds of both of these friends being agender when, until six months ago, I never even knew this gender identity existed?

When Bailey came out, I asked them how they knew they were agender instead of a masculine lesbian—I thought Bailey was just a tomboy because they had always seemed so "Girl Power!" rather than "I'm not a girl." I was unfamiliar with the nonbinary experience and wondered if being gay was an easier road that my child might still take. Bailey exhibited real strength in this conversation, and now I understand how the question itself was flawed. Bailey had always been agender, but they just hadn't had the vocabulary to express it. Since being a girl was all they had known, they had instead judiciously attempted to mold themselves into others' ideas of what being a girl could mean.

Bailey's description of their dysphoria drove this point home. The details were excruciating to learn; hearing that your child doesn't like something about themselves is never easy, but when it's about the very body they were born into . . . it broke my heart.

The next day, Bailey came out to my husband. It wasn't a perfect conversation. Before long he launched into a request that Bailey not use they/them pronouns; this particular change seemed awfully complicated to him. Even though he had missed a chance to practice complete acceptance right out of the gate, the next day he and Bailey came back together and worked it out. Luckily my husband and I ultimately both felt the same: we love Bailey and only want them to be exactly who they are.

Still, it was clear that we had a lot of catching up to do in terms of educating ourselves about what this meant for Bailey and our family. The following weeks were rocky for my husband and me. We spoke to a psychologist, an "expert" who had been recommended to us, and practically bolted from his office when he suggested Bailey start puberty blockers. Bailey had just told us about being agender the week before! None of us was ready to consider medical interventions just days into this process.

We began to seek out information about families with transgender kids. My husband noted that more often than not, the fathers in these families were the least accepting. It bothered him how other fathers' lack of acceptance hurt their children. He wanted to be open about his hesitations, but also worried that he would be playing to a stereotype if he did.

In our research, we began to understand how complicated it was for the families of transgender kids to green-light hormones for their teens, and it was clear the decision took an emotional toll on everyone involved. Hormones seemed to require a leap of faith for many reasons, not the least of which is the reality that studies don't go out far enough to have produced documentation on long-term effects. At this point we weren't sure where Bailey stood on hormones or how transition differed for nonbinary teens.

At first, we contemplated the idea that their identity might be impermanent. A small part of us even hoped for it, imagining the tough times ahead. But Bailey has been crystal clear since coming out about the fact that they are not a girl. Both my husband and I listened and tried to understand. I was frustrated that I couldn't find much information specifically about nonbinary children.

Looking back on Bailey's life, I wondered if there was a part of me that had willfully avoided connecting the dots on their gender identity. When Bailey wanted to wear a suit rather than a dress to their own bat mitzvah, I talked them out of it without much friction. Around this time, at the outer edges of my consciousness, I began to entertain the thought that Bailey could be transgender. The easy capitulation on the dress was convenient "proof" that they were only a tomboy. Bailey wasn't overly assertive in their nonconforming behavior, and in a busy life with three kids and a job, it was easy to shift focus onto other things in life. During visits with my sisters and with best friends from college, I would mention the idea of Bailey being transgender. They all said, "No, no, that's so unlikely." Statistically, it *was* unlikely. But the question remained tucked quietly in the back of my mind—otherwise, I would have been a lot more surprised when Bailey did eventually come out.

Still, I could never have imagined they were agender, since I had absolutely no cultural reference for it. Stories such as those of five-year-old Ryland Whittington showed children who were distressed by their assigned gender from a very young age, and insistent that they were the "opposite" gender. That wasn't Bailey; their distress didn't come into focus until puberty. From my cisgender perspective, one of the hardest parts to unravel with respect to Bailey's gender was, if they aren't a boy, why they want to look like one. We were unfamiliar with the all different trans identities and expressions, and how everyone's concept of being genderqueer is different. Bailey feels most authentic when their outward presentation is distanced from any association with the cultural constraints that femininity represents. I've since found multiple bloggers who are genderqueer, but present and live as masculine, and that at least has helped me to see that Bailey is not alone.

Parents of transgender kids have a lot to contend with in terms of transition and acceptance, and nonbinary gender comes with its own set of unknowns, exacerbated by a lack of resources and awareness. I was totally overloaded, working to understand my child and their needs, and bogged down with concerns about the future.

During the three summer months following Bailey's initial revelation I felt an enormous weight around the secrecy of their changing identity. I needed support, but I didn't want to reveal to everyone what Bailey was going through until they felt comfortable sharing their journey. Once Bailey was okay with telling others, I slowly began to reveal what was going on to one friend at a time. It felt like air squeaking out of a too-full balloon each time I was able to share a bit of our new reality. Thankfully, the friends I told almost universally did not blink an eye.

Bailey's sisters and our extended family have exhibited consistent acceptance as well. In the fall of ninth grade, Bailey asked us to call them by the pronouns they/them, and came out to the rest of the family. The pronoun switch came fairly easily to Bailey's siblings, but for the adults in the family the change has meant frequent slips. Although

I consistently hear others' mistakes, I'm not always aware of my own. Recently I was speaking to an acquaintance and heard her ask, "They? Do you mean Bailey and a friend?" I triumphantly realized I had used the right pronoun without thinking!

While Bailey has felt comfortable telling close friends about their nonbinary identity, they have remained calculatingly private about it with teachers and school administrators. Last year I asked Bailey if we could discuss their identity with their counselor at school as a way of getting support for their anxiety. Bailey refused, opting instead for refuge from bullying and discrimination. No matter how progressive our community is compared to the greater population, teens can be especially cruel.

Over the winter of Bailey's freshman year, a local genderqueer teen committed suicide. I awoke at midnight from a deep sleep to the sound of Bailey crying uncontrollably from their bedroom across the house. My husband and I rushed to comfort them, and at least ten minutes of unrelenting sorrow passed before we were able to calm them down enough that they could speak. Bailey finally sobbed, "I'm just so tired of pretending."

Neither of us slept a blessed wink the rest of the night, and for the next few days I was terrified to leave Bailey alone. My husband and I were completely torn up; as parents, the feeling of helplessness in the face of our child's pain was hard to take. Even though their close friends knew about Bailey's identity, Bailey still hadn't come out as agender to everyone. They clearly felt they still had to "pass" as a girl to be accepted in high school. But putting on a brave face for such a long time was taking its toll.

By the time Bailey turned fifteen the year after, we had made significant strides. We'd found a better therapist, one who was more experienced with trans teens. After many discussions with this therapist, Bailey announced that they didn't want to wait until they were eighteen to have top surgery. In the early days of Bailey's transition, I was careful to give measured responses to the topics of surgery, testosterone, and legal name change. I was uneasy with these possibilities at first, but I put on a supportive face. Bailey needed to talk about these things—these were serious, real issues in their life. My reservations paled in comparison to my desire to keep Bailey from closing us off. My husband had his fears too, and he expressed them to Bailey much more openly than I did. Surgery was permanent; was Bailey sure? How could they really know? He worried about letting Bailey make a decision they would later regret.

By next fall our roles were reversed. My husband had seen the surety with which Bailey carried their decision, and it inspired his support. Now, no longer needing to be his foil, my own doubts began to engulf me. One of Bailey's grandparents likened the surgery to mutilation. Her words pained and angered me, but I could not deny my own discomfort. I was squeamish about the visible scarring from the surgery. I didn't know how doctors, EMTs, or strangers in a locker room might react to a person with some "male" and some "female" parts. Most of all, though, I was embarrassed about my discomfort. Was I a lesser person for having these thoughts? I knew how important this surgery was for Bailey's mental health, and also knew I couldn't stand in their way. How could I come to terms with my fears? My internal conflict was eating away at me.

After weeks of sleepless nights, I joined Bailey and their therapist at the end of one of their sessions. Without warning, Bailey told the therapist they wanted to come less often. I was taken aback, as I had been under the impression that their currently stable mood stemmed from this consistent space to express their emotions. I was also concerned, and frankly a little annoyed, that Bailey made this decision without talking it over with me first. On the ride home, a reckless driver suddenly raced past us, nearly causing a collision. I snapped, seething with misplaced anger, and fell into full-throttle road rage. I leaned on the horn, spewed curse words, sped up behind him, and lost all self-control. Needless to say, Bailey was incredibly upset to see their mother behaving like a madwoman. In what was possibly the most humiliating moment of my life, the driver pointed his phone out the window and began filming my outburst. I couldn't remember a time when I'd ever felt so mortified.

I dropped Bailey at home and went to the park by myself for a good cry, devastated that I had let my own stress level get so bad that I had frightened my child. Shortly thereafter I realized that I needed to take better care of myself in order to take better care of my child. I began to make major changes to manage the built-up stress. After all, it was vital that I model for Bailey the kind of independence and self-soothing skills that I wanted for them.

One of Bailey's regular self-care practices is attending a discussion group for transgender youth at the children's hospital downtown. Regularly being in the same room with kids who can relate to a change in identity, dysphoria, and the wider world's limited understanding of transgender issues has been invaluable. In that room, for one hour a month, Bailey can relax into the normalcy of being trans. Connecting with other transgender teens makes Bailey feel less alone. And in light of the intensely difficult times so many transgender kids go through, the parent group has given my husband and me appreciable perspective on just how fortunate we are to have the strong child we do.

Yet even in a transgender youth group, it's unusual for other nonbinary teens to attend. Most teens don't feel they fit in, but most teens, even those who are binary transgender, can at the very least identify in some way with approximately half of the population. Living in a culture whose foundation assumes gender identity to be binary is intensely hard for Bailey. Not only was Bailey born with body parts that are out of sync with their brain's gender, they were born with a gender that most people still don't even know exists. If that doesn't make a kid feel left out, I don't know what does.

Of course, just as Bailey has had to adapt to living in a binary society and to being communicative and open about being agender, so have we had to adjust to new situations as a family. As Bailey has taken on a more masculine appearance, strangers now routinely see Bailey as male. It was a little odd the first time we heard a waiter call Bailey "sir." When we go to the men's department to get pants shortened, there are always references to my son's oncoming growth spurt. "No," I say, "Bailey is actually done growing." We have all had to learn when to take the time and effort to explain, and when it's better to let assumptions lie. Bailey's younger sister was once confused when a classmate at school spotted Bailey and said, "I didn't know you have a brother." "I don't," she replied matter of factly, and left it at that.

Bailey has been careful to construct a protective cocoon around themselves in public. Every parent hopes their child will feel comfortable smiling and inviting the world in, but Bailey frequently avoids eye contact with strangers, knowing that their gender could easily become a source of conflict. It's hard for me to relate given my own relatively mainstream experience. It's also proven jarring to see the confusion on people's faces when they look at Bailey, trying to figure out whether

Bailey is a girl or a boy. They don't know that the right answer is to a question they haven't even thought of.

This summer, I witnessed a brand new reaction to my child. We were all in line at an amusement park ride and I saw a teenage girl ahead of us surreptitiously glance at Bailey. I assumed she was tackling the usual question: "Girl or boy?" But the way she flipped her hair and kept sneaking quick looks brought the moment into clarity: Bailey, who once looked like a girl and felt miserable, now looked like themselves, and pride reflected in their confidence was clearly being noticed by others.

Now that Bailey is sixteen, we've been to two doctors in two different cities to discuss top surgery. Our options are extremely limited; there are so few doctors that perform this type of surgery—a masculinization of the chest—and even fewer who will operate on kids under eighteen. Moreover, the health care guidelines, which are becoming more supportive of binary trans youth, still aren't entirely inclusive of the nonbinary experience. We chose the surgeon closest to us, just an hour's drive, but we had to accept the compromise that insurance coverage was out of the question. Bailey is beyond excited to be free of their breasts, body parts they weren't meant to have in the first place.

Through fourteen years of parenting, my husband and I believed we had three girls . . . but we were wrong about something we once thought was fundamentally true. Bailey's gender identity meant a shift in course for our entire family. Our eyes opened wider. And ultimately, as a mom, I learned to reexamine what was possible for both my kids and myself. Seeing Bailey's bravery in challenging our culture's gender binary has given me the courage to challenge the limitations I thought I had for my own life. And we're all getting more comfortable with the unknowns of the future.

I look forward to fundamental relief when Bailey's struggles with insecurity, dysphoria, and isolation are in the past, when they are in a better place physically and mentally. Of course, I only have a hint of what that could look like for my agender child, gleaned through stories and pictures of those who have gone before. My greatest hope is that one day Bailey feels *truly* comfortable in their own skin for the first time in their life. When that happens, we will still have our beloved child, just a happier, brighter version. Nothing else about this journey is as important as loving our child and seeing them through it.

CHAPTER EIGHTEEN

The Name Remains the Same

KATY KOONCE

MY NAME IS KATY—not Katherine or Katrina or Kathy, not KD, KT, or Kade—just Katy. I am really attached to my name. My mother gave me Katherine Hepburn's nickname, but she almost named me "Molly" after *The Unsinkable Molly Brown*. Both names would have been fitting, because both women displayed a certain female masculinity that spoke to my destiny. After giving birth to my two older brothers, my mother wanted a girl so badly that she had a "think pink" baby shower and decorated my bedroom in every shade of pink. In an era before prenatal ultrasounds, she *willed* my genitals to take feminine form. I am not sure what her plan B would have been for a baby with a penis and a pink bedroom in 1962.

I am the child of a small town Texas football coach, and I am built more like a middle linebacker than either of my brothers. To her credit, my ultrafeminine mother allowed me to cut my hair off at the age of five and indulged my desire for a team uniform for every season. I remember rushing through the kitchen, the screen door slamming behind me. My mom and a friend sat in the early-1960s decor drinking coffee and smoking cigarettes while I circled the house in my "track uniform." This outfit consisted of a tank top, tiny spandex shorts, tube socks up to my knees, and skinny black Adidas with white stripes. Watching me, my mother didn't just figuratively bite her lip—she would chew the inside of her cheek when she was nervous or steeling herself for an ordeal. Letting me separate from her enough to be my own little person must have been very difficult, but she was also stoic; her true feelings did not betray her, or me for that matter.

One summer day, just before third grade, I was sitting on the banana seat of my bike. My dog Buford and I were watching some movers carefully hauling loads of furniture into the house across the street. I saw two girls about my age excitedly receive their bikes from the truck and jump on them. Neither girl was wearing a shirt. I was intrigued. Tomboys, no doubt. I lived on a horseshoe-shaped street, so I watched until they disappeared around the curve. A couple of minutes later they rode up behind me. The lanky, towheaded eight-year-old said, "What's your name?" I was startled but, without skipping a beat, I replied, "John, John Koonce." Without flinching or questioning, she said, "Hi, I'm Anne Wicker. This is my friend Eileen! You wanna come meet my mom?" Anne's mom said, "Hi, John."

I remember thinking that I was doing something wrong. I told folks my name was "John" or "Steve," depending on my mood. John was a straightforward guy who dug ditches and built fences. Steve was the star quarterback.

In 1970 in Texas, those folks who were deemed "girls" had to wear dresses to school unless it was thirty-two degrees Fahrenheit or below. On the first day of school, there stood Anne Wicker on the playground. She was being shuffled into my class. I remember her face. Her mouth agape. The pointing and running toward me. The screaming: "You're not a boy! You're *not* a boy!" I remember feeling mortified, but I don't remember much else until the afterschool fight in the Wickers' front yard. Apparently we were both mad and we were going to settle it right there and then. In my mind, I see Anne's four brothers and one sister yelling for her to win. I remember the goose egg under my future best friend's eye.

My two brothers were seven and ten years older than me, so they were gone from our house when I was still in elementary school. The arrival of the Wicker clan and my position as the "7th child" began what would be a rich childhood of building tree houses, laying Hot Wheels tracks, sailing, fishing, hunting, and throwing water balloons.

We staged many imaginative games in which I was usually a boy, of course. Our finest accomplishment by far was the NFL uniforms painted in fine detail on the tiny football players who comprised the teams in our electric football league. This was the time before video games: the football field was made of sheet metal two feet long and a foot wide, painted with hashtags and holes drilled to place the down markers, and it vibrated to move the tiny players toward the goal line. Ours and the surrounding streets had epic sports challenges in every discipline; Anne was the cheerleader, I was the one girl on the neighborhood football squad. We played every Sunday in full pads. I was a jock: I played highly competitive fast-pitch softball, basketball, golf, and excelled in the shot put and discus. I rode my skateboard around town and into skateboard parks of the 1970s.

Anne and I were definitely different tomboys. At Christmas, Anne "accidentally" dropped her new training bra box down the stairs of the Wickers' house. She ran down feigning embarrassment and grabbed the box with much fanfare. I, on the other hand, refused to wear a bra until my mother insisted. The first day I did, I was playing tackle football in the front yard with the Wicker boys when they started screaming, "Katy's wearing a bra!" I felt humiliated, exposed, and terrified of the near future. What was going to happen? The worst: I inherited my mother's humongous breasts. I was so embarrassed that I allowed my mother to buy my bras and feminine hygiene products rather than going to the store myself. That was back in the days of the pointy Bali bras and the Kotex belt, but I preferred to rely on tight underwear packed with a couple of pads since I didn't carry a purse. The pads also provided a secret bulge that doubled as my imagined male body part.

After one year of college, my brain slammed and barred the door to coming out. I gave it very little conscious thought. Though Rita Mae Brown's lesbian coming-of-age story *Rubyfruit Jungle* caused a stir within me, I still didn't attach this stirring to my own sexual identity. I also missed the relevance of the fact that at least 75 percent of my friends were out lesbians. Apparently no one else figured it out either. My peculiar blend of gender and sexuality made me difficult to categorize. To this day, people still say, "I just thought . . . 'Katy is Katy.'"

At age nineteen, I moved to Los Angeles to seek fame and fortune as a Kristy McNichol–style actress. In retrospect, I think I actually left Texas to find a place to come out. But coming out to myself as having same-sex attraction was confusing. I had never once fantasized about my body as anything other than male. I knew I was attracted to girls, so "lesbian" seemed like the closest fit. Just before my twentieth birthday, I met my first girlfriend, Deanna, on LA's Sunset Strip. I also found work as a roadie for an all-girl heavy metal band called Leather Angel. The glam 1980s were a fine time for me to fly under the radar, because all the boys looked liked girls too. My mother was happy to see me in eyeliner.

Hollywood was no place for a chubby baby butch with gender/body confusion; Los Angeles was no place even for "chubby." During an emotional breakup with Deanna, I moved to be near one of my good friends on the desolate outskirts of Palm Springs. Like typical twenty-one-year-old lovers, Deanna and I got back together and rented an apartment in nearby San Bernardino. It was no more than two months before we met a man named Gonzo who was doing crystal meth. He said he was doing it to lose weight, and I already considered myself an expert with the amphetamines of the 1970s. I had taken many diet pills, including black mollies and white crosses before—what could possibly go wrong?

Meth gave me boundless energy and a feeling that I could do anything. Take a child of parents with their own substance abuse issues, sprinkle that with gender confusion, and you have a recipe for a speed freak. I was unconsciously numbing the pain for which I had no words. Looking back, I believe I was literally androgynizing my body with meth, which is the ultimate appetite killer, stripping my body of fat and thereby taking my breasts along with it. Plus, with each snort or injection my dopamine skyrocketed to twelve hundred times its normal level. To put this in context, cocaine only raises the user's dopamine by 300 percent. What this means is that I got skinny and felt a thousand times more euphoric, and my body began to align with my self-image. I got thinner and thinner and my breasts disappeared! My jaw and cheekbones emerged, and I couldn't believe the person I saw looking back at me in the mirror. I saw a man, not the boy of my childhood. And everyone else began to see a man too. I started playing with facial hair at Halloween and began packing a sock on occasion.

That was the cool part. But life on meth was completely destructive and unsustainable. I stayed awake for days at a time in a drug-induced psychosis in order to avoid the real discomfort lurking just below the surface. I studied reincarnation in the wee hours of the night as a way to make sense of the jarring truth: that my fantasy life and body identity were solidly fixed on the male side of this gender system I was working with, but my genitals told another story.

Deanna and I broke up and I moved into Palm Springs proper. I spent my time doing speed and finding myself as an entertainer. The women I dated for those three years identified as straight. Years later, some have said that they thought of me as someone between male and female. By age twenty-four, after a deranged drug addict with a fatal attraction burned down my house, I decided it was time to tuck my tail and head home.

Once back at home in Texas, I slowed down just enough to realize I felt like shit. It was 1986, the year that HIV was named HIV, and I knew I needed to get checked out. Remarkably I dodged that bullet; instead, I was diagnosed with a dangerous case of Non-A, Non-B Hepatitis, which is now called Hepatitis C. Even after this diagnosis, I had some fits and starts toward sobriety. By then I had been using meth for weight control for five years. Getting clean off of speed "gifted" me with eight pounds of breasts. I was miserable. Of course the addict brain wants to turn to something at that point to numb the pain. Alcohol would be a bad choice given that the liver is compromised with Hep C. But denial had never let me down, so alcohol it was. Since I had eaten only sporadically over the past five years, the pounds began to add up. With every bra size increase, I felt increasingly miserable in my body. I assumed my misery was related to the weight gain. I wore very tight one-piece gymnastic leotards in an attempt to flatten my chest. This only managed to push them down and take the breast shape away, making me look like my belly was ten times bigger. After much begging, my reluctant mother paid for a partial breast reduction. I went to Dr. Wong at the Rosenberg Clinic. Unbeknown to me, I had ironically walked into the oldest gender clinic in the South, but my visit left me none the wiser about my identity.

I didn't realize that gender dysphoria was a thing until the mid-1990s, when I moved to Austin and met a queer artist named Venae Rodriguez. Venae had made a short film called *Male Identified*. As we talked about our childhoods and compared notes, I began to feel like parts of myself, formerly buried, were beginning to emerge. We became closer friends, and the next year we took a trip to San Francisco Pride. At the Dyke March, I met my first out trans man in Dolores Park. He talked about how he had always marched, but now he had to stay back during the march itself. I was taken by the physical transformation, and the power of testosterone. I felt excited to meet someone who identified similarly but had taken another path toward physical transition.

It was around this time that I was finishing my master's in social work. The influence of Venae and the chance meeting with the trans man at the march had left me hungry to know more. I began to learn about transgender communities, trans men, and the whole diverse spectrum of gender identities. I read everything I could find on this subject and plunged into the depths of my psychological pain in therapy. I came out as transgender in my classes at school and found this to be very exciting. I had a name for my experience, and I felt the power that comes with language. I looked around and found no therapy resources for transfolks in Austin, so I decided to learn as much as I could and eventually start a private practice that would serve the community. It was life changing to read Leslie Feinberg's *Stone Butch Blues*, Roxxie's *Dagger: On Butch Women*, Riki Anne Wilchin's *Read My Lips*, and Kate Bornstein's *Gender Outlaw*. As an emerging caregiver, it was helpful to find *True Selves: Understanding Transsexualism—For Families, Friends, Coworkers, and Helping Professionals* and Randi Ettner's *Gender Loving Care*. I also found the crown jewel for trans men at the time: *Body Alchemy: Transsexual Portraits* by Loren Cameron. Across town at the University of Texas, Sandy Stone herself handed me a copy of the movie *Gendernauts* so I could show it to my transmasculine support group. In 2000, I attended the Harry Benjamin International Gender Dysphoria Association Symposium in Galveston as my professional identity was taking some shape.[1] Within the year I was being quoted in the *Austin Chronicle* as a "gender expert." Though truthfully, I still shudder at the responsibility that comes with that title.

If I had known that it was possible to transition from female to male back in Hollywood, I probably would have. And my hunch is that I would have been happy, because my identity was not as complex as it is now. Today my identity finds itself almost square in the middle of the gender spectrum. (I don't think there's really some "ultimate man" or "ultimate woman" on each end of this gender axis. But for the

---

1. The Harry Benjamin International Gender Dysphoria Association is now known as the World Professional Association for Transgender Health (WPATH).

purposes of talking to my clients or writing a paper, I think it's an okay way to communicate, as long as we acknowledge the limitations.)

I really don't think you can separate the person from the journey. In the time of my youth, I was not fully chiseled. I didn't yet work in the transgender community and hadn't met the clients who would inspire my own freedom of expression. The world of popular culture reported nothing about transmasculine people. In the regular course of my life, I found no role models. There wasn't even a hint of a Renee Richards for someone like me, no Christine Jorgensen stories, and there were certainly no gender fucking badasses like Kate Bornstein or Leslie Feinberg encouraging me to find my own unique place on the spectrum. (It wouldn't be until way later that I found solace in the stories of Lou Sullivan, Billy Tipton, and Robert Eads.)

We can do all the insight-oriented self-examination that our time will allow, but I firmly believe it's in the mirroring of others that we truly take form. As I came out to friends, they seemed to agree with my self-assessment. The women I dated during this time helped me feel more and more comfortable expressing myself as a sexual being as well. But by far the thing that had the greatest effect on my gender journey was falling in love with Paige Schilt, a brilliant and beautiful woman whose primary attractions are to "genderful" (her term) folks like me. More importantly, she fell right back in love with me. Now, seventeen years later, she's written a memoir, *Queer Rock Love*, which celebrates love and attraction specifically to gender-nonconforming folks.

When our son Waylon was born in 2003, I realized that I couldn't imagine being called "Dad." I am a therapist to many people whose backstories are similar to mine, and they hate being called "Mommy." This is not my experience. My mother was very safe to me. She was my rock, she was the one I yearned for when I was scared. I am very attached to the vibrations of the names I have been given or have chosen, as with both "Mommy" and "Katy." By the time I became a parent, I was forty-one years old and increasingly comfortable with myself. There was not much discussion of genderqueers and I don't remember the words "gender nonbinary" being thrown around so much either. Yet I did what came naturally to me and followed my feelings to come to my identity. Some folks in the trans community criticized me as not being "trans enough," but I just felt that this was a ridiculous notion. I rebelled against people's attempts to define me again in my life.

Similarly, pronouns do not have a lot of emotional heat for me. I usually let folks decide what pronoun they want to use based on their own summation once they add together my appearance, my voice, plus whatever the unknown variable is in that equation. But if you flat-out ask me my preferred pronoun, I will say "I use 'she' and 'her' because they go with Katy." In my opinion, "Katy" goes with whatever gender is in the eye of the beholder. Increasingly, in my postmenopausal (and heavier-on-the-facial-hair years), "Katy" is sir'd a ton. Sometimes I lower my voice to stay with that assessment for the duration of a passing encounter.

Listening to trans people for a living has allowed me to compare my identity with those of others. In nearly twenty years, I have helped hundreds of people transition. That experience came in handy when I decided to have top surgery with Dr. Raphael in Plano, Texas. But it was the fear of being seen by Waylon as "Dad" and not "Mom" that cued me into the place at which my own physical transformation would cease. Although I am read as male 70 to 80 percent of the time—some days more—I eventually realized that a full transition in which I would be read as a cis-male 24/7 would mean sacrificing too many valued parts of myself. I am open to this changing. I would be surprised, but not shocked.

In the years since my chest surgery, I have found that it's often easier for everyone involved if I use the men's room. When Waylon was around eight, he started to go on men's restroom reconnaissance missions for me. He would assess the nastiness of the stalls. Sometimes he would go in with me, and since he was fond of saying "Mommy" ten times in a row while talking to me, we decided it was time to call me something else in the bathrooms. We had been reading *Percy Jackson and the Olympians*, and Waylon was taking a little quiz to determine his Olympian parentage. He determined that my wife was Athena and I was Zeus. Ha! The irony. Zeus was considered the father to all. Some things you just can't fight. We were on vacation in Hawaii when Waylon escorted me into the poolside restroom and told me, "You can take the stall, Zeus." That was one of the sweetest things anyone has ever done for me.

I can also "pass" and use the women's restroom if I choose—as long as I use my girliest voice. If I have no one to be my bathroom buddy, I have made-up conversations with imaginary friends on my cell phone. My impromptu one-way discussions are legendary. And before the infamous "bathroom bills" in North Carolina and here in Texas, it was fun for me actually. I played in the fields of unknown gender and wished I could interview strangers and ask them what factors were added together to arrive a "sir" or "ma'am." Now I have to actually contemplate if I will just put my head down and go about my business or rebelliously start using the women's room again, since it matches my birth certificate. Do I really want every piss I take to be a potential throw down in the ladies' room?

Despite the challenges that come with being in women's spaces, I've always loved a dyke gathering, and have never been able to see myself giving up my place in the community as a fellow dyke. I've listened to people who were assigned female at birth as they recount stories of feeling out of place in the context of lesbian or dyke subcultures. This discomfort was key to many in helping them to come out to themselves as trans. I have a different story. Simply put, I am the front person for the "silicone cock rock" band Butch County, and although I am a longhaired rock-n-roll butch, I love imagining myself in the butch leagues with the likes of Phranc, Leslie Feinberg, and Peggy Shaw. (Okay, we are old, maybe we are a dying breed.) Even if I transitioned to male, my Austin community would never shut me out, but that's not the point. I just don't identify as a man, whether "trans" or "cis." It would not be authentic to live a life that simply faded into the woodwork and eschewed my inner "mommy" or "dyke."

It's not easy living life in the middle. It's especially hard to navigate this middle ground in my very public roles as a therapist and an activist and (at least in my own mind) a rock star. But the people who share their stories with me—my wife, my son, my friends, and, most importantly, my clients—have taught me the most about my own gender. In the stories of my clients, once-hidden parts of myself begin to emerge. I have no idea what is left to find. I am acutely aware that my gender is ever in flux. I am lucky enough to be trusted with the most vulnerable parts of the brave souls who find their way to me. Now I entrust mine to you.

PART FOUR

Trans Enough

Representation and Differentiation

CHAPTER NINETEEN

Lowercase Q

CAL SPARROW

MY OLDER BROTHER is Queer with a capital Q. And by that I mean that he's the quintessential version of White Gay Cis Guy; he could be on the cover of a textbook, or have his picture next to the corresponding entry in the dictionary.

He was always affectionate with me when we were kids, energetic and playful. But around our adolescence, everything began to change. The other middle schoolers bullied and harassed him for being gay, though whether the offenders based their abuse on any factual evidence or an intuition, I'm not certain. Perhaps *gay* and *fag* were simply their generic insults of choice. But regardless, the effect was the same: from this point on, my brother became withdrawn and depressed. Our relationship suffered. We seldom did activities together, and expressing any kind of verbal affection became embarrassing for us both.

Our mother eventually was able to put him back into the Lutheran school we had attended when we were small before money had gotten tight. It's ironic that despite the fundamentalist lean of the school, it was a refuge from the hell of the public middle school, although I'm certain my brother's orientation was never made public. When I was in high school, I finally learned that he was gay, and by that time, getting to know my high school friends had primed me to accept it easily when I wouldn't have before.

My brother never formally came out to me. We were the type of siblings where a confrontation about personal identity would have been incredibly awkward. But I'd had my suspicions for several months, and of course, once he brought home a boyfriend, I knew my hunch was true. Since then, he's been involved in many LGBT groups, events, and pride parades. Although he was never much of an activist, he remains close to the movement and the community due to his husband's energy for politics and action. And more importantly, he's successful and happy, with little remaining of the withdrawn teenager he had been.

With him as my go-to example of the queer experience, I've found it difficult to feel like I belong in the community. My own experiences with the questioning process and my level of involvement in queer causes pale in comparison to the "real lives" of queer youth; my identities are plagued by too many "not enoughs" to fit in with the better-known queer subgroups. Am I still suffering from the "little sibling complex" of wanting to be like the cool older sibling? Is there room for the passive, the incidentally queer? Is it okay to come late, to miss the entire experience of being in the teenage queer community?

When I was in elementary school, my best friend was the girl who lived across the street. Our houses weren't exactly in a charming neighborhood, more like reflections across an increasingly busy street in a town that was in the middle of an identity crisis over whether it was rural or urban. In other circumstances, this girl and I probably wouldn't have been friends. I had a tendency toward having one friend at a time, and of dragging that one friend into all of my interests. These included drawing, stomping through muddy swamps, staring at anthills, raising tadpoles, and making homemade movies promoting environmentalism. Notably not included: talking about boys.

But inevitably, the subject would arise between us, and boytalk would ensue. *Her boyfriend was* that *guy? And they did* that *thing? Aren't we ten?! Why do you have a boyfriend, what's going on I don't understand, someone save me—*

But at ten, I already knew that I was the weird one, and of course the Popular Girls didn't neglect to reinforce the point. Staring at anthills was bad enough; not being interested in boys made me *truly* uncool. But despite the pressure from my peers, I made no attempt to change anything about how I was. I was fiercely unapologetic about my personality and convictions, even when it cost me human connection and acceptance.

Incidentally, my young age was not the only reason that crushes and nascent sexual feelings were alien to me. Somewhere in the developing stew of the person I was growing up to be was a notion festering and solidifying into a very real truth: I wasn't going to experience sexual attraction when I was older. It occurred to me, even at this young age, that I may never understand the tingling pull of sexuality that others were feeling all around me. Still, I was mostly unbothered by this. I just kept being me, staring at anthills and stomping through swamps.

Then at eleven, puberty struck. I was so embarrassed by menstruating that by the second time (I kept it secret the first), I couldn't even utter the words to my mom and had to make her guess the reason I was in tears. I felt a great shame in the whole experience and wanted to hide it as much as I could—as if by denying it, I could make it go away. Of course, my mom was delighted and hugged me and called all her women friends, and they all wanted to congratulate me and tell me secrets about being a woman. I hated all of it; I wanted to crawl under a rock every time the topic came up.

Once I realized my body had sexual implications, I grew a modesty that bordered on the fanatical. I couldn't own the fact that I was turning from a girl into a woman, and even worse, a sexually capable one. I wanted to go back to being a child, a state in which I perceived I was allowed to be asexual without drawing notice and concern, and I wouldn't be called a *woman* like it was a fact of the universe.

I was sixteen when I first heard the word *asexual*. I was deeply immersed in a blurry period of baggy, androgynous clothing and a few cautious but precious friendships. The disdain that I'd always harbored for my peers' sexual and romantic coupling was slowly softening. I was becoming used to being on the outside of their rituals, resigned that I was simply missing a piece of the human puzzle, but certainly not longing for it. My mom couldn't settle on whether she thought that I was perfectly normal or that I was weird and incomprehensible (her indecision continues to this day). Then I stumbled upon the homepage of the Asexuality Visibility and Education Network, and there, right on their front page, was the definition of asexuality—the definition of *me*![1] When I finally learned about asexuality as a term and a real orientation, it represented so clearly what I was that it seemed foolish not to adopt the label, especially if it helped me connect with others like myself.

But discovering that my lack of sexuality was, in and itself, a variation on sexuality left me with a burning question: Was I *queer*? Ironically, I was in a relationship of sorts with another girl at the time; it was not exactly romantic, but exclusive and intimate beyond a typical friendship. But *lesbian* is not a label I had ever considered for myself. *Women* were lesbians, and I wasn't a *woman*. But I sure wasn't a man. I had long settled on thinking of myself as a "tomboy" kind of girl, or just avoiding the subject entirely. I still hadn't seen past the binary; I just thought of myself as me and ignored the labels that didn't feel good, even if it meant I had none at all.

In the process of sorting through my internal conflict around my own queerness, I eventually encountered a variety of nonbinary terms to describe gender: neutrois, agender, genderfluid. But I wasn't yet ready to give them much more than a cursory consideration. I thought these identities were reserved for those who changed their body. And although some part of me was intrigued by the idea of having a body that lacked the sexual organs and characteristics I had never been comfortable with, the notion felt too wild, too unattainable for my reality.

Beyond that, medical transition seemed an admission of defeat. If I were to physically alter my body, taking the time, effort, and expense to transition, I would be giving up my agency. I'd be letting society chase my sense of self into a corner from which I would never escape. I wanted to believe that I could silence my own despair over my curvy hips, high-pitched voice, and petite *cuteness* by sheer force of will. I would simply not allow society to tell me that these things meant I had to consider myself a woman.

But the seeds of realization continued to sow. Years later, I found myself watching videos online of trans men on hormones and feeling painfully jealous of something . . . something I couldn't define. I was pretty sure that I wasn't a man, so why did I feel so compelled by their experiences? A number of things intrigued me: the androgynous look of the early days on testosterone, the experience of not feeling like a

---

1. More information available at www.asexuality.org.

woman, the plain honesty and acceptance these guys had about who they were, and the joyous optimism they had about the future. This jealousy moved me to examine my own feelings about gender once more, and to imagine being brave enough to experiment with testosterone.

Shortly into my foray with gender exploration, I met a new friend, Skyler. Also asexual and nonbinary, they were the first one like me that I had ever personally known who wasn't resistant to the idea of transition. Skyler made nonbinary transition seem normal, and that normalcy made it easier to think about whether I would ever want to pursue hormone therapy or a name change. It was through meeting Skyler, and our nightly conversations online, that I took the step of choosing my preferred name. And it wasn't as though Skyler didn't also have reservations about hormones, but these were things that we could discuss with each other openly without fear of misunderstanding and judgment. We talked about the parts of trying testosterone that we wanted, and the things we didn't want. We wondered how being ace and nonbinary were related, if they even were.[2] Our friendship was brief due to simply falling out of contact, but it helped bring me into the LGBT experience more personally. Here was someone like me who considered themself queer. They weren't ashamed about it, nor did they feel they were sitting on the edge of what it meant to be LGBT. Knowing someone like that gave me permission to begin to consider myself queer too.

Despite finally finding words to describe me and others to connect with, I was still left floating in the ether. I felt little momentum pulling me toward transitioning. And could I *really* trust my childhood sense of self, audacious enough to claim my gender and sexuality so early, naive enough to think it would never matter?

Sometimes being nonbinary feels like "not man enough to be transgender" and "not woman enough to be cis." Sometimes being asexual feels like "not gay enough to be queer," even while in a relationship with someone of the same sex or gender. Sometimes I worry that I mistake a general feeling of tomboyishness for being transgender, and that it's something I need to get over instead of embrace. I worry that because I joined the queer umbrella so much later in my life than those

---

2. "Ace" is slang for asexual.

who found it as middle schoolers—like my brother, who grew up in the arms of PFLAG and support groups—that I'm hopping on a bandwagon only after it's gained momentum and a degree of acceptance. I don't want to water down our small nonbinary movement with my indecision. What if I'm just affirming the opinions of our detractors, who believe we're all just confused?

Even my parents, supportive as they try to be, have told me in times of strain that I am being ridiculous and militant about my clothes, that I am embarrassing them by not blending in with my peers, by fighting about putting on a dress for a wedding. Although they are familiar with LGB issues because of my brother, the T remains a mystery. They want to be supportive, but they don't take the time to understand. I also don't talk about it much with them because I feel a little bit of guilt: two for two, they got two queer kids. I don't think they will ever get a blushing bride in a wedding dress. They don't say it much, but I know they hope I marry a man and have a family so they can have at least one experience of normalcy. Perhaps they even wonder whether I allowed myself, as the younger sibling, to be influenced by my older brother. I suspect that, deep down, they feel a little cheated; maybe they even blame me, just a little.

They'd never say it aloud, but I can see the doubt in my parents' eyes. *Nonbinary* and *asexual* are not the same as the inborn gayness of my brother. They are, instead, conscious choices, avenues for an early adulthood rebellion. But how can I expect them to know what's going on with me when I'm still suffering from doubt and confusion myself? I can't even answer whether asexuality caused my discomfort about having the body I have, or if I was uncomfortable about my body first, which led to an aversion to sexuality. Maybe they grew simultaneously from a single underlying sense of self. I'm not sure. I think this confusion is a common experience when trying to navigate something as complex and arbitrary as gender; those who have never questioned their own identities, like my parents, may not understand this process.

We spend years posing as something we're not because we don't know what we are. All we know is, we don't feel like the gender we're supposed to be, yet we can't find an alternative either. Everywhere we turn we get reminded that most of the world has extreme trouble with thinking outside the confines of binary labels. Furthermore, many of us who have not made movement toward social or physical transition have vulnerabilities—labels based on feelings rather than actions can have a tenuous confidence.

I now have the benefit of having multiple nonbinary friends and a discussion group at a local queer resources center, and all of us are hiking the trails of self-discovery. We do not need to navigate these paths alone. We have collectively suffered varying degrees of isolation, inferiority, frustration, and a longing to be "normal" in order to make friends or escape bullying. Among my queer peer group, I've found so many more people I relate to than I have ever found among heteronormative America. It's a testament to how much our gender or lack of gender, sexual interest or lack of sexual interest, implicitly impacts our life, since we are continuously drawn to those whose experiences match ours even if we haven't come to terms with them yet.

It has taken me a few decades to accept that when it comes to gender, I'm further outside the norm than most, and to realize that this difference has a name if I want it to. Even though I grew up in a family without strong gender expectations, binary gender seemed like an unshakeable paradigm before I was old enough to learn that things could be another way. Until we learn otherwise, those of us on the borders walk under more familiar labels that are not quite right, like a pair of pants that are too short or cut for someone else: tomboy, femme, butch, lesbian, gay, fairy, transman, transwoman.

Sometimes I feel like I'm desperately clinging to the guide rope of the community I'm hiking with so I don't get left behind. The feelings of community, the friends I've made, have been valuable and precious. Maybe you, like me, have trouble pinning down an identity that seems to always be in flux, and you wonder if you belong under the nonbinary or queer umbrellas. Maybe someday you'll realize something new about yourself and head off on a new trail with a new community. In the meantime, give us the gift of your perspective and hike with us.

CHAPTER TWENTY

Not Content on the Sidelines

SUZI CHASE

AM I A WOMAN? I take female hormones, giving me breasts and a more feminine face. I have had my body surgically altered to be physically shaped like a woman's. My macho voice is gone, replaced by sweet feminine music honed by hours of practice. My closet is full of feminine clothes, my bureau brimming with beautiful jewelry. Feminine walk, movements, and mannerisms have become so well practiced that when I'm in public, no one notices that I once was a man.

Does that make me a woman? It certainly makes me adept, something that I've never been before. My clumsy, oafish, uncoordinated, socially clueless self is, as if by magic, shown to the world as a bold, beautiful, confident woman. I marvel at my own accomplishment. But that doesn't change one's gender. And if I need to be honest about the way I think of myself much of the time, I would have to say that I feel . . . male.

I envy those women who can say that they always knew they were female, who knew in grade school they wanted the pink tricycle and the Barbies with full wardrobe. I can't imagine what that feels like, knowing for certain you are the opposite gender from the one you were born into. My being transgender was experienced differently—an intense, unshakeable, and unquestionable but completely unreasoned belief that becoming a woman would be the most wonderful thing that ever could happen. That was accompanied, unfortunately, by the equally unshakable understanding that, despite what I might want, I was and was fated to remain a male.

I took to manhood reluctantly. My constitution lacked the bluster, the confidence, the savvy, and the stoicism that seemed to be required. I had to develop the necessary skills, often faking and too slowly learning, until I managed to be a reasonable facsimile of a male. As a kid, I fooled few. Every real boy saw through my façade and took maximum advantage, subjecting me to the usual taunts and humiliations afforded to those boys whose nonconformity becomes evident. *How* they knew—I still can't fathom. But during those awkward school-aged years, I was noticed everywhere as the one who was different, who couldn't hold his own, who could be cowed and exploited. Summer camp, a new school, even a vacation at the beach all threw me in with children who seemed to have received a forward communiqué from headquarters alerting them to the vulnerable soul in their midst. The names they called me even eerily matched, as if a common lexicon had been agreed upon by a symposium of bullies worldwide.

By the time I reached adulthood, I had developed a mask that hid my discomfort with my gender. I could attract women by exuding highly practiced masculinity. With my children, I was the father who demanded their best, and who would not tolerate misbehavior. I would have preferred instead to be the nurturing one, who told them there was no one in the world like them. But I did what was expected.

The main effect throughout my adult years was a steadily increasing discomfort with my place in the social world. The sort of friendships I seemed to form with other men tended not to be satisfying. With women, it was often easier. They were more likely to be comfortable with allowing an emotional vulnerability that I'd found much rarer in men. However, approaching women for friendship as a married man proved fraught with awkwardness. Misread intentions abounded despite my best attempts at sincerity, and suspicious nature overwhelmingly won out over willingness to connect as friends.

Entry into my fifties drove me finally to seek the source of my struggles and pursue relief. That year, I summed up my goal in two words:

fit in. The more I examined my life and resolved to know myself better, the more my explorations became increasingly focused on gender.

As I put together the puzzle pieces, the picture slowly emerged that I was transgender. Movies and books that featured females fascinated me. The company of women calmed and comforted me, whereas the company of men made me uneasy. And from my teens on, I discovered a fascination with having a woman's body. It galled me to the point of pain that I would never experience the sensation of breasts or female genitals. When I fantasized about being a woman, a feeling of wonder and amazement overtook me, placing womanhood on par with a lottery win or landing my dream job.

My understanding of being transgender is that I have a structure in my brain that really wants me to be female. Some would say that means I'm female and have always been female. But my gender is the sum of my experiences, my physical being, how people see me, how I see myself, and the role I am accustomed to play. I've lived for more than fifty years as a male. I've been a father for more than eighteen years, was a husband for twenty years (until transition shattered our marriage), and was looked up to as a male schoolteacher by generations of students. Did I think I could erase that in three short years by taking pills and asking everyone to call me by a new name, however feminine and beautiful?

———————

Early on, psychological "help" proved to be anything but. I had a famous psychologist—a recognized expert in transgender treatment—sneer at me when I claimed I had dysphoria. I had confessed to him that I didn't mind having a penis (though I would gladly trade it in a minute for girl parts), and that I'd enjoyed a lot of what it allowed me to do. "I've had patients," he told me, "who couldn't urinate standing up because they couldn't bear to handle their genitals," as he gave his opinion of what a "true transsexual" should feel. Luckily his patronizing manner and disdain for my condition did not deter me. I'd waited so long for an appointment to see him that I forged ahead alone. By the time the long-awaited appointment came, I'd already gone out several times as female.

The residual disappointment left by that doctor's disparagement was short lived, but I still had a period of internal conflict ahead. At first, I resisted the possibility that I could be transgender. From everything I'd heard in the media (whose ignorance I was yet to discover), to be transgender meant that you had to feel like a woman in a man's body. I didn't feel like a woman at all; I'd never felt the slightest desire to cross-dress, and I didn't abhor what hung between my legs. No, I did not feel female. But neither could I tune out my heart's message that life as a male was so dreary that I couldn't allow it to continue that way years into the future. Amid misgivings, I started to consider living full time as a woman.

I viewed transgender women with awe and curiosity. I understood why someone might transition and live as a female: they spoke of the music of hearing their new names, and were I fortunate enough to have one of my own, I knew I would hear its sound in that same way. I began to toy with the idea that I could begin to live a female life, even if I didn't feel as they did. Nobody had to know that I wasn't a woman inside.

Possibility became plan, and plan became destiny, and before I knew it, I had a transition strategy mapped out. It even entered my mind that an entire year of such pretense might make me eligible for sex-reassignment surgery and for the female anatomy I'd always craved. That notion was as tempting as it was sobering. Yet I had a healthy respect for the changes transition would bring. Could I keep up the pretense of being a woman when I didn't fully feel like one? Would I even like it? Would I miss living as a man? And if I followed the secret desire of my heart and changed my body surgically, would I feel comfortable in my new body, or would I discover it was a disastrous decision after it was too late to go back? I wasn't sure I could even manage a convincing female presentation.

One of my transgender friends suggested I try it, to go out into the world and be seen as a woman. If I discovered I was not transgender, I could opt not to repeat it; I was risking very little. Those first few outings were tentative and scary, but the lure of transition dragged me forward. I had never before worn a single article of female clothing. The very idea revolted me. I wouldn't go unless I actually looked female; being seen as a man in drag held no appeal. How could I go about that? A former engineering project manager, I treated my first cross-dress outing as a development project, and approached it accordingly. I drew up a checklist, classifying items as critical, important, or nice to have. A wig, makeup to cover beard shadow, breast simulation, shoes and clothing that at least appeared unisex—those were critical. Shaving the exposed parts of my body was important. Jewelry, purse, and watch all made the nice-to-have list. I spent weeks preparing. I obtained the hardest items first (the wig and makeup, as it turned out), and then filled in the rest. Finally, I ventured out.

Anyone could have picked me out as male-bodied, but only if they gave me a second look. To the casual glance, I was a woman. I hated it. My clothes didn't fit well. I feared something would slip or open up, and a displaced wig, tufts of exposed body hair, or a makeshift undergarment would reveal my identity. I found makeup smeared across clothing in places so far from my face that I can't imagine how the transfer occurred. The whole outfit felt unstable, constructed from duct tape and bailing wire, as fragile as the dream it was trying to realize.

And I didn't feel female. I was deceiving the world into treating me with a deference I didn't deserve. The whole enterprise felt forbidden and dishonest.

Afterward, the experience called to me again. Leaving the house each morning with wallet and keys tucked male-style into my pockets, I would spot my purse on the dressing table. Immediately, conviction would seize me that I should be carrying that instead. And the sight of the form-fitting women's blue jeans hanging in my closet brought forth visions of my adventure into that colorful, tenuous world of fantasy, now in the past. Both were frequent reminders that I remained stuck in my monochrome life.

I tried several more outings, expanding my wardrobe and getting better at assembling my disguise. After a few weeks, I felt natural, even proud, going out in public. However, I couldn't escape that my internal gender identity had changed little. I was being accepted by nearly everyone in my life as a female, except myself. Deep down inside, I had the intuitive sense of being stuck as a male.

I had so perfected my man-mask that it had fused to my being, becoming such a part of me that none saw behind it. The veneer was opaque to the point that dumbstruck looks greeted me when I disclosed my plans to live as a woman. To those who knew me, the mask *was* me, the only me they had been allowed to see. So fast was it stuck and for so many years that its tendrils had burrowed deep into my skin. I no longer needed this visage, and often even detested it, but it became impossible to tell where the mask ended and I began. Male habits and perspectives were so ingrained that seeing beyond their tint was impossible. Even when I happily donned the trappings of my new life—wig, earrings, bra, skinny jeans, and knee-high boots—I still felt like I was girding for a military adventure in a foreign land rather than dressing for everyday life.

This sense of maleness saddened me. To me, femininity means the beauty and harmony that so many of the women I admire bring to the world, despite the forces that would see it overgrown with the utilitarian and the competitive. I see the capacity for nurturing, for generosity, for giving without thought of receiving, for pure love. These qualities seemed to come naturally to so many of the women I knew, while I could only yearn for them and pretend. I burned for just a taste of that true feminine spirit, amid the daily subterfuge to hide my origins.

My eyes are open to the ways femininity is not an unmixed positive. I've seen and sensed the angst from so many women who have crossed my path. They face condescension. Assumption of passivity. Society's disdain. The impossible standards imposed by our culture can lead them to feel jealousy and self-doubt. Add those to a parade of other pitfalls and trials of womanhood. Strange as it sounds, I wanted those pitfalls and trials for myself just as much as I wanted the joys, as part of a true female experience. I'd gladly have taken all of them and more to be able to drink from the cup of genuine womanhood, rather than sip from the imitation flavors I'd brewed for myself.

These concerns led to worrisome questions about my future. Would I make the rest of my life onerous and artificial only to realize that fantasy did not match reality? Would I grow tired of the constant subterfuge? I needed expert guidance. I chose a counselor more carefully this time.

My new gender therapist was the one calm spot in this maelstrom of longing and change. She told me we all experience our transness in different ways. I am no less transgender, no less deserving of a satisfying transition than the four-year-old who begs his mother for a dress. The person who can say, "I wish I were a woman" need not allow herself to be eclipsed by those who say "I've always been a woman." There is no one right way to be transgender and no one way to transition. I understood that people whose gender doesn't fit neatly into the binary boxes of "male" or "female" are still entitled to transition into the presentation in which we are comfortable. Being nonbinary does not mean we need to be content to sit on the sidelines and cheer on others as they transform their lives.

Living more than three years as a woman has highlighted the truth of those words. I do not yet feel like a woman, yet my gender experience has shifted. Now, I have momentary flashes of certainty about my femininity, and periods of time pass with no awareness of gender at all. And sometimes, in the company of folk who are entirely binary, be they men or women, I even have an occasional sense of differentiation from them, where I sense my gender to be entirely removed from the linear spectrum that stretches between male and female. But most often, I still feel decidedly male.

This persistent fluidity, however, has had no impact on my comfort with the feminine presentation and expression I have chosen for myself. I still delight in my image in the mirror, unmistakably the woman of my yearnings. I relish the rituals of traditional femininity, celebrating my body by adorning it with jewelry and clothing, carefully selecting colors and textures. The sisterhood of female-with-female friendships feels like settling onto a soft couch, especially when compared to the hard surfaces of pretransition connections I encountered with my fellow males. And the transformation of my physical body through hormones and surgery feels miraculous, but at the same time deliciously subversive. I have a satisfied sense of having "gotten away with something," persuading the medical community to allow me my dream body despite a gender identity that might seem disqualifying. Indeed, that same subversiveness comprises some of the pleasure of my daily feminine living. I am unbothered by the seeming dishonesty inherent in a presentation at odds with my internal gender experience. On the contrary, I derive excitement from fancying myself a spy under deep cover who has infiltrated the foreign country of femininity deeply enough to emigrate and pass seamlessly among its citizens.

Do I still wish I were completely female? In my most authentic moments of reflection, yes; I sense glimmers of discontent that the opportunity to be a binary female (transgender or cisgender) was not offered to me. I am not sure about God, but oddly, I've found prayer amazingly helpful. Instead of praying to the Almighty, I pray to my inner strength. It works just as well, especially when all I ask for is the peace that comes from accepting myself as I am. If I am a male who must willingly live as a woman, that is far better than a male who reluctantly continues living as a man. After all, my transition has brought moments euphoric beyond my wildest imaginings. Seeing myself with breasts, with smooth shaved skin, with avant-garde attire that brings out my body shape perfectly—all these were experiences whose rewards no cisgender person could ever understand. There is no question in my mind that transition was the right decision, my gender identity notwithstanding.

Near the end of my time with her, my therapist asked if I occasionally wished I were still living as a man. My answer came quickly: "Not for a split second." Will I someday be able to say, "Okay, am I finally a woman now?" I can't see into the future. For now, I need to be satisfied with enjoying my transition as a dream come true. I still marvel at the strangeness of the journey taken by a man who now lives happily as a woman.

CHAPTER TWENTY-ONE

You See Me

BRIAN JAY ELEY

Content Warning: This chapter contains themes related
to suicide and sexual abuse.

WHEN I was a kid, I wanted nothing more than to be an X-Man.
I hoped every day that I would be startled by the discovery of an ability that would distinguish me from everyone else. I childishly believed
in a just universe. I believed that life would unfold like the predestined
arc of superheroes and that hidden in my story was the reason I felt so
alone. Even in the universe of the X-Men, powers have an insidious
nature; most mutants' powers range from useless to detrimental. We
hope for flight. We hope for strength. We hope for teleportation or heat
vision. What most of us get is invisibility.

Invisibility is useful in woefully few instances. If you're talking super
powers with friends and someone says they want invisibility, you need
to get that friend help. That person either wants to do something highly
unethical or is in serious need of a self-esteem boost. When invisibility
occurs in real life, it is a transfer of power—clandestine powers pre-
serving and growing their dominance over a group of people being
silenced. It is easier to silence people when they doubt their own valid-
ity to the point of questioning their own existence. How do you cham-
pion what you are when you aren't sure that it even exists?

I was always a weird kid. I remember people being concerned that I was so sad. I didn't know how to hide being sad but I quickly realized that it wasn't normal to picture my own death frequently throughout the day. Soon after that, I realized that it was unusual to be a black, Christian child at a Jewish preschool. Next, I found out that I didn't speak the way people expected a black person to speak. Being from the South gave that experience a sequel when people started asking why I didn't have a Southern accent.

Everyone looked at me and told me I was going to grow up to be a football player. I hated that. I didn't care for sports. I wanted to play with my big sister, Danielle. I thought Danielle was the coolest person ever. She's still in my top five, if I'm being honest. She seemed so much more comfortable existing than I did. I thought I could follow her lead. I wanted to be like her. I wanted to be *liked* by her. I wanted to like all of the stuff that she liked. I remember being so happy playing My Little Pony, even though I didn't have my own. I could tell I wasn't supposed to want those and that was fine because I could ask for other toys and play with hers. Perfect. Well, it was perfect until she didn't want to play with me anymore and that meant I stopped playing with My Little Pony because it never was *my* little pony.

I believed the rhetoric I was told as a child. I believed America was great. I believed God was good. I believed that all people were equal. I believed that it was wrong to be mean to people based on who they are. I believed that anyone could grow up to be anything. No one told me explicitly that I couldn't play with toys for girls. I grew up with the implicit bigotry that surrounds us all.

At a young age, I felt the weight of the invisible oppressive forces in society. It guided me into toxic masculinity and away from things I actually enjoyed. R & B, pop, folk, songs that I now love would spark a rage in me. I was angry at myself for liking the Spice Girls or Mariah Carey or Jewel. I was angry at myself for wanting to be friends with the girls more than the boys. I was angry at myself for the times I wanted to be one of the girls. I was angry that I wasn't a normal boy. All of that anger was set to the tune of the pop hits of the 1990s and I wanted to get rid of it all.

A lot of people say that it is wrong to call people homophobic or transphobic because they are hateful and violent rather than afraid. I hate to say it but fear is what leads to anger and violence. The anger inside of me when I realized that I had a "song for girls" stuck in my head is the same anger that builds up in the men who murder trans womxn whom they find attractive. For many, the violence of toxic masculinity is a horrifying and futile attempt to kill parts of their true self. It's an attempt at suicide.

In high school people thought I was gay. One night I was in my mom's room and I was wearing her wig. I thought I would get a laugh if I kept it on and pretended to be surprised by her. My mom walked in and then I shouted, "I'm not gay!"

"IT DOESN'T MATTER IF YOU'RE GAY! IF YOU ARE JUST SAY SO AND BE DONE WITH IT!"

Wow, um . . . okay. I wasn't expecting that response. I was looking for more of a surprised laugh. Maybe a "Boy, you are ridiculous!" General reverence for my teenage, comedic genius and flawless timing would have been about right. A hearty guffaw in response to a silly, one-off bit that I had clearly constructed moments before seemed more than appropriate. Instead, I got the passionate response of a parent who has been left in limbo for too long.

I thought about being gay a lot. I never ruled it out. I told myself that I wouldn't let gender get in the way if I ever met the right guy but I generally wasn't interested. I loved women. I lusted after women. I would later find out that a lot of those women were lesbians. I just thought that I was awkward and bad at flirting. My high school friends later gave me shit for being attracted to women with masculine features. I thought that traditionally attractive women could be attractive. I also thought that people who weren't traditionally attractive could be attractive.

I grew up in Houston, which is beautifully diverse. I was exposed to people of different races all the time but I grew up in a predominately white and Jewish part of town. I thought dark-skinned black women were the most attractive people in existence. The black women I met always told me that they only dated white guys; they didn't want to date me. Similarly, I wasn't supposed to think black women were attractive because the colonialist powers that wrought havoc, laid waste, and then staked claim the world over had every interest in enforcing the beauty standards to which they adhered. I'm still intimidated by black womxn when I want to flirt.

I had terrible self-esteem and didn't think I was going to be attractive to anyone. I was more interested in personality than looks. I liked weird girls. I liked nerds. They were beautiful. I watched enough movies to realize that a nerdy or weird hot person is still hot. I was nerdy and weird. I dated nerdy and/or weird white women. It worked.

In college I tried harder than ever to be a normal cis, straight dude. I told my friend Scott once that I was thinking about being celibate for a while. According to Scott, every guy who decides to be celibate for a while comes back later saying he is gay. So I didn't take a break from sex. I just kept on being a dude to the best of my abilities.

In America, we pressure eighteen-year-old children to sign legally binding contracts worth more money than they have ever earned in their lives just so they can get an education. These children, freshly indebted and now fully legally responsible for themselves for the first time, then leave home and cohabitate. They are supervised by a handful of adults who are preoccupied by succeeding in academia and by another handful of slightly older children who mostly don't have experience outside of being a college student. The majority of these children haven't been taught about self-care, consent, intersectionality, or why house parties are actually better than bars and that a big part of that is not having to hang out with any random jerk who walks into the bar.

I had a rough go of college. My bipolar was undiagnosed. Worse, I was on antidepressants and my life began to spiral out of control. Suicide can be an infrequent side effect for people who, you know, have depression. But for those of us who are bipolar and misdiagnosed, suicide is a more frequent side effect. I had a thinking spot at the top of a parking garage near my dorm. I would go up there to disappear. I would skip class sometimes and look out over the city. I felt like I could see all of Madison. My friend Matt didn't know that was my thinking spot when he jumped. The people at the crisis hotline didn't know I was up there, literally sitting on the ledge, when they put me on hold and I got disconnected. I cried myself to sleep on that roof that night. I never went back. I stopped going to class. I wasn't sleeping at night. I was writing and recording three songs a day. I still managed to go to my job. That's where I met Emily.

Emily was a cute, short, white woman. Emily was my first work flirt. After weeks of flirting, I invited her to hang out. I thought we could have a few beers and it would be nice to be off campus for a while. I was glad that I wouldn't have the temptation to binge drink while I was trying to charm Emily.

Emily wasn't of the same mind. Emily brought a large bottle of disgusting vodka. She said we had to finish the bottle because she couldn't take it back to her dorm. I felt weird. I felt pressured. Whatever. I figured it would be fine. Her encouraging me to drink negated my inclination not to get too drunk in front of her. It gave me a pass.

She got me very drunk. I walked her back to her dorm. Her dorm was next door to mine. It wasn't a problem. She took me up to her room. We kissed. We made out. She had already told me that she was a virgin. I didn't want her to feel pressured and I didn't want to be uncomfortably drunk for her first time having sex even if she were fine with it. I told her that I should go home. I was drunk, tired, horny, and riding that new crush high. She insisted that it was safer if I spent the night. My dorm was next door. I woke up with her on top of me and I was inside of her. She stopped when I woke up and I said that I thought she deserved a better first time than that. I felt violated but I felt like I couldn't tell anyone. I had known so many women with stories of sexual assault that seemed more valid to me. I was worried that as a guy, I would be perceived as lucky to wake up to sex whatever the circumstance. I believed that my story would only detract from the horrors to which women are subjected. It was years before I told anyone. It was years before I processed that night and understood that it was sexual assault.

I moved back to Houston shortly after.

When I was nineteen, I got caught trying to kill myself. I tried to say goodbye to friends who I thought were too far away to do anything, but Facebook already existed and those friends found friends who found Danielle who called my mom who called the cops. I remember sitting in the hospital looking at my doctor. At that moment I realized that I could either tell him what he wanted to hear and get out and try again without any farewells, or tell him and everyone else everything they *didn't* want to hear, get stuck in that hospital way longer, and have a shot at living. I decided that if people didn't want me dead, then they had to deal with me living.

I didn't think it would make me feel better. I thought it would wear everyone else down. In the beginning, it worked just how I thought it would. I was admonished for being too vocal about private issues. I lost contact with people I had known. But I didn't lose anyone who had actually been there for me in my most difficult times. Instead, they sat in my pain with me. I didn't get handed the easiest circumstances or personality but I got really lucky with friends and family.

For the first time in my life, I had made space to discover myself. The women I became romantically involved with all identified as lesbians. At first, it confused us both. None of them could explain why but they told me they felt oddly comfortable with me.

I fell in love many times and every partner dropped me off further down the road than the last. I understand now that it is best to lead people to their own realizations about themselves. A woman who had not been with a man in many years first introduced me to the concept of "queer" as an umbrella term for not being straight or for being transgender. We were together for many years before I admitted that I thought I might be transgender. She took me to a store and we shopped for clothes. I got a pair of shorts, a bra, and some makeup. We pretended that it was all for her. When we got home, I gave myself my first clean shave. I put on the shorts, the bra, and the unisex shirt. She did my makeup. My body didn't look that different but my face was so new to me. I looked beautiful.

As beautiful as I looked, I didn't want to begin a transition. I didn't want to change my name or my voice. Sometimes, I even felt right in my own body. I wasn't confident enough to be seen in public. I never thought that I was a cross-dresser. I couldn't explain what I felt. I left the idea behind until I met a partner who identified as nonbinary.

At twenty-six, I started identifying as nonbinary and genderfluid without any real changes to my expression. I knew that I felt less like a man than I presented. I wasn't a full-on woman but I definitely was not a man. It was very confusing for many but I was steadfast. I demanded to be seen for who I knew I was. During this time I started gaining some traction in my music career. I had the largest stage I had ever known to tell people who I was. I was dedicated to presenting a persona larger than myself that encompassed all of me. I was Biz Vicious. I proclaimed that I was "genderfluid, new to it, and still just a tad bro" and that I wasn't "tripping on what's in between your legs."

Though I was staunchly and vocally nonbinary, it still took me a long time to accept the idea of identifying as trans. I still lived with the convenience of passing privilege. I didn't want to co-opt the term from binary trans people who are in so much danger of physical harm and so regularly subjugated and denied opportunity as well as basic human decency. I still lived with the convenience of passing privilege. If I could hold my tongue and fight the urge to declare my identity, I could be seen as a man in a "man's body." I was encouraged to identify as trans by an older trans woman who was an activist and told me that she feels deeply for nonbinary trans people because we suffer erasure from cisgender and transgender people alike.

Despite acceptance from someone further along in her journey, I was still apprehensive. I realize now that it was fear: I was suffering from internalized transphobia. I lived in the treacherous space between recognition and true acceptance. Honestly, I still find myself wondering where I am on that journey. People don't expect transphobia in trans people, but how could we completely shed something so constantly reinforced when we spent so long oppressing the trans person in ourselves?

Over time, I began playing with my wardrobe. Though I always had great dysphoria over my upper body, I came to love my legs through dancing. Tights were a patch to a hole in my heart I didn't know existed. I never would have guessed that the answer to the awfulness of pants was to keep the shape, make them tighter, and make them stretchy! The other fix to pants was to cut off as much of the leg as possible. The magic of short shorts was a gateway to a new gender.

I had started rapping in Austin and gained my small acclaim after returning to my hometown of Houston. I felt like the conqueror upon a triumphant return. All of my shows were either headlining or as opening support for nationally recognized acts. I joked that my career was going just well enough that I had to worry about joining the illustrious "twenty-seven club" with Kurt, Janis, and Jimi.

The most important show I played that year was not for the largest audience. I was asked to play at Trans Day of Remembrance on the steps of City Hall in Austin. I composed a brand new song called "Invisible We," meant to be an anthemic declaration of intent to never again succumb to erasure as trans people. For the backing vocals and chorus of the song, I sought out Doomstress Alexis, a trans musician and activist with her own day celebrated in Houston. I believed that it would be a symbolic bridge between an older generation of binary trans people and a younger generation of trans people that continues to push the bounds of gender. As I performed the song, I heard abrasive shouting from passing cars and I thought, "I am currently a target. I may be murdered for identifying as trans right now." That was the moment that I truly knew I was trans.

A year later I realized that my gender is fluid but spends much more time on the feminine side of the spectrum. I wanted to be the same awkward, pseudopunk, low-maintenance person who I am, but read as femme. I didn't know how to present on the other side of the imaginary line when my natural features are associated with men. I slowly started to wear more and more "women's" clothing to see how far I had to go before people stopped calling me "sir." Instead, I was being perceived as a gay man. This simply would not do.

When performing on stage, you should perform bigger than you think you need to—so big that you think it is too much. This is because performance seems smaller from farther away, and also it is much easier to scale back than it is to increase incrementally. I decided to go big. I went shopping for my new full femme look. My stage persona is built to be a braver version of me so if the look failed it was okay, because that persona is ostentatious and unafraid of failure. I was new to dressing femme, but thanks to my years wearing pants marketed to women, I already knew the importance and luck of finding a dress with pockets. My partner's sister was throwing away a cheap wig. My partner cut it for me to make it complement my features. We bought makeup. I had colorful eye shadow, a bright purple lip stain, and plenty of glitter.

My friends and family struggled with my pronouns. It had been a battle to be consistently recognized as something other than a man. I was so worried about what this new dimension of my personality would bring to my life. I thought that surely there must be limits to what people would accept from me. I was completely wrong.

I was surprised by many things. I was surprised by the rappers who didn't seem to be phased at all by their peer taking on a new aesthetic. I was surprised by my unsurprised exes who told me that they were waiting for me to figure out that I was a lesbian. I was surprised by my boss pulling me aside to tell me that she liked when I dressed up for work because she thought I seemed happiest and most comfortable that way. I was surprised by my mom and sister telling me they finally felt that they really understood and could see me as a son and a daughter, a brother and a sister. I was surprised that presenting full femme felt good because of the support I received, but it still didn't feel like me.

I've been asked many times what my coming-out story is. I mean, how do you come out as a genderfluid, bipolar, autistic, HSV-2 positive, weird, black person with radical social views based on treating all people like people? The truth is that I didn't have to do it. I came out when I was nineteen as a person who wasn't going to be invisible anymore. I now see more people like me, more than I ever would have hoped. I'm still figuring out how to present my gender in ways that feel right to me. I'm twenty-nine. I'm still figuring out a lot about myself. It's scary not to fit into one of the archetypes we are offered. But I find it infinitely scarier to try to look myself in the eye while hiding from everyone else.

CHAPTER TWENTY-TWO

Clothes Make the Gender/Queer

AUBRI DRAKE

Content Warning: This chapter contains themes related to
family-of-origin abuse experienced in childhood, including graphic
descriptions of verbal, physical, and sexual abuse.

MY THREE SIBLINGS and I spent our years before high school
living near the poverty line, before my blue-collar father landed an aero-
space engineering job that pushed us into lower-middle-class existence.
I remember what it was to be hungry, to not have enough food. I got
excited when people from church would give us black trash bags full
of clothes because they felt sorry for us. It was always a bit strange to
open up that trash bag and be overwhelmed by a wave of scents that
made up the donating family's smell: a hodgepodge of fabric softener,
perfume, cologne, pets, body odor, and sometimes cigarette smoke.
This led to a very patchy, hit-or-miss wardrobe that *never* passed
muster with my peers. They knew me for what I was: a poor, weird,
gender-nonconforming religious kid.

My first memory of life was hiding in a closet with my older sibling,
listening to my father scream profanities at my mother while she
sobbed. When my father wanted to make a point about how unhappy
he was, he would grab our sixty-pound dog by the neck and throw
the dog down the stairs. He once locked me out of the house on a
twenty-degree night in nothing but a T-shirt and shorts until I gave in

and let him see me cry. He would press his body against mine when I was cooking at the stove, wrapping his arms around my belly right under my bra and wetly kiss my neck right under my ear. His lips were always wet. He once snuck into my room at night and rubbed his erection against my back as I feigned sleep. My father followed the cycle of abuse like a script: first sweet and kind, trying to erase the painful memories, then building tension like a ticking bomb until . . . explosion! Rinse and repeat. At nine years old, I was rewarded for my audacity to beg for peace and mercy by being told I would amount to nothing, good only to be a prostitute. I was nothing but unsatisfactory property to him; he often told me I was useless, worthless, and unlovable.

My mother's abuse was more subtle. My mother taught me my worth in this world was entirely dependent on always saying yes and pleasing those who had power over me. She would manipulate me and my siblings, telling each of us lies about what the others had done or said. She held me up as proof that she was a good mother. She'd say, "*You're who I would have been if I wasn't abused growing up.*" She completely ignored my youngest brother and withheld any affection from him; he began displaying signs of suicidal ideation at age six. My older sibling had documented learning disabilities, which my mother refused to acknowledge. She would keep my sibling at the kitchen table late into the night, screaming at them because they didn't understand their schoolwork. As an eight-year-old child, she would regularly keep me up past midnight, crying on my shoulder about my father's abuse and insisting she would leave him. Like my father, she viewed us as extensions of herself: "*I brought you into the world, I can take you out.*"

I believe my parents would have been abusive regardless of their religious beliefs, but their religion fed and encouraged their abusive behaviors. Most days my parents' abuse wasn't bad enough that Child Protective Services would have stepped in, had they known about it. And my parents were white, college-educated, conservative Christians, so they received more slack from the system. My parents just celebrated their thirty-fifth wedding anniversary. But white picket fences and jade anniversaries are not always what they seem from a distance. Sometimes, they're downright sinister.

My parents were very focused on ownership; they insisted that anything they bought for us belonged to them and they could take it away from us whenever it pleased them. But if I bought something for myself with my own money, it was mine and they couldn't take it from me.

That's why I began working under the table early. I started a lawn-mowing business at age eleven where I earned as much as $600 in a year. I used this money to pay for gymnastics team and to send myself to sleepaway summer camp for a week each summer. I was receiving paper paychecks by age thirteen; I transitioned to a job that removed state and federal taxes as soon as I was legally allowed to work at age fifteen. With my first official paycheck, I bought my first piece of new clothing ever. It was from the Old Navy outlet, a deep-sky-blue rugby-style polo shirt with a white collar and a coat-of-arms patch on the left breast. It has survived the test of time well; it's still in my drawer at home.

I deeply enjoyed going to thrift stores; it was freedom to find clothes I wanted to wear at a price I could afford. The local Goodwill was the next town over from an upper-middle-class town, so they always had good options. One time, I got a ratty, incredibly comfortable black and green zip-up University of Hawaii sweatshirt for $3. My younger brother bought it for me when we were out biking and it was unexpectedly cold and windy. He and I would ride our bicycles for dozens of miles just to escape our house, especially on holidays—my father's abuse always escalated on holidays.

My parents' intense religious convictions instilled them with a deep disdain of almost all television. To protect us from the secular world, we never had a TV in our home. When I was six years old, we were allowed to watch occasional G-rated VHS tapes through a Commodore 64 monitor. For the most part, my access to movies that were not conservative Christian propaganda depended entirely on my local library or thrift store.

Books were the same. One winter, my parents took us four kids down to Florida to a superconservative Christian camp (just like the one where we spent a week every summer). On the one day we left camp premises, I found a book at a church thrift store that I bought and hid from my parents, reading it in the attic when they weren't home. *As Nature Made Him* was the story of David Reimer, a person who was assigned male at birth but was raised as a girl after he lost his penis in a medical accident. His doctors believed that gender was entirely social (nurture) with no biological influence (nature). His parents were convinced by these doctors that raising him as a girl would make him feel like a girl. But he transitioned back to male in his teens, and after a troubled life, he died by suicide at age thirty-eight. It took me years to figure out why I was so interested in intersex people, David Reimer, and the question of gender and nature versus nurture.

As a prepubescent child, I didn't think about gender and simply inhabited my body in ways that pleased me. Sometimes it was the green cotton print jumper dress with tiny pink and yellow flowers and a pink silk ribbon around the middle over a white blouse. Sometimes it was pants and my favorite red triceratops T-shirt. My outfits frequently involved yellow or red rain boots because I wanted to be a firefighter.

Although my parents' conservative Christianity punished me for many aspects of myself, it also provided odd pockets of relief. As I grew older, my overall disinterest in dating anyone was perceived as me being chaste and "waiting until marriage." Wearing boys' clothing was moderately acceptable because I was being modest. I had long brown hair (because my parents believed girls shouldn't have short hair) but I would jump off of playscapes with it streaming behind me like a tail. I hated pulling my hair back so it ran wild and free, just like me.

I was happy to run around, ignoring the gender people kept trying to force on me. My body was my sports car—stylish, lean, athletic, fast. It had purpose and function, and it felt right to me. My body looked like all the other boys', my clothes fit the same way as theirs. Then puberty arrived with a vengeance and my body turned into a minivan; all curves with no get-up-and-go, meant to be filled with children. Clothes started clinging to my body in all the wrong places; they stopped being a form of expression and instead became material to hide in. I began wearing increasingly baggy clothing, trying to cover my betraying body.

My complex relationship with my body and clothing was compounded by my participation in competitive gymnastics. Tight spandex was required, putting every inch of my body on display. Despite that, I would lose myself in the motions and simply bask in the strength and purpose of my body. But the competitions encouraged self-judgment: I started from a perfect ten, waiting for the judges to acknowledge me just so they could take away points as I made mistakes.

Gymnastics also exacerbated my tenuous relationship with food. I was cursed with early puberty; my chest began growing at age ten and I had my first period at eleven. Kids didn't want to be partnered with me for strengthening exercises because I was taller and heavier. I remember overhearing my coach tell another gymnast that she needed to do more cardio or she would end up looking like me. I was already obsessively exercising but it seemed food was the one piece of the body horror puzzle I could control. Being thinner meant my chest would be less substantial; I knew that if I could get my body fat low enough, my period would stop. But my body never shrank the way I wanted it to shrink; I've always been built like a linebacker and it takes a lot to make a musclebear disappear.

During middle school, I tried playing around with makeup once or twice. The end result was closer to circus clown than anything else. It always left me disheartened that other people seemed able to do "girl" so much better than me (and make it look effortless), no matter how hard I tried. I remember reading Judy Blume's *Are You There God? It's Me, Margaret* and being horrified at these strange creatures who thought puberty was something wonderful that couldn't come fast enough. I couldn't believe girls in real life were like that, while being terrified that they really were. I felt betrayed by the boys who suddenly seemed to realize I was a girl—a creature that could possibly procreate—and didn't want me around anymore. I would look at photos of myself as a younger child and feel a deep sense of loss because that confidence was gone.

As I grew older, I became despondent that no boys were interested in dating me. I spent a good three months wearing women's clothes and makeup, trying to become something boys desired. I felt immensely uncomfortable; it made me want to peel my own skin off and run away screaming. And it made no difference; no boys wanted to date me.

In between these occasions of gendered effort, I would give in to my internal rhythm, to what felt most comfortable. In those years it meant a soft masculinity, a gender of teenage-boy athlete: tank tops, cargo shorts, T-shirts, jeans, sports shorts, sweatpants, and sweatshirts. During those vacillations of gender presentation, I would eagerly modify my wardrobe, made possible with thrift store shopping.

My favorite thrift store was, and still is, a regional chain called Savers. Imagine Goodwill and Salvation Army had an obsessively organized, philanthropic, secular baby; that baby is Savers. Savers is a nonprofit that donates their profits to other nonprofits. They have T-shirts, suits, blouses, dresses, pants, jeans, shoes, sportswear, couches, tables, tablecloths, jewelry, pots and pans, silverware, toys, books. . . . Savers really has it all. Each item is clearly marked with its price, organized among its compatriots of a similar definition. And heavens be praised, glory of all glories, Savers has a block of bright red, genderless changing cubes. The only requirement for changing cube entry (which I regularly ignore) is six items or fewer. I have never once had a negative reaction from staff when I've bought clothes that directly clash with my apparent gender.

I left home at age nineteen and never returned. After college I mostly gave up struggling with my gender presentation; I decided that masculine woman was the closest gender that fit. I found a few men who would date me, though they would encourage me to dress more femme, especially for special occasions. I still felt disquieted at the idea of being a masculine woman who wasn't attracted to women; I longed for a non-queer representation of my gender and could not find it.

One night, while browsing through an online dating site, I stumbled on a profile of someone whom I found aesthetically pleasing, and who offered up hir gender identity as *genderqueer*. I'd never seen that word before! It was like I had been struck by a bolt of lightning; I knew deep in my soul as soon as I saw the definition that it applied to me—*was* me. Soon after, I dove headfirst into Tumblr and inhaled all the information I could find. I received my social justice warrior degree online; my conservative religious cobwebs were brutally scorched away with hours of reading intense online debate. I reconsidered everything I thought I knew.

As soon as I realized I was genderqueer, the next crisis hit. Was I, or was I not, transgender as well? For me, to accept I was transgender was to accept that I wanted to take steps toward presenting socially as a gender. If I wanted to transition, how did I want that to translate into my life? The world is set up on a binary: Where would I pee? What would my driver's license say? What pronouns did I want people to use? What would my name be? I was also dating a heterosexual man and knew transitioning would be the eventual death knell of our relationship.

After months of intense soul searching, I came to the conclusion that I would maintain two genders: a social gender and a personal gender. My social gender is the one of two binary options that feels less uncomfortable; for me, male is more comfortable than female. So it's the men's bathroom and an M on my driver's license and health insurance. My personal gender is my own internal gender, my true gender. And that is unabashedly genderqueer.

Pronouns were something of a task to figure out. When I came out at work and I told people they could use they/them or he/him, everyone used he/him (when they weren't misgendering me entirely by using "she" or "her"). For many people, it simply takes a while to get used to hearing their new pronouns. But it's been more than four years of he/him pronouns, and even after years of strangers and acquaintances reading me as a man, I have yet to feel comfortable with people referring to me as "he." Every time someone uses he/him pronouns to describe me, I look around, trying to figure out whom they're talking about. It feels like when I forget to cut the tags off of my T-shirt, scraping my skin and making me itch all over. It's become overwhelmingly obvious to me that they/them *are* my pronouns.

After my initial gender realization, I saw a therapist for six months. She was decidedly unhelpful, except perhaps in giving me an opportunity to practice setting boundaries and discontinuing services. She insisted I was really a straight trans man, and that nonbinary genders, bisexuality, and asexuality were not real. She pressured me to break up with my partner because he was cis and struggling to integrate my identity shift; she wanted me to start dating women. She pressured me to start hormone replacement therapy (HRT), even though I wasn't sure whether hormones were right for me.

It took a lot of internal debate and discussion to see another health provider. Luckily, I found a lovely, trans-affirming endocrinologist who was onboard with starting me on low-dose HRT, letting me direct the speed of medical transition. I still wasn't sure if it was what I wanted or needed. I went to the doctor's appointment, filled my prescription for transdermal T, and started T, all without being sure. Yet within a few days of starting testosterone, my body felt better, felt more like home.

In my moments of intense gender questioning, when I felt like I didn't know anything, I would make lists of things I did know. And one of the things at the very top was always top surgery. Within six weeks of top surgery, I started wondering why I had gotten rid of all my femme clothes. I felt so free; clothing suddenly fit how it was supposed to. As people began to read my masculinity as "man," I felt the need to adjust my expression to better reflect my gender in whatever way it wanted to manifest. And as I had done so many times before, I returned to Savers.

Even after I started a salaried job that solidly placed me in middle-class territory, I still couldn't abide the idea of paying more than a few dollars for clothes. Despite having a financial cushion, my brain would not let me forget: all it would take for me to be homeless was a few bad things hand in hand with a work layoff. Unlike many of my peers who were raised in upper-middle-class families, I didn't have well-off parents to bail me out if things went wrong. My parents' hold on their lower-middle-class status was always tenuous. My class insecurity snuck into many areas of my life. I found myself stocking up on nonperishables when I was stressed; I always picked the item I needed based on how cheap it was; I bought only sale items; I stayed in the motels with the most "value"; and, in general, I hoarded my money for that day when disaster would strike.

Despite these life changes, I always returned to Savers: my own private genderqueer boutique. My first necktie, the red tie that goes well with everything, came from Savers. It's silky soft, a rich crimson. It first adorned my sweaty neck the first time I wore pants to a wedding, complementing my navy blazer and khakis. It snuck its way into my work wardrobe, adding formality to black pants and a white dress shirt. It was worn at parties, around a bare neck, sitting on a bound chest. In time, it was accompanying me to work yet again, but as part of a different ensemble: a men's white dress shirt with the favored crimson tie, matched with a black skirt and ballet flats.

Savers also provided me with beginning attire for trapeze and circus arts. I started doing circus arts a year ago and it's been transformative. I'm getting to do similar things with my body as I did in gymnastics, but with a body that is mine. I'm still unlearning the toxic messages from gymnastics. In contrast, circus celebrates everyone; all bodies and all gender expressions are welcome. Circus has always been a refuge for the freaks and weirdos; people are celebrated for being their funky, unique selves. My expansive gender is encouraged. People have offered me their makeup before performances when I somehow neglect to bring mine. And performing has been brain-breaking for me; I perform to entertain people, not to attain technical excellence. Unlike with gymnastics, I don't start from perfection and then fuck up. I go out, perform tricks I enjoy accompanied by music I love, wow the crowd, and give them a window into what it can look like to be genderqueer and trans and at home in one's body.

CHAPTER TWENTY-THREE

The Flight of the Magpie

ADAM "PICAPICA" STEVENSON

2005

I am twenty years old and studying philosophy at the University of York. I have been cornered in the passageway between the toilets and the Student Union offices by my friend, a third-year linguistics student who had recorded my phone calls to study for their dissertation.

"You gave me a lot of work. I had to write a whole page about one of your conversations."

"What do you mean?" I asked.

"My dissertation is about gender in language. You broke the rules."

"How?"

"You managed to tell a whole story without revealing at any moment whether you were talking to a male or female. "

"I suppose I didn't feel the need to."

"All the other subjects did."

2006

It's July and I am going to my graduation. If it were my choice I wouldn't be here, but my Granny really wants to see it. I don't even know who the person next to me is, despite studying alongside them for three years. I barely know who any of the other philosophy graduates are. I'm not friends with any of them.

On my first day at university I had invited one home for a cup of tea and he'd told me he thought stupid people should be sterilized. I'd not mixed with philosophy people after that. I hated philosophy with a passion but I had been too stubborn and too arrogant in my intellectual abilities to change my course; instead I'd spent my time trying out new roles, without much success.

I entered wholeheartedly into the university's student drama society since I had always enjoyed performing. I catalogued props, painted sets, ran the box office, booked workshops, flyered shows, and acted in plays. I also wrote little pieces that I performed; on one memorable occasion where the script called for a mother feeding her baby, I found myself in a housedress feeding minidoughnuts to a middle-aged man with a large wooden spoon—the usual student drama stuff. Yet for all my work and effort, what I really wanted to do was direct a play, which was never approved; I was a philosophy student and couldn't talk the right drama-people language.

I had a go at student politics. I didn't really want to but a friend plied me with Southern Comfort until I agreed to run with him. Before long, we were tight pals and in charge of the hundred societies. He was the person with the ideas and I was the person with the talk. We changed a few things to make them more efficient and were hated for it. Later I stood for president, which I lost comprehensively, publicly, and embarrassingly.

At another point I was in a sketch show; I was in a horror film where I played an alien seed pod (laying on the floor outside a gents loo at three in the morning, wrapped in bin-bags and covered in KY jelly); I was in a band that split up before the first gig because we all caught mumps. I made my living dressing people up in old-fashioned clothes and taking their pictures. I spent all my money on trying every new kind of beer I could find. I ballooned in weight.

Living independently from my family, I also started to experiment with women's clothes, wearing women's knickers and socks daily. When I moved into a shared accommodation (with both men and women), I wore these clothes openly (except the dress, which I flounced only in private). I wore my pink pajamas when we sat and watched telly, my floral knickers drying on the rack alongside my housemates'. I didn't know why I was doing this at the time; they never asked me and I never asked myself. Like everything else I had done at university, it was unplanned and inconclusive.

So I sit at my graduation feeling like an utter failure and, worst of all, celebrating that failure in this stupid, public manner, wearing my dumb grey robe and silly square hat.

The only success I feel I really have achieved is writing a novel. I enjoyed doing it and the process made me feel like *me* in a way I couldn't describe. My plan after graduation had been to stay in York with some other literary friends and work on my writing, but I was evicted before I could move in because one of the flatmates didn't want to live with "too many males."

Instead, I'm forced to decamp to my parent's house in Coventry, a city of permanent drowsiness. I find dull work in a toyshop but it isn't long till they let me go. Soon, I find myself doing the same job I had when I was sixteen but, due to a change in labor laws, for less money. I am stuck and going nowhere.

I hadn't lived in Coventry long enough before I left for university to have built up a good network of friends, and the ones I do have are dispersed throughout the country. I console myself with Internet chat rooms. Online, I can converse and enjoy myself better if I pose as female. This small activity begins to worm into my consciousness. I begin to wonder, "might I do a better job navigating through real life as a woman, too?"

2003

I'm standing around a piano wearing a maroon gymslip and my hair in bunches singing "It's Raining Men" by the Weather Girls. I'm seventeen and I've only been at this school a year. I know a few people but not very well. This is the dress rehearsal for the school play. It's called "Daisy Pulls It Off" and it's a pastiche of schoolgirl stories of the 1920s. The school is a mixed-gender school, there are only three males cast in the play but only two male parts, so I am playing a schoolgirl called Monica. Around me are twenty girls, all in the same gymslips and black tights and singing.

It's not the first time I play a woman. When I was eight, I played Miss Marple in the school's creative interpretation of *The Wizard of Oz* (to oomph out the cast, the teachers had cleverly written a subplot about fictional detectives on the hunt for Dorothy). I had been specifically cast as an old biddy. The skirt had itched.

When I was thirteen I played a cross-dresser . . . in Latin. Going to a state school in Cambridge, we took our Latin play-reading competitions very seriously, as we wanted to beat the posh schools. The Latin teacher was a big *Rocky Horror* fan so I had been cast as a doddery old man who wanted to be a *salutatrix*—a slave dancer. Under my toga I wore a mini white dress and a pair of fishnet tights. The Latin teacher said I looked better in the dress then her daughter.

But right now I am a schoolgirl and someone has got the giggles and we are all laughing together.

"I like you," says the girl on my left, "you're just one of the girls."

EARLY 2007

I am back at home for a double funeral.

The previous year has come to a close and my dad's father has died of an illness, followed shortly after by my dad's mum. The atmosphere in the house is understandably gloomy. Everyone is cut off from everyone else by their own emotions. It's a dark Sunday evening in January and we sit in our living room watching *Antiques Roadshow* trying to guess how much the antiques will be worth. The phone rings and my mum picks it up. There is a noise, barely human to hear—a pure emotion, a wail—the saddest noise I have ever heard. My granny, the one who had forced me to go to my graduation, has died suddenly.

Of course I pick the wrong time. A fortnight after the funeral and the house still filled to the brim with sympathy cards. My emotions are churning in my stomach so much they hurt, but this is the way forward. Over Sunday dinner, I come out to them: I want to transition into a woman.

They are supportive at first, and ask gentle questions while my sister cries quietly to herself. But as the weeks go on, the support wanes. They don't believe that I really am trans. They think that the emotional turmoil in the house has mixed with the general depressed malaise of the last few years, that, rather than answering the questions of who I am in general and what I am going to do with my life, I have focused on gender, because although the way out is neither easy nor usual, it is at least mapped out. People who feel useless and lost due to their gender have a definite course to steer; people who feel useless and lost in general do not.

My friends say the same thing. Nobody agrees I am a woman. Even *I'm* not sure. I email my old housemate and political pal, who saw me in girl's PJ's most nights for a couple of years, and he gives me his opinion, that "everyone has some sort of conflict between male and female in them. It could be that this is just more pronounced with you. I think it points more to you being fairly 50/50 actually (even though that sounds silly)."

I agree with him. Being 50/50 sounds silly.

And yet . . .

1992

I am seven. Our teacher is sick and we have the school's standard supply teacher. I hate her as I have never hated anyone before. She makes the boys sit on one side of the classroom and the girls on the other. It's not her I hate, it's that line, the invisible one between the girls and the boys, the one I had never really noticed before. Nobody could straddle that line, could they?

Among the children there are three groups: boys, girls, and others. I am in the "others" group. We are a ragtag group of children. There's Fraser who needs an extra adult to help him, Ameeth with his clock-stopping stutter, Debbie in her dungarees, and Steph with the long, black eyelashes—and me, more interested in puppets, plays, animals, and stories than the boy and girl stuff.

We all like plays. We improvise plays in the playground, giving ourselves different parts and changing the plot until it's how we want it. Then we bring in pages of typewritten script and share them around, learning parts and bringing props and costumes until we have a full play to show. Rarely there's anybody to be an audience but we show one another and that's good enough for us. It's good being one of the others.

LATE 2007

I'm up a hill in Barcelona. Montjuïc.

With the money my granny left me, I have been able to fund an MA in writing at Middlesex University, with some leftover to go on holiday. The plan was to spend a month going around Spain, but as usual my plans have gone awry. After being pickpocketed twice, mugged once, and fleeced by every traveler's check cashier in town, the month has shrunk to two weeks and the whole of Spain has shrunk to Madrid plus a handful of cities in the north.

I'm flying out tomorrow, my trip half-finished, half-failed again. As I look back on those things that have befallen me, I look out at the sea, I look back at the good things I experienced: the Parc Guell, with its snakelike benches, a sight I had long wanted to see; wandering around the galleries of Madrid and discovering the weird Breughels I stared at in books as a teenager; meeting people as a lone traveler— from Guido, who had pointed me to good places to eat, to the girls I played cards with, to the French tramp with whom I'd shared my lunch when I was stuck all night on a park bench because it was a holiday and there was no room in any hotel or hostel. I can pick those golden moments, the shiny ones, and keep them to myself. As I sit here on the top of this hill watching the seagulls, I feel a wave of self-acceptance and a strange kind of forgiveness that never completely leaves me after.

And it helps that I have a new word—androgyne. After I came out earlier in the year, I explored what a person with a 50/50 gender split might be. I happened upon a website where I could discuss gender and gave myself the handle Pica Pica. It is the Latin name for the European Magpie and I chose it because of its fame for collecting shiny objects. I was going to do the same, fly both sides of the gender divide and pick all the shiny things for myself.

2008

I get back to England, move out of Coventry, take my masters in London and explore what this new word "androgyne" means.

I am now working on that masters; working on the next novel, working ungodly hours in a local pub and spending much of my spare time chatting androgyne stuff with others online. I love being an androgyne, though I haven't really learned how to pronounce it. Suddenly, I know why I didn't use the proper gendered language structures, why, when my breakdown shook the rocks of my identity, my gender was the weakest point that took the most damage, and why I hated the line the supply teacher placed between boys and girls.

I've adopted my new identity like the convert of a new religion. I am zealous in telling everyone the good news that it is possible to be both male and female or neither male nor female. I am didactic and dogmatic, I decree what is in the realm of androgyne and what isn't. I make videos where I lay down all my great insights into androgyne. It seems clear to me that I am an androgyne from birth and my inability to get hold of my life before is because I hadn't understood myself. I compose androgyne anthems in my head, I hold imaginary androgyne rallies in Trafalgar Square, where the great masses of the other-gendered are enlightened by speech. I alone have the message of androgyne-ness and I can heal great mental suffering and pain. I may be a little mad.

2017

Now I am thirty-one and I have calmed down. I no longer think or worry about why a person would have a nonbinary gender identity or what that exactly entails. Nor do I worry about how I represent that identity to the world. It's a bit like walking a long way and putting a heavy bag down.

I live in London and work as a primary school teacher, where I am often called "Mr." or "Sir" (although most of the younger children call me "Miss"). I still dress in my female pajamas and lounge around, just as I did as a male student. I have not changed my name, my body, the language others use to identify me. I recently cut my hair into a short, boyish haircut for the first time since my teens. To the outside world I am a slightly eccentric male.

But I have transitioned.

I have transitioned in the relationship with myself; I am comfortable with the male and female inside. It's been a slow process—a gradual 'getting-to-know-you.' I used to hold on to "androgyne" like a shield but as I have gotten used to myself, I've not needed it anymore. Sometimes I go back to the forums that shaped those feelings, or watch my old videos, but I do not connect with that anymore because somewhere along the way I have dropped that burden.

I can allow myself to chat with "the girls" as one of them and "the boys" as one of them. Since I am neither girl nor boy, I still get a lot wrong, but I no longer beat myself up about it. I can shrug my shoulders and say that I manage pretty well as an androgyne. I don't feel I have to hide parts of myself. I can talk with people honestly, can reveal both my masculine and my feminine passions and, most importantly, think of them not as one or the other, but as part of the androgyne whole.

Since becoming more comfortable with myself, I have found it much easier to make friends, although I am still working at keeping them once they inevitably move somewhere else. I never tell people I am an androgyne but sometimes *they* tell *me*. Every now and then someone will inform me that there is something different about me than other men, or that I have quite a pronounced female side. Sometimes they'll flat out say I am a girl, and instead of shriveling up inside or feeling strange, I can tell them that to me, male and female aren't all that important.

CHAPTER TWENTY-FOUR

An Outsider in My Own Landscape

S. E. SMITH

MY ENTIRE LIFE has been a politics of defiance. Teeth bared, claws out, tongue sharpened, ready and willing to defend myself from all comers—including those of my own communities who feel I am not *enough* of whatever they want me to be. This ferocity, this chip on my shoulder, is the thing that keeps me alive, the thing that gives me the strength to fight back. I will not cower in the corner, apologizing for my very existence; I will be messy and difficult where you will be forced to look at me, no matter how uncomfortable you find it. You should be uncomfortable. It is discomfort that makes us human.

I'm queer as in "fuck you."

I have spent over a decade living in conflict not just with my own body, but with cis and trans people alike who tell me my experience is insufficiently trans. At times I feel like a tree felled by expectations, waiting to be swarmed with chainsaw and axe so I can be chopped apart into neat, digestible rounds. But there are spikes inside me, waiting to throw the chain.

Here is a secret: sometimes I am very morbid.

It is a survival tactic for those of us who live in the between space, neither/nor. At a time when conversations about gender nonconformity are going mainstream, there is still no clear role model for what gender nonconformity *is*: What it means to be genderqueer, agender, bigender, genderfluid; why some of us also identify as trans and others do not, why some of us pursue transition and others do not. We are all navigating uncharted waters, drawing maps as we go. At times it is terrifying. Who am I? Who are you? To outsiders—including binary trans people—our uncertainty and struggle are sometimes read as evidence that we're just "special snowflakes" putting on a performance. And sometimes we are pitted against each other: for example, those who choose to transition, like me, are used as evidence that those who do not aren't "really" trans or gender nonconforming.

You can be a gender-nonconforming person who is perfectly happy in the body you're in. You can also be someone who needs to transition, and both of these things are equally valid. These are the things I remind myself of when I wake up in the morning feeling bitter and fractious. Sometimes society needs to be told to stuff it.

Say it with me: "Stuff it, society."

But at the same time, let's not pretend that society doesn't influence the way we think about our identities, doesn't imbue us with a sense of alienation as we struggle to belong in a world that rejects us at every turn. As I thought about transition for myself, and what it would look like, I wondered how much that vision was mediated by society, pop culture, and even the trans community itself. I wanted to disentangle who I knew myself to be from the pressures I experienced both within and without my community. What does it mean to be "genderqueer"? What do "genderqueer" people look like? If existing outside the binary is supposed to free me of specific gender constructs and pressures on body image, why do I sometimes feel as narrowly trapped as women and men do?

I want to say that I have this vision of myself on my own, but that would be a lie, because clearly my idea of what a genderqueer person looks like is drawn straight from what people tell me we are supposed to look like. The idealized body I visualize when I glare at myself in the mirror is thin, flat-chested—a long lean whippet of a boy who might be a girl or who might be something else entirely. Gender-nonconforming people are depicted as "androgynous" in pop culture, but this mysteriously seems to mean "masculine." It might seem unfair to turn to supermodels and magazine spreads as models for body image, but men and women do it too: our beauty ideals as a society are shaped by these pressures. It's easy to say that we should move beyond beauty, as Jane Pratt once famously said, but it's harder to put into practice.

We aren't shown with breasts or curvy bodies; we tend not to be depicted as large people with stacked muscles and beards, either, but the spectrum leans toward the popular cultural perception of the epicene masculine-as-neutral. Those of us born with internal genitals are supposed to be short, cute, and slim—or lanky, with dramatic cheekbones—with short hair and tough, wiry bodies. Media darlings like Ruby Rose and Tilda Swinton are angular, defiant. There is no softness to them. To be socially acceptable, to be *successfully* gender nonconforming, one must be thin, narrow, tomboyish. Tomboyish—there it is, right in the name: boy. The depiction of our bodies in pop culture often falls into that of a femme man crossed with a butch woman—observers do a double take, asking themselves whether that person is a boy or girl.

They don't ask another question: Why does it matter so much to them?

From the start, my fear and fascination with my own transition became bound in the limitations of my own body. I am irredeemably short, fat, round-faced. I was once big-breasted and big-hipped, more 1950s pinup than 2010s genderqueer ideal. Could you be a fat genderqueer? A femme genderqueer? The ethereal genderqueer aesthetic was never achievable for me. It led me to wonder if I belonged anywhere at all.

I wish I could wear clothing tailored for cis men, but it doesn't fit right on the shape of my body. I cannot button suit coats over my chest, pants are too long and trail on the sidewalk behind me. Shoes are comically large, vests look ridiculous, ties make me feel like I'm choking. While I love the idea of specialty fashion houses that cater to gender-nonconforming people, they are way beyond my budget. To wear the "men's" cuts I can afford is to be a sad, pathetic clown flopping in clothing that obviously doesn't fit my peculiarly proportioned body, one that such clothes were never designed for. Gender expression becomes a matter of cold cash realities.

I love wearing drag—which for me is skirts and dresses, paired with close-cropped hair, bare face, and big earrings, a mixture of elements to confuse the observer. But to dress in women's clothing, even when

I am having fun and enjoying it, is to be forcibly read as a woman by the people around me unless I explicitly clarify otherwise, which leaves me uncomfortable and nervous. Sometimes I settle for the American uniform of ambiguity, jeans or slacks and a tee. But even then, my swaying hips give me away. No matter what I wear, my body outs me.

When most people look at me, they see a woman, and when most people gender me, they call me "she." Even after years of HRT and long past top surgery, people still feminize me, though the further into transition I get, the more uncertain they become. This, in turn, upsets them, turns them hostile, particularly when I refuse to provide the answer they want when they wonder, "which one are you?"

I want to stand for other genderqueers like me, who struggle in their bodies, who might at times feel conflicted about whether they are entering transition for themselves or for the sake of performing gender the "right" way. Early in transition, I was featured in the *San Francisco Chronicle* as an example of what a genderqueer person looks like, how we live our lives. But in the photo essay that accompanied the article, all I saw was a fat woman squinting into the camera lens. I felt like a pretender. My friends told me to avoid the comments.

Would I have been as unhappy in the body nature and genes saddled me with if society and some corners of the trans community could move beyond their notions of embodiment and gender? Even as I ferociously defend the right to present and perform gender in any way you want, I am gnawed at by this question. I will never really know whether I hate myself because I experience a conflict between my gender and my body, or if my relationship with gender is in conflict with what society says "genderqueer" is supposed to look like.

It took me a long time to come into an understanding of my own identity. I grew up right at the cusp of this era of abundant resources, where discussions about gender and identity and queerness and the wide spectrum of human existence are only a few clicks away, featured on shelves at the local bookstores, advertised as public talks on signboards at universities. I had to learn many gender lessons on my own. I furtively read trans memoirs and tried to find myself in them. I sat around living rooms with my trans friends and watched them shift through their identities and become something new.

It took me even longer to tentatively label myself as genderqueer, to shyly present this as my gender, to advocate for myself. Longer still for me to begin to assert myself, to enter the endless struggle many of us have with pronouns. Sometimes I want to call myself "it," in defiance, in rage, to make a point. On those days I am feeling monstrous, something burdensome and heavy that stalks through the hallways of life. I know that so many people feel "it" is dehumanizing, that the word is actively used against trans women to marginalize them. I have been there when my friends are called "it" and "she-male" and I wonder if it is even my word to reclaim. Am I freak enough, in my genderqueer, queer, disabled body? Am I freak enough when people shout "tranny" at me in the street of my small town?

Many of us are pressured to just "pick a gender" by the people around us; I must either reluctantly embrace femininity or perform masculinity. An Internet commenter says that I "look like a woman" so that's what she's calling me, regardless of what I might "claim" to be. Society has no method of dealing with people who are neither, and rigidly insists on slotting us into one category or the other, no matter how hard we struggle or how loudly we scream.

I cannot deny the pain that trans men and women experience, the risks they experience on a daily basis, the climbing death toll for trans women, particularly those who live on society's margins. At the same time, I watch their conversations unfold, cringe as they tear me apart, perpetuating the medicalized gatekeeping of transgender bodies and identities.

I scroll through a politics of exclusion, the very thing our forbearers fought against for so long. Some of the things they say remind me of the things cis people say. They reinforce my own fears that I am not good enough. That I am a faker. That I am being difficult. Dan Savage, creator of It Gets Better and gay icon to so many, mocks my pronouns on Twitter. Many others join in. It becomes a multiday affair spread across the Internet, spilling into a hit piece on *Gawker*. *Yes*, I whisper into my pillow. *Yes, genderqueer people are constantly challenged over our identities. And maybe*, I say, *it doesn't get better.*

I overhear comments that being genderqueer is just "fashionable"—as though my gender is like an infinity scarf, something to be picked up for a season and then discarded when it's no longer in vogue. People accuse us of having "passing privilege," which is a bit of a double-edged sword. Can and do I pass as a woman? Yes, though less so these days. But I also do so at great personal cost, for to pretend to be something you are not is painful, and it is even more painful to deny a hard-won and hard-fought part of your identity. Sometimes I am exhausted, coming home from social events where I've spent the whole night pretending to be a woman, or silently allowing people to decide I am one. And I am not always touched with "passing privilege." I've been run out of bathrooms, stared at in dressing rooms, asked to cover my upper body when cis men are not—reminders that my body is unknown, other, unsettling because it defies assumptions and expectations.

We are dreaming things that a previous generation never imagined, but those dreams are sometimes night terrors, too, frustrated visions of our oppression. I think of Sasha Fleischman, the agender teenager set on fire for wearing a skirt while they slept on the 57 bus in Oakland. I think of Gwynevere River Song, a twenty-six-year-old shot to death in their own Texas home, and of Jamie Lee Wounded Arrow, a two-spirit Oglala Lakota woman murdered in South Dakota. I think of *A Gender Not Listed Here*,[1] a study from 2012 documenting the increased incidence of physical and sexual violence, harassment, unemployment, and health care discrimination in gender-nonconforming communities.

It is painful to be called her, she, girlfriend, lady, woman, gal, even when these things are said with affection and love. It is painful to know that correcting these things would require a long, complex conversation that not everyone is ready or able to have—that sometimes, it is easier to clench your teeth, to smile and nod. "Sure," I say, "I'm Joe Smith's daughter."

Sometimes I feel like a superspy, flipping through my passports to decide who I am going to be. Am I going to go out in high femme drag with queer friends who will be careful to avoid gendering me, where I can inhabit myself to the fullest, wearing skirts and dresses because they are fun and part of my gender expression? Or am I going to strap myself into those same garments to miserably endure forcible passing as a woman at a dinner party with people I don't know well who would be confused and alienated by who I really am? When I don a formal dress to avoid spending an evening being interrogated about my gender by strangers, who incidentally take pains to explain how they

---

1. J. Harrison, J. Grant, and J. L. Herman, *A Gender Not Listed Here: Gender-queers, Gender Rebels, and Otherwise in the National Transgender Discrimination Survey* (Los Angeles: eScholarship, University of California, 2012).

don't "get" it, it feels like a concession. Okay, you won, fooled ya, guess I was a girl after all.

There is, too, the passport for paneling at a conference where I will be derailed by another panelist who realizes I'm not the woman she thought I was. She asks me to give a thumbnail explanation of gender-nonconforming identities. She will place me in the situation of speaking for every gender-nonconforming person ever. When I am trapped behind that microphone, I will watch half of the room go deathly still with embarrassment, while the other half will lean forward with prurient curiosity. The panel is supposed to be about heroines in fantasy.

Sometimes I just want to be a person, not my gender.

I wonder whether superspies ever decide to stay in bed and read under the covers in the distant light of a lamp glowing through the top sheet. The cat purring beside me doesn't care about gender one way or the other, as long as I give him his dinner on time.

Gender, they say, is a social construct. As though this radical statement erases gender altogether. Gender is who we are raised to be, it is who we become, it is who we are, it is who we are perceived as. Gender is the thing that gets me interviews because my name looks like a man's and then gets me "thank you so much for coming in, we'll be in touch" because my body is indecipherable, or is forcibly classified as feminine. Gender is the thing that gets us male politicians and female secretaries and long, lengthy discussions in feminism and social justice movements where there are only two genders, where even social progressives tell us to wait our turn, it's not time for "fringe issues."

Gender is the thing on the bathroom doors that leaves us out. Gender is the tick box that doesn't exist for us. Gender is the question some of us struggle to answer. Gender is the thing some of us must explicitly out; "yes, I know I look like this, but I'm not." Gender is the uneasy silence that hits the room when someone says "but what about people who aren't men or women?"

In a world where so many people grapple with the very *idea* of gender-nonconforming identities, where people are obsessed with instantly categorizing other people, we are an upsetting unknown. We are the antimatter that defies explanation. "Why can't someone look at you and declare that you're a woman?" they want to know.

When we are acknowledged at all, we are told by society—even our own trans community—that we are supposed to look this way, act this way, talk this way, as though we are uniform, as though there aren't cascading identities within the gender-nonconforming umbrella. I see this dismissed as internecine squabbling, as petty arguments over identities and labels: Does it really matter if someone is genderqueer or androgyne or genderfuck? Agender or nongender? Why can't people just be quiet about their genders already?

Why does it matter so much to us?

I hear from some feminists that we hate ourselves, that, as a genderqueer, I'm just trying to distance myself from an identity as a woman because I'm self-hating, secretly misogynistic, suffering from internalized sexism. I just need to come to terms with my womanhood, they say, with the stinking hateful betrayal of a body that continually reminded me of the parts I was born with before I carved them away.

People ask: "How can you struggle with body image when there is no clearly defined social standard for what your body is supposed to look like?"

My reply: Your willingness to completely ignore who I am, to erase me instead of facing me, yes, there, that, what you just said, *that* is why I struggle with body image. As long as people forcibly label me as someone I am not, I will forever be an outsider in my own landscape.

PART FIVE

Redefining Dualities

Paradoxes and Possibilities of Gender

CHAPTER TWENTY-FIVE

Not-Two

AVERY ERICKSON

"DILIGENTLY, ARDENTLY."

The penetrating, heavily accented voice of our "teacher" booms over the loudspeaker in the meditation hall, shaking us from our wandering fantasies and sleep-deprived nods. The recorded voice of S. N. Goenka, a celebrated yet deceased Burmese meditation teacher continues to encourage us in our practice: scanning our bodies with awareness from top to bottom and back again, hour after hour, day after day. It is a practice of becoming deeply intimate with the reality of this present moment.

It's day four of ten of total silence in a Buddhist retreat. I walk from the main hall to my room on the men's side of the sex-segregated compound. I'm walking slowly, paying close attention to all the physical sensations as my legs move—the shift of muscles across bone in my hips, the extension of my knees, the feel of the earth under my feet, the tightness of my shoes as my feet have swollen from sitting for fourteen hours each day. I broaden my focus to include a swirl of the ever-present chatter of thoughts and feelings inside of me, which surprisingly sped up when everything external quieted down. And what they've been speaking—shouting, sometimes—is confusion, despair, and fear around my recent awareness that I have mixed feelings toward my body; I don't feel totally at home or authentic there.

I recall looking at the men in the communal bathroom earlier that morning. I had felt familiarity, but not identity. *I know this body, but something about it seems . . . not me.* Fear and a sense of otherness started to rise up inside me; I wondered if these men could sense that someone or something different was in their midst.

I wondered if they could smell it on me.

As the men went about their business, I became bashful, sheepish, grateful that no one was allowed to speak, not now and not for days— that I didn't have to interact, that they couldn't hear my voice.

That I couldn't hear my voice.

I snap back out of memory and stop for a moment halfway up the hill. I look across the compound to the women, wondering what the same situation would feel like on that side. I search my feelings and my body for a sense of recognition, of home, as I imagine myself on that side of the line, as a woman—or at least among women.

But, nothing.

No revelation, no epiphany, no clarity. Just the realization that I feel equally puzzled by the lived experience that is "woman" as I do "man." I know that spiritually, emotionally, I identify more with what our society says is the domain of woman—vulnerability, emotionality, wisdom. But beyond that I have no idea what it means to be a woman either.

Huh.

Back in the meditation hall, I sit with close-eyed awareness. It must be around five or six in the morning, though it's impossible to know for sure since there are no clocks or watches. All I know is I've been sitting here since 4 AM, repeatedly scanning my body. I intentionally hold my awareness on the parts of my body that the world says makes me "male."

At first, all I'm aware of is blankness. I can't (or don't want to?) be in touch with those parts of my body. I can feel and visualize my hands, my feet, my limbs, my face—but I can't feel my genitals, my chest. No imagery comes to my mind's eye. I'm curious and alarmed about this, and my head is flooded with questions, one after another:

Does this mean I'm trans? Do I have to change my body?

What will the people in my life think? Will they accept and love me? Will I be abandoned? Will I be safe?

What would it be like to have breasts? Do I need any of that? I don't feel like a "woman." What's a woman anyway? Or a man for that matter?

I'm so scared. Oh my god.

God damn it.

Fuck.

Question upon question, racing thought after racing thought. And no answers.

This cacophony of fears rising up out of the ether inside of me starts taking the form of future-tripping—scenario after scenario that I may have to endure, navigate, and confront with this new opaque realization; it is all instantaneous, rapid fire, relentless, never ending, like only the mind can be.

This torrent harkens back to the first day of the retreat. Usually folks don't fall apart until halfway through a long retreat. For me, it was immediate; I broke down staring at the forest, praying for help and guidance, feeling totally alone, isolated, terrified, and enraged at god, because who I seemingly thought I was was being turned over on its head in an instant.

But that's why I came to this retreat. I came for the same reason that anyone meditates, whether they realize it or not: to see what is true. To be aware of this life and be with this moment, just as they are. As I drove up to the retreat, I knew something was there, though I couldn't put my finger on it. From some inner mystery, I felt the intensity of feeling, the pressure of some force inside me pressing outward . . . It was just a matter of time, a matter of arriving, of being with my experience in a concentrated way, free of distractions.

As the days of sitting go on, things come more into focus, literally. I continue to pay extended attention to my chest and genitals, and find that I can feel them physically against my clothes and seat, but they don't feel like an integral part of my body. They're there, but not there. And my range of feelings about this goes from despair and what I would later identify as dysphoria to neutrality and disconnect and, occasionally, acceptance. My feelings about my own body are not consistent; sometimes I feel embodied and at home, sometimes it feels terribly wrong.

I don't know what to do with this. This is not the trans narrative of "born in the wrong body, hate my body" that I've heard and seen.

It is day seven of the retreat, traditionally the point in which most or all of the participants have cried, laughed, broken down, or broken through. The collective air is distinctively marked by a palpable settled-ness. Weighted silence, like the air between Christmas and New Year's.

Seemingly out of nowhere, all goes quiet in my busy mind, and a single word bubbles up, like the soft beginning of a simmer.

Avery.

I know in my heart and in my body that this is my name, my new name in this life; a name to reflect my new, slowly coalescing reality and identity.

And from then, I have been Avery.

Days and days of meditation later, I'm back at home in San Francisco. This city is the nominal mecca for all things queer and trans. It's the place where LGBTQI+ folks know to go when they need to find them-selves, find community, or find resources for survival, for thriving. I start my research, "diligently, ardently," and find myself in two com-munity support groups.

It's not easy—the trek across the bridge to other side of the bay after a full workweek on a Friday night—but the Pacific Center in Berkeley is the place that hosts an ongoing support group for trans women. I show up my first time alone, nervous, hopeful. I park, casing the build-ing out from afar, before finding the courage to enter.

I sit in the circle of our cramped room with women in various stages or manifestations of their transitions. I've taken to wearing a beanie over my short hair, a little tuft poking out the front of my head, which has traditionally sported an almost crew cut suitable for martial arts and wearing a motorcycle helmet. The tuft is one of my first intentional attempts at signaling externally that I'm more feminine inside than oth-erwise meets the eye. I've never grown my hair out before, and each new millimeter feels like a mile on the road to authenticity.

We go around the group as is customary, introducing ourselves, our identities, how we're doing that week. I listen intently. When it comes to me, I say, "Hi, my name is Avery . . . and this is the first time I've introduced myself by this name."

A wave of heat rushes up my body, into my face, a wave of fear, excite-ment, and shame, as well as relief as I say this out loud, to the world—as I testify, as I claim my seat. There are smiles, nods, calm congratula-tions, recognition and appreciation in their eyes. And just as quickly, the moment is over, the focus passes to the woman next to me. The usual discussion begins, and I listen intently, seeking to identify, seeking answers, seeking belonging and clarity.

I continue to do this, week after week, Friday evening bridge commute after Friday evening bridge commute. I get to know these women, sharing pie and shitty decaf coffee at the diner down the street. I find that I identify with what they say about their bodies. I identify with dysphoria—that feeling of pain around the "male" characteristics that I have, the feeling of pain of having my femininity not seen or acknowledged by others. The pain of wishing I had been born female.

And at the same time, I don't identify with being a woman.

I'm confused—how can I feel dysphoria about my body, want feminine physical characteristics, but not feel like a woman?

In contrast to me, the women in my group are very clear: *"I am a woman."* I wonder at first if I just haven't come to acceptance, if I don't feel I can legitimately stake that claim yet, but eventually will. But the longer I sit in that community room, and the more stories I hear of them asserting their womanness in a world that doesn't always accept it, the more I find that it's not me. I share the body experience of these trans women, but I don't feel like I'm a woman. I don't feel like I have any idea what a woman is.

On Thursday nights, I walk to the Gender Spectrum group at the Queer Life Center in San Francisco. I sit in a similar room, feel the same end-of-the-week exhaustion at being in yet another group, but this time I'm with a small group of fairly androgynous AFAB (assigned female at birth) people who unanimously use gender-neutral pronouns. They're all so hip and dapper, all young urban queers who look like they're in line for a Tegan and Sarah concert. I envy them.

I feel relief when I get to say that my pronouns are "they/them." There is a sense of recognition, of belonging, that in this group to be "they/them" is the norm.

The conversation then proceeds to the frustration at not being recognized as nonbinary, of constantly being misgendered as a "she" (or as a "he," for some of our more masculine-presenting members). We also speak about not being seen within the trans community, of not feeling that our identities are known and honored. Some speak to the joy that they felt upon getting top surgery, bringing them to a place of outward-presenting gender neutrality.

As I listen, week after week, I'm struck by a similar sensation that I experienced with the transwomen in Berkeley. In this case, I identify with what they're saying about their spirits and their identities, but I don't identify with their feelings about their body. In fact, I look around the room, and only see people with bodies that started "female"—a body I'd rather have, and don't. Over the weeks there is no one that is AMAB (assigned male at birth) like me. I feel lonely, isolated, confused.

Again.

I don't understand how I can relate to them wholeheartedly, in my spirit, but feel different and apart in regard to my body.

Is there no group for people like me?

Zen is very skeptical of words and ideas.

"Zen" brings many images to folks' minds. People share with me that Zen means to be calm, collected, skillful, focused, mentally clear. It can evoke East Asian imagery, feelings of settledness, a figurative mountain amid a storm.

For me, Zen is sometimes these things, but it is also rage, fear, confusion, despair, love, obsession, delusion—and any other experience or sensation that naturally arises in life and in consciousness. It is about being aware of and totally experiencing what is, about leaving our judgments at the door and dropping into direct experience. It is about practices that help one drop below, or break out of, our conditioned thinking and limited perception.

It is about seeing beyond dualities.

In Soto Zen, a spiritual practice that has developed my ability to *be* in all of my life, sitting meditation is the main practice. Sitting with a focus, but oftentimes just sitting. Lots and lots of sitting. Just sitting, and being aware to the best of one's ability of all that shows up. Just watching it, letting it be, not pushing it away or holding on to it. Bearing witness and embodying.

Loving unconditionally by simply allowing.

I was graced to have this practice before gender showed up in a big way in my life, and it has allowed me to fully experience and live all that entails my being a nonbinary person. To be nonbinary means to embody qualities that our dualistic minds say are oppositional or in conflict—feminine and masculine, outgoing and introverted, assertive and receptive, yang and yin. I'm a femme-presenting and -identifying person who competed in martial arts and rides motorcycles too fast. I'm assertive and ambitious, a working professional; and, I long to be a housewife that makes lunches and takes the kids to school. I have been part of both men's and women's groups, and have identified with parts of both. I've also felt isolated and not part of either.

I have breasts and a penis.

Textual studies—sutras and koans—are another part of Zen practice. They are designed to confound our normal discursive thinking, to see beyond the "normal" appearance of things. There is a very famous Buddhist poem called *The Mind of Absolute Trust*. Realizations through this teaching text have brought me great peace, ease, and joy around being nonbinary. It starts by stating:

> The Great Way isn't difficult for those who are unattached to
>   their preferences

In other words, living a life of serenity, acceptance, and contentment is the natural result of letting go of one's mental preferences and judgments. As I became aware of my transness, I at first preferred—wanted, longed—for it to fit in a box, to be one or the other. If I wasn't male then surely I had to be female. This was the concept I was familiar with.

However, as time went on, I found that I didn't fit that model, and the more I tried to define and label it, to prefer part of my experience over another, the more pain I felt. Only as I softened my internal grip, as I let my gender arise and express itself as it would naturally in each moment, did I feel peace and ease. It became just a flow of experience and activity with no beginning and no end, unfettered by my mind's judgments and commentaries.

> Dividing things by opposites is a disease of the mind
> The more you think about these matters, the farther you are from
>   the truth
> Step aside from all thinking, and there's nowhere you can't go

Freedom and ease in my gender authenticity have not been a matter of figuring it out, but instead have been about stepping aside from thinking, about letting go of my preconceived ideas about gender and its relationship to body and spirit. I have had to drop into my body, into my gut—the place where guidance and acceptance live. In the body there is no gender conditioning or training, there's no "yeah, but . . . ," no masculine or feminine—just simply what *is* in a given moment.

> If you want to describe its essence, the best you can say is
>   "Not-two"
> In this "Not-two," nothing is separate, and nothing in the world
>   is excluded

One thing at a certain time and place is "feminine," at another time "masculine." It is all relative and therefore unreliable in providing an eternal, abiding, or unchanging label. The binary, the duality, the either-or, ends up limiting us rather than liberating us.

There are no limits in my gender, the only the limitations are in my own mind and what/who I give myself permission to be. The only limitations that have ever truly existed were within me. Paradoxically, one can argue that there are external limits on gender—safety, societal acceptance. But, if there are no internal limits, nothing anyone else thinks, says, or does can keep me from manifesting and embodying my own authenticity, this little sliver of the divine, the Beloved.

> With not even a trace of self-doubt, you can trust the universe
>   completely
> All at once you are free, with nothing left to hold on to
> All is empty, brilliant, perfect in its own being
> As vast as infinite space, it is perfect and lacks nothing
> The mind of absolute trust is beyond all thought, all striving, is
>   perfectly at peace

In being nonbinary, there is nothing to figure out, nothing to get to—it's already within me. I came to trust my own experiences and conviction along all the dimensions of what we call gender—presentation, roles, bodies, sex—"diligently and ardently," but I was also fraught with confusion, despair, fear, and excitement.

> In the ultimate freedom there are no doctrines
> When your mind merges with impartiality, both making and
>   being made disappear

Meditation and Zen study allowed me to not need to be in a box, to see the labels and boxes as transparent, flimsy, as just tools—useful to a point, but ineffective or dangerous in the wrong circumstances or the wrong hands. It challenged me to be in touch with whatever showed up in a given moment, and with the space and opportunity to fully embody and love all of myself totally, regardless of how my mind or others gendered that behavior or experience.

When I eventually left both the trans women's and gender spectrum groups, I wondered where *my* group was. Turns out that part of it was here all along, in the form of my Zen sangha. *Sangha* means community of spiritual practitioners, other people on the path with you who are committed to living an awakened life. It is considered an essential and irreplaceable element of a spiritual life.

My sangha teacher, with whom I share most everything, knows my life, my struggles, my thoughts, my patterns. She supports me and holds me accountable. She guides me to live my life fully and in alignment with my principles. She has seen my journey around gender in all its facets.

It is to her I first bring my needs around gender pronouns in our community. We sit face to face on cushions in our temple zendo, or meditation hall, for dokusan, or formal discussion between teacher and student. "I really don't identify as a 'he,' anymore," I say. "I'm really more of a 'them,' someone's whose gender is both male and female and neither male nor female, unknown at times, fluid, changing."

"No separation, not two," she says with a smile. She asks me more clarifying questions, truly excited and curious in her inquiry. She also thanks me for my practice, for giving her something juicy to likewise practice: her own mental conditioning around gender, her habit patterns around language and the limitations of language, and the call to constantly return to the reality in front of us. In this case, me. "I feel both grief and a sense of excitement," she confides. She affirms her commitment to supporting and honoring who I am and who I am becoming.

I feel overwhelming gratitude and a sense of belonging not only to be acknowledged and seen, but to be thanked and honored. I tear up and feel my heart under my robe, the Zen robe I've sewn by hand that acknowledges my formal entering into the stream of our lineage.

What I found over time, and came to embody and love, is that it wasn't about finding my place in the trans and queer community, but a matter of *making* it, of making a place for myself in all of my communities.

It's been a matter of creating and sharing concepts and new terminology that are roomy enough to include all of me—someone who is nonbinary but also transfeminine. Someone who doesn't identify as a woman but presents like one most of the time, and moves their body toward female. Someone who sees the ideas of women and men, male and female, masculine and feminine, as just words and concepts that can limit our ability to perceive reality and live our authentic lives. Someone who by simply being alive and authentic explodes the duality between the physical and the spiritual, who demonstrates that one's spiritual sense of themselves and their physical manifestation are at once independent and inseparable—what Zen calls "simultaneous inclusion" of the relative and the absolute.

Through this realization and this actualization I have found freedom, contentment, joy, and presence. I am infinitely grateful to this practice, this community, and for the opportunity to be alive and to be nonbinary.

My Zen teacher then suggests that our sangha could use my gender and pronouns as an opportunity to practice. She gives me a platform at one of our study nights to come out formally at group level, and to make my needs known.

She thanks me in front of the others. The others thank me for my vulnerability and offering. They tell me they love me.

CHAPTER TWENTY-SIX

Kitchen Sink Gender

NINO CIPRI

I SHOWED UP in a pink tank top that said "SEAHORSES AGAINST GENDER ROLES." I'd shaved off two-thirds of my hair the week before. I was covered in tattoos and body hair and attitude: my normal public armor when venturing into potentially hostile territories. I signed in and stood awkwardly next to a pole, waiting for class to start. When everyone was ready, the instructor called, "All right, ladies, ready to begin?"

I bought the pole-dancing class Groupon with the idea that I'd someday write an essay titled something along the lines of "I, a Queer Trans Nonbinary Weirdo, Took A Pole-Dancing Fitness Class So You Don't Have To." It was going to be an adventure into the mysterious world of straight yuppie ladies who wanted something edgier than Zumba. I was misgendered on the phone before I even got there, and then again once class started, despite my customary polite "heads up, I'm trans" email: "my name is Nino, I'm nonbinary and trans, my pronouns are they/them/their; if you need any explanation of these terms, I recommend the following sites . . ."

I wish that misgendering was not a unifying experience among transgender and nonbinary people. But I'm thirty-two, and I've realized that no matter how artfully I wield signifiers of my gender—hair, clothes, tattoos, attitude, THEY/THEM buttons—these still miss their mark on some cisgender folks. Context (like a pole-dancing class or a customer service job) adds weight to the physical characteristics I can't or don't hide: narrow shoulders, boobs, wide hips. That tips the scales for most people, in one direction or another. Both directions are wrong, but how much time I'm willing to spend correcting the inevitable misconception is its own equation. That same context + how often I see this person + how much of my time I think they're gonna waste = *fuck it*, more often than not.

After the instructor finished calling all of us ladies again, we started our warm-up. The teacher put on "I Like It" by Bruno Mars, a song that seems tailored for my own existential despair.

It all seemed to be going according to plan, and I expected to continue to hate the rest of the class.

But I didn't. This is not an essay about how pole-dancing "freed me," or any such pseudorevelatory nonsense. What I felt was more complicated than love/hate, triumph/failure, or any other binary can encompass.

As a kid, I remember watching my best friend's tumbling routines during gymnastics meets. I secretly thought that I'd be good at the sport, but I never signed up. There were a lot of reasons for that: money, time, preferring the fantasy over the twisted ankles. Plus, I had firmly fallen into the role of *tomboy* by then. I was not graceful. I was nobody's princess, and couldn't manage the regal posture, nor could I imagine wearing that much makeup. Gymnastics, dance recitals, playing the flute or the violin—I had a sense that these weren't for me. There was a prerequisite delicacy that I felt I lacked. Instead I spent my time on softball fields, in martial arts dojos, and in music practice rooms, blowing long, leisurely goose-shrieks on the saxophone.

As a part of this voluntary exit from the realms of femme, I was inevitably embedded in groups of cisgender men, where I occupied a liminal role: not a dude, but dudely enough to have my disruptive presence accepted, or at least utilized. I was often treated as a visiting scholar from Planet Woman, and was routinely used as the Google of female mysteries. I'll never forget the day when one of my fellow bike mechanics asked me what a hymen was, followed by another wondering aloud if virgins could get their periods. It's a special experience, having a group of male coworkers—who are ostensibly grown-ass adults—delve into such personal territory out of sheer ignorance.

But I picked up some bad habits in those all-dude spaces: most particularly, the art of refusing markers of femininity. American masculinity currently seems to center on saying no. It so often looks and feels like gender by process of elimination. Knowing that I wasn't a woman made me think I had to eschew anything that might lead anyone to think otherwise. It's a constant bargaining when it comes to being nonbinary, a trade-off between transparency and protection.

It took years to understand the depth of alienation I felt from both masculine and feminine spaces. I eventually mapped out my own liminal terrain, a space that overlapped both and neither. It was my body, my gender, and my life, and I could define those things for myself. I didn't have to be a woman, and I didn't have to transition to being a man. I could carve out an identity that fit me, rather than an abstract.

I had a friend who went hard into pole-dancing a few years ago, to the point where she had bought her own pole. It stood proudly in her living room, and during a pregaming session before a bar hop, she showed us some of the moves she'd learned. Prior to that, my understanding of pole-dancing was relegated to the trailer for *Showgirls* and Club Super Sex in Montreal, which I went to with a group of friends when we were eighteen. (Because of course we did.) Club Super Sex was a better education than *Showgirls*—someone actually *licks* a pole in that, which is (a) gross and (b) counterproductive when you're relying on friction to do your moves. The five of us sat awkwardly close to the stage, laughably young, clutching our overpriced beers to our chests. We were obviously Vermont hicks, dressed in worn jeans, boots, and T-shirts. The dancer came on stage, yelled at us in French (which none of us understood), then rolled her eyes and began her routine. We figured out what she'd been saying quickly enough, once her high heels skated in the air just above our heads: *move back and give me room to work, dumbasses.*

That night in my friend's apartment reminded me of those long-ago gymnastics meets. As I watched her show off her spins and climbs, I could acknowledge my own yearning, but instinctively dismissed it.

Pole-dancing was firmly affixed to the feminine realm: attractive, but not *for me*.

I surprised myself in that first class by actually enjoying it. Despite the misgendering, despite the worst songs that Spotify's Top 40 list could offer, despite being in a room full of mirrors and feeling deeply uncomfortable with what I saw when I looked in one, I liked it. It felt good, and oddly enough, I was sort of good at it. By the end of the first class, I had most of the moves down—not the ones that relied on flexibility or strength I hadn't yet developed, but even those, I could see the map to getting them. The teacher called me a natural. It was more complicated than that, though: it was (or would be) a lot of practice, and letting my body do the work it was capable of.

The second class was even better. It was taught by a different teacher, who described movements in, how shall I say, *earthier terms*.

"I think about body rolls like vomiting," Sylvia said, undulating from her hips up to the crown of her head. "Heeeuuurrrgh!"

Sylvia put no effort toward pretending that any of this was delicate. She showed off her bruises, and pointed out the places where she'd ripped off her skin so often that she'd lost feeling. It was like taking a dance class with Deadpool—which is to say that it was *great*. She reminded me a little of an acting teacher that frequently yelled at us to unclench our assholes, although Sylvia was more encouraging.

Pole-dancing isn't that different from hapkido, a martial art I practiced for four years. Except instead of flipping someone twice my weight over my hip, I was swinging my body into the air. The Juliet Spin, the Fireman, the Carousel, back and front hooks, body rolls, climbs, slides, sits. Walk with your chest high and shoulders back, steps languid. Loosen your death grip, use the muscles in your legs and not your arms, don't hold your head and neck so stiffly. Relax into it.

Relax.

That's where I ran into trouble.

I have an exquisitely tender relationship with my body: pain and pleasure and love and disappointment. I love my body for the things it does: carries me up mountains and flights of stairs, holds purring cats, makes silly faces, touches other bodies in all sorts of pleasing and enjoyable ways. I admire my long fingers, my facial hair, the bone structure of my face. I flex my arms in mirrors. I've tattooed my body, rubbed lotion into its skin, iced its joints, and applied liniment to its sore muscles. It hasn't always been easy, and our relationship has had its ups and downs.

And there's the dysphoria. I've worn binders and compression bras that press against my ribs like a slow asthma attack, but I'd take them over creeping anxiety and dissociation that pop up when I gaze down at my chest. I love my body, but strangers misinterpret it, as have friends, family members, and lovers. They see my breasts and soft belly and hips as something different than I do, *someone* different.

I often think of my body as a gift from my family: like several of the gifts they've given me over the years, it's really not what I would have picked out for myself.

My gender and my body are at odds with each other. Never is this more apparent than when I'm wearing booty shorts, falling into a spin like a trust exercise, knowing that these moves were created in appease- ment of an invisible hetero cis-male gaze. On good days, I'll flip off the male gaze and make *fuck me* faces at my own reflection. I can dance for myself, and for the music. I can channel that long-ago Quebecois dancer who shooed us out of the way: *get out of the way, assholes, I'm here to work.*

Other times, I can't meet my own gaze, can't get out of my own way. I've left some classes feeling like a stranger in my own skin. I'll struggle out of the sweat-soaked gear, stumble into the shower, and dig my fin- gers into my bruises until I feel like I'm back at home in my own body.

What exactly is feminine about pole-dancing, besides its traditional connection to burlesque?

Most of the pole-dancers I've met look like they could bench-press sleeper sofas from IKEA (it's currently the heaviest thing I can think of). And pole-dancing is not gentle on your body. In two months of pole dancing classes, I grew calluses on my hands the likes of which I hadn't seen since I was a landscaper. I collected bruises in unlikely places: inner thighs, outer ass cheek, armpits, the top of my shoulder, the backs of my knees. I lost several layers of skin off the top of my feet and shins from doing climbs, from relying on friction to hold myself aloft. I'd emerge from classes walking bowlegged as a cowboy after using the skin on my inner thighs to hold my body weight. Sylvia, in one class, introduced a particular move by saying, "We call this move *The Dislocator*. You can probably guess why."

I think the most feminine thing about pole-dancing is that it's a lot of pain, sweat, torn calluses, and bruises, but dancers are expected to make it look effortless. Women are not to be seen exerting themselves. Men can scream out their exertion and frustration, sweat puddles, and grunt like horny tortoises, but Heaven defend the femme accused of "trying too hard."

What I have learned from the femmes in my life (including the pole-dancers) is how to deconstruct this notion of that which appears effortless, of being a *natural* anything, rather than someone willing to invest resources into an action, a look, a creative or intellectual pursuit. There's something daring about *femme* that refutes postmodern coolness, in which we can only like things ironically or half-assedly. Caring is vulnerability, and vulnerability is a cardinal sin.

Vulnerability, I believe, is the first and foremost object of masculine refusal.

I had to disguise my own initial interest in pole-dancing under this banner of irony and disdain. When I liked it, I had to do some hard thinking about why I'd brought that baggage with me. Yes, part of it was due to getting misgendered almost immediately. But that was a regular part of my martial arts practice as well, where I was too nervous to even come out.

So where had this hesitance stemmed from? Was it a disdain for the feminine that I'd absorbed from the culture around me? I think that's part of the answer, but not all of it. My initial refusal might have originated in my time in all those cis-male dominated spaces, which I used to my own ends, as a trans and nonbinary person navigating a frequently hostile world. Saying no was a measure of control that I could exert over my identity: no to high heels, no to makeup, no to push-up bras, no to colorful clothing, no to long hair, no to jewelry, no to perfume, no to spa treatments, no to glitter, no to all of the fun shit that had been marked as femme. I wore a lot of gray and blue in my twenties: urban camouflage. I drank a lot of straight whiskey. I had a lot of unsatisfying sex that felt dirty, but not in the fun way. Looking back, I think it was a matter of caring too much about the wrong kinds of things. I'm not saying that I was doing gender wrong (there really is no such thing), but a lot of my actions were protective, not proactive.

It took me ten years to come to a new conclusion about my gender: that it could be a process of addition instead of subtraction. That I could, in fact, say yes to a particular kind of dress. That I could wear a dress and still feel comfortably masculine, or rather, that I could still feel comfortably *myself.*

I've started taking a kitchen sink approach to my gender: it all goes in, except the things that don't. Motorcycles are, in fact, part of my gender. So are boots. Whiskey is still a part of my gender. Eye shadow and blue lipstick have gotten mixed into it, but red lipstick and nail polish feel like drag, and not the fun kind. Turtlenecks might have been part of Steve Jobs's gender, but not mine. Practicing martial arts has been a long and complicated part of my gender. The kind of shirts that your gay uncle wears on his yearly visit to Key West? Definitely part of my gender. Cats are integral to my gender. The necklace my mother gave me. DIY haircuts. Calluses, scars, and tattoos. Gray dresses cut in the same style as a burlap bag. This one pair of high heels I bought last month. Baking, but not cooking, and definitely not reality TV shows about cooking.

How can these things be part of gender? I can hear some snarky critic getting ready to school me already. *Motorcycles are not inherently masculine.* I agree! My gender isn't inherently masculine either. It just really fucking likes motorcycles.

My gender surprises me—it dressed down for a long time, in gray corduroy and a peacoat. It kept its eyes averted. Now it has all kinds of demands.

I wanted to make pole-dancing mine, to absorb the practice into the liminal terrain I've mapped for myself. My gender looked up from a walk through the college town where I'd be spending the summer, and it saw a pole-dancing class, and it said, *yes, that.* One of the few times my body and gender actually agreed on something.

Pole-dancing is not unproblematic, for many obvious reasons. It can thoroughly fuck up your body: tear muscles, erode joints. The practice prizes particular body shapes over others. The space that I was in, at least, was annoyingly heteronormative. But once I ignore the top-forty music and the exhortations of the instructor, I can just concentrate on what my body does, on how my mass and weight shift and move. It satisfies the same need that my martial arts practice once did. Everything turning in circles, momentum and centrifugal force, friction and leverage. Forces meeting in a fluid exchange of power, a conversation between the body and its environment.

CHAPTER TWENTY-SEVEN

What Growing Up Punk Taught Me About Being Gender Nonconforming

CHRISTOPHER SOTO

AS A TEENAGER, I would buy women's jeans from the department store and sew the inseams. I would sew my pants as tight as possible, from the crotch down to the cuff. I would tighten the cuffs to a point where my feet could barely slip out of them. These were the days before skinny jeans were sold at stores, when everyone would sag their pants. These were the days when assimilationist fags couldn't even get married or appear on Ellen DeGeneres's talk show. To be brown and have jeans so tight that your cock and balls were showing was to be a target for street harassment in my hometown.

In PE class, I would have to ask my friends to help me pull off my pants because they were so tight. In those days, Levi's didn't sell skinny jeans and nobody in my friend group was "out" as queer.

The cis girls in our friend group would sew their jeans, too. We would put patches on them and on our jackets. We had cuts and dirt stains on all of our clothes. We visited homes in empty prairies where our friends would host backyard parties. The prairies with abandoned homes, homes that runaway youth would occupy, homes where folks would cook meth. There were coyotes fighting with house cats, grapevines, and orange trees. I would be charged ten dollars and go into a backyard party where hardcore and grindcore bands played. Someone called the cops. Someone started a fight and the next thing I knew there were gunshots outside. Our shirts were from thrift stores or from bands that we liked. Our hair was dyed bright colors— straightened and oddly cut.

One friend, Allie, cut my hair diagonally at the bangs. I had shaved bridges into the sides, and I was growing a rattail in the back. I had long sideburns. I pierced my septum with a safety pin, punching myself in the face so I wouldn't feel the pain. I tattooed my thigh at age fifteen in a stranger's living room. I smoked a bowl and pretended I didn't know my next tattoo was done by a white supremacist.

In my hometown, there were goths, cholos, bros, skaters, the blacks, the tongans, preps, and my friends, the punks.

For the most part, everyone minded their own business—except for the bros, who were always starting trouble with other groups. They even beat up a couple of the girls in our clique because they thought our pants were too tight. White people are violent and it's seldom seen that way. I grew consciousness around my race before I knew anything about gender or sexuality. I knew that police harassed me because I was brown. I knew that classmates would tease me because of my accent. My gender and sexuality were confusion that I could suppress or ignore. I thought all the boys liked grabbing cocks. I thought all the boys put on their sister's thongs and bras, tucked back their dick, and arched their backs. I remember the men looking at my prepubescent body and saying, "gay guy's a girl's best friend" when I was the only "boy" at the party, waving in my then-love for the Spice Girls.

Our parents assumed that we were always high, all us punks, though we were actually straight-edge (most of the time). The police would always follow us, but we weren't troublemakers.

I was a smart kid, but the teachers never respected my ideas.

To be punk was to resist, to accept the burden of being gawked at in return for living a life of self-determination.

Being punk meant being an outcast, and it taught me how much society can isolate people that are different. First because I was a femme kid, then because I was a brown femme teen, then because I was a brown femme punk teen, now as someone who sometimes identifies as brown and sometimes trans or gender nonconforming or trans-femme or gender-fluid or gender-confused or agender or post-gender. I miss the days before any thinking about race, gender, sexuality. I miss being five years old and ignoring the cigarette burns on my baby sister's carpet. I miss playing with the brown girl down the block who had pigeons for pets or the old drunk man who carved a wooden cactus for me. I'm forever pressing flowers into perfume.

Someone might ask, *why put up with the burden, the harassment?* I'd tell them, I have no interest in being part of the "normal" world or communicating with people who cannot accept my differences. Honestly, normality is something that is not even obtainable for me now. I'm brown and have my hands and neck tattooed, my tongue is still wild, if an employer Googles me they'll know I'm an anarchistic prison abolitionist. Normal is a faraway thought.

The punks accepted me for who I was, despite how I looked. The punks loved my differences, my thoughts, my weirdness.

———————

It's more than a decade later: I don't really talk to punks anymore. I moved across the country and found new interests. I started focusing on my poetry writing and I identify as gender nonconforming sometimes. I started talking to QTGNC POC (Queer Trans Gender Non Conforming, People of Color) activists and then I stopped.

My struggle to understand my gender has been a long process, and it still continues. Lately, though, I've been thinking about the relationship between my teenage years as a punk and my reality as a gender nonconforming adult-ish now. How was my gender outside of the binary then and how is my gender outside of the binary now? What does it mean to be non-cis? What does it mean to be not-trans either? How has the false binary of cis versus trans limited the ways that we experience and can express gender? Does gender have to be stagnant or can it move? Why is gender so policed? Why can't gender fluctuate? Why can't we be illegitimate in our genders? What does it mean to call someone illegitimate in their gender? How have confines of the English language limited the ways that we relate to our genders? Why is gender not about fashion or presentation? Why is gender sometimes about fashion and presentation?

Can gender be a narrative instead of a word? I would like my gender to be a narrative about the experiences that I've had as a brown person who is often not granted the privileges of existing in spaces with "normal" white cis-men or cis-women. I'm a brown person whose narrative is not about the same experiences as binary trans men and women.

I've often been told to think within binaries. People regularly say, "You're either male or female" and "You're either cis or trans." I don't think it's that simple.

I've come to understand that I have *always been* gender nonconforming. To be punk is to be gender nonconforming, to fall outside cis standards of gender and beauty and acceptability.

To be punk is to understand street harassment, job discrimination, police profiling, and other costs associated with presenting yourself as outside of the gender binary. Yet being gender nonconforming should not be defined by experiences of violence. Being gender nonconforming is about more than experiencing violence—it contains laughter and joy and various formations of liberation.

Currently, mainstream definitions of trans-ness create trans identity as a destination to be arrived at. Trans becomes a place where one can find a stagnant, permanent home. There is a narrative around trans people—"I was a man born in a women's body" or vice versa—that is easily digestible to mainstream audiences. There are words to describe feelings separated from one's body: gender dysphoria. It is falsely thought that in order to be legitimately trans one must experience gender dysphoria, that one must arrive at their new gender like a destination. This is some people's narrative but not everyone's. Here, again, the discomfort that one feels around gender or the violence of one's gender becomes the definition of their experience.

I don't identify as trans (most of the time, anyway) because trans is often thought of as part of a binary. Those definitions don't relate to me: I don't pass or identify as a woman or a man most times. Sometimes people try to tell me what my gender is, but it's really just their ignorance showing.

My gender has a billion different opportunities for how it wants to present itself: I don't think of male as the antithesis of female, because that dichotomy in and of itself erases intersex people. And I don't think of trans as the antithesis of cis; that's limiting and erases the experiences of gender nonconforming people.

I identify as gender nonconforming because I've never been privileged by white cis-gender constructs. I have never seen a space for myself within the confines of cis manhood. What is cis-manhood? Am I a cis-man in a dress, in a shirt, with short hair, with a wig? What if I was assigned male at birth but I don't feel like there is a man *or* a woman inside of me? What if I was assigned male at birth but I feel like there is a peacock on fire flapping its wings on the beach inside of me? What if tomorrow the peacock is dead but a baby fawn walks out of the ocean of my gut and that is how I feel? Can that not be my gender? If not, why not?

Maybe someday this feeling, this resentment toward such strict notions of gender, will change.

Being a gender nonconforming youth, the main thing I loved about growing up punk was that I could fail the binary and still didn't have to put up with any trans-misogyny. Being punk, I could fail cis standards while also failing trans standards of legitimacy. I didn't have to prove myself as "legitimate." I could just *be.*

Now, I feel so many expectations about my gender, from cis and trans people alike. Like when I was punk, or came out queer, I'm still told that my existence is just a phase.

And I'm finally in a place where I'm okay with that. Even if my current gender presentation *is* just a phase, and shifts into something new, that's exciting. That's an opportunity for me to learn more about myself.

––––––––––––

It's been a year or two since I have stopped presenting outside of the binary. I have thrown away all of my femme cloths, my blue wigs, my nail polish and lipstick. I sometimes identify as a man (though it doesn't feel right to say cis) and I sometimes identify as gender nonconforming (though I am hesitant about saying it publicly too often). Maybe I don't want to lose the privileges—respect at work, walking down the street without fear—afforded to me when people assume that I am cis.

Right now, I would rather not identify with any gender at all.

I walk down the street and I feel the peacock kick inside my stomach, I feel a little girl inside of me dead. I walk down the street and I imagine my breasts growing after estrogen. I want to keep them hairy. I have a dream where I'm pregnant and then give birth in a bathtub. The whole bathtub is filled with my placenta. There is a dream where I'm more brave and I look the way that I feel. There is a dream I have where to be brown and to exist outside the binary does not feel like I'm being hunted anymore.

Yes, I know that most of the reason why I present within the binary now is because of fear. When presenting outside of the binary, I am catcalled and yelled at and have my photograph taken by strangers on the subway. I am laughed at. I am before my father as he calls me the wrong name. I am the wrong pronoun. I am scared to go in the bathroom. I am scared my partner won't love me. There is work discrimination; the LGBTQ non-profit I worked at was all white except for one person. They talked about trans lives but then fired me, the only non-cis employee. They talked about LGBTQ homeless youth and then fired me, a staff person who has experienced teenage houselessness. It was because of the cis-heterosexual white woman that I was fired. I made her uncomfortable. I know it.

Nonprofits—even LGBTQ ones—are not safe for brown nonbinary people; nor are public spaces, nor the home, nor the heart of a lover. When my gender has no destination, when it is always in transit from one place to the next, when it is punished so severely for transience, I would rather let you believe that I am cis. I feel safer here. Safer, but not home.

I tell my friend who still presents outside the binary that I want to be alive. I want to live. And so this is my gender: a desire to live. And if trans and gender nonconforming people were not killed and incarcerated and starved so constantly then maybe I would be more legitimately trans or nonbinary. Maybe if it weren't for capitalism then I wouldn't be so afraid of existing outside the binary. I wouldn't be afraid of dying poor and young.

I'm wearing pants today, my hair is short, you can call me sir. I know what's in my belly. She'll wake up someday.

My gender is and is not about fashion. My gender is and is not about the ways that I experience violence when presenting outside the binary. My gender has everything and nothing to do with how I was assigned at birth and how I am perceived. My gender is a private narrative that is unique to me and I'm only nonbinary because I think that might be an accurate feeling for right now. To call myself nonbinary feels, at times, like a haircut, where I look up and say, "yes, that's how I feel inside." To be nonbinary feels, at times, like when I was punk and looked up and said, "yes, that's how I feel inside." Definitely this is not how everyone experiences this narrative. I like that. I'm done writing now.

CHAPTER TWENTY-EIGHT

Rock a Bye Binary

JULES DE LA CRUZ

I DIDN'T ALWAYS PLAN to be married. It just happened. Much as I didn't set out to be a parent, but that is where I now find myself. Firmly knotted and about to be with child. Technically I am not carrying—my wife is the one who has endured the years of shots and prods and pokes and endless examinations, blood samples, and biological humiliation, as we have sought the miracle of life through the assistance of a fertility clinic. The care we have received these last few years has had a profound effect on both of us, but in turn, I really believe we have impacted them as well. There is always a sterility to the doctor/patient relationship, but when one is dealing with matters related to procreation, things get intimate. Really intimate. Obviously more so for my spouse than me, but in regard to a same-sex couple seeking to start a family, I think we might have trailblazed a bit. Not in the *Heather Has Two Mommies* arena—as that frontier has been breached a long time ago—but rather in a "How do you treat people that don't fit your gender box?" kind of way.

From the get-go I made trouble. I wasn't trying to be a pill but there are things that I notice that others don't, because they live and move in a comfortable world where their expression of gender is validated and encouraged (albeit to the point of being destructive) on a daily basis. These things that pigeonhole and bind and restrict, they get under my androgynous skin and I can't let them go. My wife knows this about me and has come to accept that I stick my foot in the door as it is being slammed. I'm lucky I still have two legs.

For example, I haven't legally changed my given first name from the flowery, significantly feminine "Juliet" to my now exclusively used gender-neutral name of "Jules." And despite the many requests on forms for me to indicate my "preferred name" in most every place that proudly asserts their progressive nature by bothering to ask me, they promptly go on to completely ignore my answer and instead call out as loudly as they can in any given tiny waiting room, "Juliet? Juliet? Is there a Juliet here?" This is generally followed by me reluctantly rising from my seat and being capped with stares and whispers along the lines of "Um, did you make a mistake there buddy? They called Juliet, not Romeo." In the instances that I have held my ground and said, "Do you mean Jules?," they inevitably doubled down right then and there and called out twice as loud, "MISS De La Cruz. Are YOU Miss De La Cruz?"—head cocked like they couldn't absorb the information coming out of this male figure that stands before them. Please. Just don't ask if you aren't going to check the answer.

I cleared this hurdle right away at the fertility clinic, only to immediately encounter the other side of the coin. When you are one-half of a couple seeking assistance to scientifically place a blastocyst inside a receptive womb, the partner without that womb is unintentionally disregarded. Not out of malice, but as a result of my wife's card-carrying birthing potential, she was listed as "intended parent #1." She is Quixote. I am Sancho. All eyes are on her and the role she will play.

Come appointment time we would wait together in the anteroom until a nurse appeared, beaming with kindly delight and hope, eye contact wishing all things pertaining to Motherhood to befall this sacred vessel. She would call out my wife's name and smile at her and her alone and rightly so, as she was the "primary" uterus. But for gosh sakes, I too will be changing dirty diapers and getting up in the middle of the night and, last I checked, we are in this together so maybe a small squeak of acknowledgment is allowed? Instead, they would call her up and I would anxiously wait to hear my name. *Any* name. But alas, there would be silence after she was called and I would rise begrudgingly, trailing behind as I carry the luggage, not the embryo. Factual, but that's beside the point.

I really shouldn't complain. We were there because we wanted to be. A deliberate act with the hopes of a deliberate result to alter the course of our deliberately planned lives. In some nearly imperceptible way, it seems as though the entire mood of cisgender couples in a fertility clinic mirrors a sense of failure and resignation, in contrast to those of us that are eagerly ordering up fertilization soldiers from a cryobank. It's as if same-sex couples long ago accepted that we cannot, so we are perfectly determined to figure out a way, to do. Like so many other marginalized groups in this world, we start out with the default doors closed and it is up to us to figure out how to get them to open. For many others, however, medically defined infertility is a blow to everything they have ever dreamed and believed their life could be. Every visit to that waiting room is confirmation that they couldn't do this alone. I'm sure that many of those people sitting there in that waiting room felt strangely out of place, slightly embarrassed, as if they didn't quite belong or wished they didn't have to be part of this club. Off kilter in a room full of people looking down at their shoes. As I have felt in every waiting room for most of my life. Hoping to not be singled out and humiliated. I empathize, truly I do and I can most assuredly say I know the heartache involved, if only because it has taken us so long to conceive, and for other reasons as well.

But there we were, all of us, crossing paths. The medical staff were seasoned professionals, extremely proud of the work they had done with same-sex couples, as well they should be; they were as warm and accepting and supportive of a place as any could be, but there was still a learning curve. They genuinely wanted to get this right, but had limited experience breaking a binary box. It's a wonder anyone in the business of babies is receptive at all, what with the overwhelming pressure that exists to immediately tie a pink headband around the crown of a day-old infant, lest anyone mistake the girl for a boy. The binary will not be strong with my little one.

From the very beginning there was a form. A blue form that went to male patients and a pink form to the females. In traditional couples seeking an answer, one of each is handed out requiring a full health history disclosure. Don't get me started on the pink and blue color assignment—I can spend days in places like Target pulling baby cards out that say, "Who's a big boy now, oh the things you can do!!" with trucks and sports equipment and tools and projects on them only to compare these with the nauseatingly pink ones with flowers and hearts and fashion designs that say, "What a pretty girl you are." No mention of any accomplishment other than the fact that this little girl is blossoming in looks. Nothing like improperly shaping a child's outlook on life with a pasty 4 x 6 paper. But this form in this place was standard procedure and my wife and I were each handed a pink one.

As I took the form from her, my wife's pleading eyes said, "Please for the love of g-d, don't make a scene. It's just a formality. Don't you want to have a baby?" I took the form with a silent scowl. Pink. Ugh. But then I looked at it. It was clearly designed for a person who would be medically carrying a baby. It asked everything about the recipient's lady parts that could possibly be gleaned from a piece of paper. Last period date, gynecological history, pregnancy history, etc. "What is this?" I stammered uncomfortably. Why do you need to know all of this?" And then, a nonchalance, tinged with just a hint of pride at having the opportunity to interact with yet *another* same-sex couple: "this isn't our first rodeo, don't ya know." "Oh, we give this to all of our female same-sex couples. You know, in case you decide to carry the baby." I thought my long-ago forgotten uterus placeholder would fall out on the floor right then and there. No chance of that, I said mentally. Never. Going. To. Happen. Really, just not my thing. And why the assumption? Not all cars race at Daytona. The parts are present, but don't assume that makes me a possible great nesting place for human cell formation. "No, no, I'm sorry, I'm not comfortable giving you my full health history for no apparent reason," I said. I'll take the form that you use for "intended parent with no chance of carrying the child." Um. Blink. Blink. Well, um, we don't have one of those. You get pink or blue. My wife was already nervous enough so I took the pink one. I felt a closer affinity to that one than the one that asked if my testicles had properly descended in puberty.

My wife, who often absorbs my discomfort and files it away for later action, told the doctor at a subsequent appointment what had transpired. She explained how uncomfortable it was for me to be pigeonholed into a pink or blue form that asked for information about my biologically female body. A form that assumed the things that apply to people who are cisgender and possess an identity that fits neatly and nicely into a color or one of two very rigid boxes. I have my own box thanks.

The doctor agreed. As a clinic, it never really crossed their mind that being asked questions about body parts could be uncomfortable for some people and just striking out a pink form and writing "not applicable" can still isolate and reflect a disconnect with society. That hurt could run deep. No matter how practical a two-form system might be, the binary form had to go. And so, a few visits later, the doctor gleefully presented the new "purple form" for me and people like me titled "Intended Parent #2." No digging around for history. Just acknowledging you as part of the process, in the medical chart. *Now* we were making progress. We brought it home and I filled it out with utter gratitude at having my own color.

———————

We have literally been trying to conceive since New Year's Eve 2014. That's how we celebrated the ball dropping. No alcohol the whole evening and on January 1 at 12:30 AM I gave my wife a "pop-shot" to force an egg to release, which in turn would allow for her egg to be inseminated within thirty-six hours. Intra Uterine Insemination, known as "IUI." That didn't work and we've been trying ever since. I can't say it is always this difficult for most people, but I know for some the dream never materializes and they move forward in their lives, grieving and regrouping as best they can. Some don't make it. This concept of being parents is really all that they shared, and when that is no longer possible, they aren't either. That wasn't ever a risk for us, my wife and I. We are pragmatic and rational and practically emotionless when it comes to things like this. Both on the same page, making the hard decisions, not letting life get in the way. So when it didn't work the first time or the second or the third, and we found ourselves implanting our last viable embryo after almost three years of trying IUI, IVF, multiple rounds of FET, tens of thousands of dollars later, we knew that if it didn't happen now, we were done. We gave it our best and there was no more to give. We mulled over adoption but not to any degree that could be called a plan. There was no other plan. We talked about what ifs and said the are you okays and slid right on into "I guess the furbabies will have to do." We will go on, we reassured ourselves.

The night before the last embryo transfer we grieved once more in advance because after this many disappointments we didn't dare hope. We had a note in our overflowing medical chart cautioning everyone, from receptionist to the doctor herself, from uttering a single positive thought within our earshot. It was strictly forbidden to give us anything that could then be taken away in an instant. Our hearts were calcified. The day of the final procedure I went to work afterward. My wife worked from home. We used to both take the day off, like it meant something. Not this time. The obligatory waiting week went by filled with my wife's off and on mournful utterances of "I don't feel anything." "I just know, I can tell . . . it didn't work." What could I do or say that could counter this? It wasn't my body. How could I feign hope when I had none? We found ourselves verbally reminding each other, "don't think positive, just assume it didn't work."

We waited almost ten days—well past the time you usually check your blood for signs of pregnancy—and the first blood test revealed an elevated level of hCG. Human chorionic gonadotropin, a hormone that is produced by the placenta that increases when implantation occurs. The numbers were high enough to indicate "something was happening." It's a good first sign, but we'd been there before only to have the number decline and, just to draw out the misery, linger long enough to ensure yet another distasteful medical procedure. "Pregnancy of unknown origin," they call it. Nothing really there but enough to be something that forces medical intervention. Another blood test a few days later and, yes, the numbers were still climbing. That's a very strong indicator and in any other situation would be warmly welcomed news, but in our world, not nearly enough to celebrate. I don't think I even smiled. When will the other shoe drop, we said. Plenty of rapidly developing cells just stop and don't make it past the first few weeks, elevated numbers be damned. We joke that it won't be until the head is crowning that we will believe.

Finally, weeks later an appointment for the first ultrasound. Another invasion of my vulnerable wife's personal space and quite possibly the most heartbreaking exam of them all, depending on the results. More ambiguity with our emotions. The doctor comes in and we hold our breath and I watch the screen. And then, amid electronic lines of white and spaces of black emerges the strongest, most beautiful heartbeat I will ever not hear. But I can see it. On a screen. Flickering, "hello, here I am." There is life inside.

We breathe. The doctor is pleased, my wife is overjoyed and tears stream down her face. She dabs at her eyes, beaming at me. Holding my hand. And at that very moment in time, immersed in an experience that defines many women the world over and binds them forever more to the species ritual of motherhood, I am filled with dread at being called "Mother."

Motherhood and all of the social construct that this word and act entail do not give much permission to those of us who are transgender to do such a thing. Oh, I know plenty of male-identified people that have birthed children, but in my experience, most were conceived in a time and a place too far back to recall exact details of how and why. First marriages, social pressures, identities that had yet to be established resulting in mistakes with a yet to regret beautiful son or daughter, or multiple kids as the outcome. Loved and cherished, all of them, despite the impetus. Even now with trailblazers like Thomas Beatie, the much publicized "Pregnant Man" appearing in the tabloids and even on the cover of *People* magazine, the image of a masculine-gendered individual voluntarily choosing to carry, suckling infant at the breast, is not publicly comforting. Visually represented as Madonna and child, Motherhood evokes femininity and flowery hearts and tender touches that are not acceptable territory for society's understanding of male-cored women.

One could argue that these traits are inherent in all of us and that, properly fostered, they will manifest in varying degrees, but I suspect that most cisgender men, as is the case with little girls that grow up doing boy things, get the short shrift on being the role models for what are considered "mothering" skills. This will change—of this I am certain—but for those that fully exhibit the XY, there is currently a path to parenting redemption. Assuming the role of the Father. Those that have fully transitioned to men often relish this title and if ever the word "daddy" meant something straight and narrow, it is as uttered by a child that knows nothing of the complexities of sex and gender identity. Some aspects of these rigid roles are showing signs of waning and inevitably every parent is called upon to "Mother and Father" at various times, interchangeably delivering the duality of soft and hard. This is really where we should all strive to be, no matter the circumstance, to whatever degree in which our chi was forged. A whole nurturing entity, unafraid to tap into both halves of our gender duality.

But to really get down to brass tacks, I am struggling with literally what to be called. The title of "mother" is still only seriously applied to the one that has the proper goods regardless of whether or not you birthed, adopted, or married into that role. I don't like the term "mother" applied to me any more than I currently like being called "lady," "ma'am," "girl," or any other feminine pronoun. Although I am equally as likely to respond to "sir" (or the newly found "boss") as I am to swivel my head if I hear "excuse me, miss," these words do not reflect that which is within. Sometimes both will happen within the realm of a single interaction and it's actually more comfortable, for I *am* both. Female and male. Balancing, yet likely to be tipped either way for any number of reasons. At least until the occasion is over. Should someone introduce me to my child's teacher as "this is Lemonseed's mother," well, I just don't know if I want to go there. And I am equally as certain I am not Lemonseed's father either.

There is much to be said about the need for and use of a new lexicon to describe that which has always existed but has heretofore not been acknowledged. An entire essay might be written on the blossoming of gender-neutral pronouns such as ze/hir, or *hen* in Swedish, or the honorific "Mx." instead of Mr. or Ms. With the introduction of words into various authoritative dictionaries such as "ginger" and "supercentenarian," I would argue that the least we can do is find a word that conveys the same awe and reverence of mother and father, without the binary connotations that inherently come along. Technically, the word "parent" has all the necessary ingredients, but it completely lacks the reverence that I desperately seek. A parent is detached and legalized. It carries no warmth or wholehearted sacrifice that defines a person that fills the shoes of a child's physical as well as emotional lifeline. I need a great title, like mother or father. After all, since I waited fifty-three years to become one, I demand an aptly assembled greeting card section. It can be well stuffed come Mother's Day *and* Father's Day. This should readily satisfy consumerism's marketing libido. It is not enough to tell me, "well there's only two to choose from so pick one." I refuse. And a plain, hollow, generic absence of title on the well-meaning card is not enough either.

What is a *mamsir* to do in situations like this? I of course turned to my wife for answers. For years now my wife has called me Mužy. It's pronounced "moo-gee" with a shoosh sound before the "gee." Not a hard "g"; more like "zshe." Don't worry if you don't initially get it; it is a uniquely Czech pronunciation, which is like rolling your r's in Spanish or a German *eszett*. Mužy is basically the Czech word for man

(Muž) with a feminized ending as denoted by a "y" in the language. Muž with a y. Mužy. And it had to be something Czech because well before I met my wife she had developed an obsession with Prague and the Czech Republic. I know it's her happy place, the place she calls her home away from home. It means the world to her. And so, after our first trip there together, she developed a little pet name for me. Mužy. I like it and it's easy and short and cute and it reminds me of her being in her happy place so that makes me happy too.

So, when I approached her with this mother/father dilemma of mine, fretting as to what to be called after the birth of our child, it was a relatively easy solution for her. "You will be known as 'Mamuž,'" she decreed. Wow, that was easy. It seemed familiar and comfortable and everything I had hoped it would be, full of love and admiration for my equal parts male and female. The only disadvantage is that no one outside of my little soon-to-be-expanding family will know what it means. Well, and all of you of course, but for the most part it isn't a well-known title for nonbinary folks like me but, heck, it's a start. I mean, someone had to utter the first "mama" or "papa" so if you should find yourself in this situation, searching for a word to denote the reverential mother- and father-ness in your persona, try it on. Mamuž. I'll share. And some day, there might even be a Hallmark section. All kidding aside, it fills the void for me now and most likely will be my trademarked name for life. My child will come to know me and call me by a name that is societally neither male nor female in force but will instead contain all of the best of both. This is the advantage to starting fresh down the path. No burdensome footprints of baggage ahead. No images of "Mommy Dearest" will precede me and I am free to forge (and ruin) my own reputation. What relief! I readily admit it is a disappointment to not have a perfectly established title waiting for me at the end of my wife's hours of labor and I'll feel somewhat distanced upon reading the congratulatory new mother (and possibly father) cards that are sure to be sent, but in the end, it isn't about a word. It is about the love that has persevered against all odds to bring us to this place. This threshold of parenthood. A Mother and a Mamuž.

We aren't out of the woods yet. We are just under the eight-week mark. Hardly time to start turning on the oven light to see how it's rising but the ingredients are there and the miraculous building blocks have all come together. We struggle every day to believe and to find joy in that which has so long been out of reach. There will be additional ultra-sounds for which we will be eternally grateful for the reconfirmation, right on up to the point where we might dare actually tell our loved ones the news. There are no plans for a traditional "gender reveal" party because in all honestly, what would we say? It's up to this little entity to declare their intended path and discover just the right reflection of that which is regarded as "male and female" in this all-too-often-binary world. And anywhere on the spectrum this Lemonseed finds them-selves is absolutely where we think they should be.

Author's Note: Less than forty-eight hours after writing this essay, we found out that our little Lemon had stopped growing and no longer had a heartbeat. There's really no explanation at this point. It's just the way things turn out sometimes. I wish I could say we were surprised but after all we've been through, it seemed par for the course. Reflecting on the impact this turn of events has on my identity, I struggled with whether or not to submit this piece but with my wife's permission and encouragement I believe that what I have written captures a moment in my life that may not ever be repeated and therefore honors the little girl that never came to be and the Mamuž that might still.

CHAPTER TWENTY-NINE

To Gender and Back

KORY MARTIN-DAMON

IT TOOK both my parents dying for me to realize that I could not please anyone else save myself. I went from an only child, juggling the expectations of two people, to being an orphan and hearing only my own voice. Suddenly, I found myself in a desert of grief—empty, yet full of emotions I didn't know what to do with.

Theirs were not the first deaths I had experienced. I come from a large Catholic Cuban family and almost every year saw the death of someone I knew. Sharp memories from childhood are of freezing funeral home viewing rooms filled with the sickly sweet musk of flowers and quiet weeping. By the time I was ten years old, I was no longer afraid of caskets or dead bodies or the interminable night that preceded the long drive to the cemetery the following morning.

My young life had been dominated by dichotomies. My parents practiced two faiths, one in secret and one in the open. My father was not only a Rosicrucian, but he was also a Santero, a healer who practiced the faith that was brought to Cuba from Africa by slaves and that later integrated aspects of Catholicism. My father held séances during which he "channeled" a spirit guide that healed people or gave advice. This was done in secret, for not everyone understood Santería or approved of it.

On Sundays, I went to Sunday school at the local Catholic church and later attended mass with my family. On my tenth birthday, I took Holy Communion wearing a stiffly starched white dress and veil. I wore white, lacy gloves and held a small, beautiful white Bible with exquisitely drawn pictures of Jesus, Mother Mary, and saints. My patent leather shoes were also white, as were the frilly ankle socks. I remember being extremely proud to be at church for Holy Communion. So proud was I that I blurted to my mother that I would grow up to be a priest. She narrowed her eyes and gave me a firm shake, rattling my teeth.

"You are a girl, young lady," she hissed. "If anything, you can be a nun." But nuns did not give sermons or wear the handsome collar. I knew I did not want to be a nun.

Before the moment I told my mother about my first secret wish, I had gone through life blithely unaware of what it meant to be a girl. I knew there was a difference between men and women. Women were softer, kinder, and liked to hug and kiss instead of shaking a hand to greet you. They had soft breasts against which I could pillow my head. Men were narrower, harder of body, and liked to rub their bristly beards against the soft skin of my cheek, burning it as they laughed. They also liked to hold their fingers out so I could pull while they let out gas. In other words, men were disgusting.

I found nothing interesting about boys; they were smelly and loud and teased mercilessly. My friends were incomprehensible and slightly nauseating as they became increasingly giggly and moon-eyed for boys. A year later, I was the first girl in my class to get a period and grow breasts. I then became endlessly fascinating to the boys.

My body's betrayal shook me to my core. My first period initiated me into the world of women; with it came expectations to suppress my masculine tendencies. Outwardly, I indeed conformed: I was slight and feminine and shy. Inwardly, I was seething with confusion and contradictions.

By now, it was ingrained in me that I could not be a priest, but letting go of that dream did not hurt too deeply, since I had discovered the public library and the joys of reading. Instead, I wanted to be a writer. For a long time, I held on to this second, secret wish, as I voraciously read anything that came into my hands. I was an exemplary student. I could not be any other way—my parents worked hard to send me to private school. My mother worked seven days a week, ten hours a day; I hardly ever saw her and missed her terribly. My only solace over the years was the books.

In 1984, I turned twenty-three and I moved out of my parents' apartment to my own. Although I was unsure of what I was looking for, I returned to books and began to do research on gender. I started with sexuality, since I at least had a term for my orientation. I felt ashamed of being a lesbian but I hungered to know more about it, perhaps meet others like me. Eventually, as I combed through the shelves of the Miami Public Library, I came across the DSM (the *Diagnostic and Statistical Manual of Mental Disorders*). I found homosexuality firmly entrenched within its pages. I also found the term "Gender Dysphoria."

The same drive that pushed me to read the Bible in its entirety when I was a child now drove me to learn all there was to know about transsexualism. Almost all the articles and book chapters I found dealt with male-to-female transsexuals. One small paragraph spoke about a female-to-male transsexual but had no pictures of him. The book went on to explain the steps that could culminate in surgery. Even though the whole process seemed insurmountable to me, the next day I opened the yellow pages and began to look for a psychiatrist.

It took months and many referrals before I found a team of psychiatrists that functioned as a gender team. I quickly learned that I had to conform to certain behaviors if I was to be considered a candidate for hormones and surgery: I had to identify as a man; I had to identify as straight; I had to live full time as a man for at least two years; and I had to want marriage and children, the whole nuclear family façade. None of those things was true of me, but the more I tried to convince the psychiatrist of the veracity of my lies, the more I began to internalize my story, until I came to believe it myself.

Two years later, I began hormones. The changes happened fast—too fast.

My first transsexual role models were trans women who were on hormones and lived full time as women. They ooh'ed and aah'ed over me, expressing complete confusion as to why I would want to become a man while at the same time taking me out to men's shops to purchase a new wardrobe. But I did not dress in men's shirts and pants and shoes unless I came to the clinic. They knew I did not feel safe doing so and they understood. Wearing men's clothes would mark me in the eyes of others as suspect; I would be "read" as a lesbian and bullied by others. Sometimes I would accompany friends to lesbian bars; only then would I slick my hair back and wear men's clothes. None of my lesbian friends knew I was transgender. When I did tell them, many expressed frustration and anger and ended our friendship. The butches were especially angry that I was "betraying" who I was by becoming the enemy.

I knew that I could not continue my transition in South Florida. I didn't feel safe transitioning openly, so close to my ultraconservative family, and in a city with traditional views of gender roles and sexuality. I had heard there was a gender center called Ingersoll in Seattle, Washington, so I used the money I had saved up for surgery and moved across the country to the Pacific Northwest. The night before my flight, I said goodbye to my trans women friends. They cried and hugged me, peppering me with kisses. The next day, my parents put on brave faces and drove me to the airport, where I boarded a plane.

I arrived in Seattle in the summer of 1989. I set my dreams of transition aside while I got a job and a place to live. Once I found an apartment, I crawled onto the small mattress on the floor and proceeded to break down emotionally and psychologically. I missed my parents terribly. My grief felt like a wound I carried inside. I spoke to them once a week and hungrily listened to their tear-soaked voices. I knew how much it pained them not to ask me to come back home. Not that it would have done any good; I had learned from them how to be independent, driven, and stubborn.

At this point in my life I began a series of jobs: I worked as a transcriber for the department of oral biology at the University of Washington; I worked as a housecleaner with a well-known company out of Capitol Hill; I did temp office work. Ironically, the one job I held the longest is the one job I never told my mother about. It would have broken her heart that I, a college graduate, was cleaning houses, just as she had done most of her life in the United States. Yet she had done it out of necessity, and I did it because it granted me freedom.

Once I had a place to live and an income, I set out in search of Ingersoll. The first time I saw a female-to-male transsexual was like coming home. I sat in a group of trans men in awe. I rarely spoke, I was yearning to hear their stories.

As I sat there, week after week, a niggling doubt began to grow within me. Horrified, I pushed it down—I was a trans man, a straight man, one with a genital condition that could be corrected with surgery and hormones. Within days, I found a therapist, got on hormones, and began to save for surgery. I drove myself so hard I barely found time to breathe. I spent my time either working or at Ingersoll. I continued to read about gender, fiction and nonfiction, but nothing that would cast aspersions at my choice to transition. The books I read reinforced the story I was telling myself.

I woke up after my mastectomy and shifted on the small bed, weighed down by pain and weariness and the odor of old blood. Friends came to see me, to wish me well and rejoice over this milestone in my transition. I swallowed back confusion, pushing down the doubt that now dominated my thoughts. I smiled at the right moments and said all the proper things, all the time feeling like an alien in my own skin. My identity as a trans man was fragile and paper-thin.

As soon as I was alone in the hospital, I sat up slowly and made my way to the bathroom mirror. There was a bandage around my chest and a clear drain filled with pinkish fluids poking through the skin. I wanted to get into the shower and scrub until I bled. I hated the smell, a mix of stale blood and antiseptics. I grimaced. The face that looked back at me was that of a stranger. The beard felt like a disguise, but I knew that, even if I shaved it off, stubble would remain. It was thick, worthy of praise and envy from my trans men friends. I shook my head and shuffled back to bed. I had recently turned twenty-eight, and the niggling doubt had turned into a roar. Still, I would not face it head-on for another decade.

In the meantime, I met a gay trans man and we became lovers. My identity shifted again. As with changing clothes, I quickly accepted these aspects of myself. Except the clothes I changed into did not quite fit and felt odd on my skin, yet change them I did. I embraced a bisexual identity with pride and fervor. I traveled to Vancouver, BC, and then to San Francisco, to march with the bisexual contingency in the Pride Parade. I faced biphobia and transphobia full on. People could not accept that I was attracted to both men and women. They found the concept of bisexuality confounding and suspicious. I found that, if I filled my head with fighting the injustices outside, then I could ignore the increasingly insistent voice inside, telling me I was not living authentically yet.

I found myself arguing with detractors, yelling until I didn't know what I was saying anymore. I recall walking in the Seattle Pride Parade, holding up a sign for an upcoming trans male conference that I had helped organize. One woman called out mockingly, holding her crotch, "Hey! I like what I have!" I yelled back "Good for you!" and shook my head.

First my father died, then my mother. I journeyed back home for both funerals and was met with disgust, shock, and condemnation from my family. My godmother demanded that I leave the funeral. I was a sinner, she said, a sick pervert who had no place in the family. She was the matriarch of the family, so I opted to leave. My cousins, who clearly did not understand my choices but loved me despite them, rallied around me and demanded that I stay. I left anyway. The only link to my past—my parents—was now gone. Leaving did not break my heart, nor did it break me, yet I did not allow myself to break down until I came back home to Seattle.

By now the suppressed doubt had morphed into depression, fueled by voices in my head urging me to find an end. There was nowhere else to go. I was diagnosed as bipolar and prescribed mood stabilizers and an antidepressant. I absorbed this new identity, further complicating my already crowded self. But this time when I looked in the mirror, I saw despair and exhaustion. I had to find who I was at the cost of all else. The result was that, now, my very *being* was paper-thin.

I started researching suicide. I came to a point in my life when death seemed preferable to fighting. I was exhausted from years of lying to myself and others, of working incessantly to pay for hormones and surgeries. I was forty years old, and the idea of forging ahead alone did not appeal to me. I had friends who were loving and supportive, yes, but they did not understand what I was going through. One night I sat down and told my best friend that I wanted to die. He gave me a long, warm hug, and told me he would be there for me if this was what I needed. I sobbed inconsolably. He rocked me back and forth and rubbed circles along my back.

Perhaps I had only wanted to hear someone say they would be there for me; perhaps I had just wanted to declare out loud that I was spent. Whatever the reason, I woke the next morning and knew that I would not kill myself. I knew I would reach inside of me one last time and face my last gender journey with the same determination I had used in the past.

Since I could find nothing about retransitioning on the web, I began to read about trans women and their transition to female. I had not had lower surgery, so I still had ovaries and female hormones. The first step I took was to throw away the testosterone and begin electrolysis. The second step was to tell my friends. Within a month, I had my period again. Two years later, the beard was gone. I began to incorporate tunics and tights into my wardrobe. It became a game to me, reminiscent of those days in high school when I was part of the drama club. Each tunic and legging combination, each man's pants and shirt I wore, was an outfit for a play. I even bought a mastectomy bra with padding that gave the impression I had breasts.

One evening, I stood naked before the bathroom mirror. I had no breasts, but I had wide hips. I had no facial hair but I had a deep voice. I had feminine thighs but I shaved my head. I existed somewhere in the middle of a gender. No one else, as far as I knew, could fully appreciate this new place I now lived. I had reached the inevitable and paradoxical final destination of my journey: uncertainty and nebulousness.

I am now on the cusp of my fifty-sixth year of life. I have no concept, no idea, no definition of gender. To me, women and men are equally strange and fascinating creatures. How can you *not* question gender? It seems so artificial to me. I feel like I have been around the world and back again. I speak to friends about retirement and they ask me if I want to travel. I smile at their question and tell them no. No, I've been places few have been to and many more will never know. When I retire, I will write and read and walk and enjoy the sun on my face. I am not driven anymore. Although I am still exhausted from my journey through gender, I have a deep sense of peace, fulfillment, and joy. I've carved paths for myself in my search for language to define who I am, only to finally realize my sense of self cannot be caged by a word. There is nowhere to go but inside, nothing to be but a human being.

I was once asked if I considered my choices a mistake. I can honestly answer, "No." I am the product of my choices and their consequences. If my journey has been a mistake, then so am I. But I am no mistake. If anything, I am a wonder, a question, and an answer. I no longer seek a face to mirror mine. I no longer seek a label. I am Kory. It is enough.

CHAPTER THIRTY

Rethinking Non/Binary

ELI ERLICK

THE TRUTH of my gender wasn't always safe to reveal. Over time, that truth was changed through outward lies.

In fourth grade, my teacher made us write a paragraph about ourselves in the third person to hang on our classroom wall. I wanted to refer to myself with "they" pronouns, but my teacher told me that it wasn't possible and grammatically incorrect. I had already figured out "he"— the pronoun assigned to me at birth—didn't fit me; but "she" didn't feel quite right either. I knew I didn't belong in either of those categories. "They" felt like a good place, separate from the cisgender men and women whom I couldn't relate to. However, when I attempted to write about myself using these pronouns, the other students forced me to "pick one" and concede that there were only two options.

That day, my classmates harassed me into silence; the girls rolled their eyes at me and the boys kicked me in the groin to try to figure out my assigned sex. I was too scared to argue. Asserting a pronoun that wasn't assigned to me at birth angered the other children. They hadn't met anyone like me before. I was forced out of negating the male or female label, even if neither was correct. During this experience, I felt like my self-perception was somehow wrong or broken.

As for the paragraph, I used my name instead of pronouns and refused to provide any information about myself. If one part of the statement wasn't truthful, none of it could be.

As with so many youth, the enforcement of gender normativity shaped and limited much of my gender expression and identity over time. Every day, I was told that certain actions, such as leaning with my foot against a wall or looking at my nails the "wrong" way, proved I was truly a boy. At the time, anything was better than "boy," so I let them call me what they wanted. I had never met another trans person nor had I even heard the words "transgender," "nonbinary," or "queer." The inability to speak about my gender or how I wanted to be referred to led me to withdraw from my social circles and gendered programs. I knew they would reject the notion of simply not separating students into binary genders, so the only other option was to not participate at all. To escape the humiliation, I pretended to be sick. Simply using the restroom was not an option and I would have to miss a whole day of class to keep myself safe from the brutality of the gender binary.

Trans, gender nonconforming, and nonbinary students face appalling treatment every day. As I quickly learned, it only gets worse when you're assigned male, because the other students thereby deem it more appropriate to physically assault you. After hearing about a bully who had been expelled for assaulting another student, I saw subjecting myself to violence as my only option to fight back. I hoped for the more physically violent students to attack me in front of a teacher or faculty member so they would get expelled. However, when they did attack me, nothing happened. In one case, a student threw me to the ground and kicked me until I couldn't breathe. A teacher monitoring the schoolyard saw what happened and simply ignored it.

Educational policies are intended to manage rather than protect those students not conforming to norms. I was repeatedly thrown down and punched for as little as trying to talk to classmates on the playground, and it led to no institutional or interpersonal changes at the school. In fact, the teachers smugly denied that they could do anything about it. My gender nonconformity was deemed to "provoke" the other students; therefore, it was my fault I was being assaulted. The teachers' apathy toward the violence they witnessed gave me a sense of hopelessness that continued for years.

In fifth grade, my class entered a multiweek academic competition between girls and boys, physically splitting the room in two. Correct answers to trivia questions and good behavior earned us points and prizes like candy, stuffed animals, or toys. But as soon became clear, "good" behavior was contingent upon gender normativity. Immediately after the competition was announced, a student asked, "which side of the room will Eli be sitting on?" To my disappointment, the teacher promptly retorted, "the boy's side of course." But I was unsafe on either side: with the boys, I would be at risk of attack, and the girls would tease me relentlessly for merely "wanting" to be one of them.

With my assignment, I began sabotaging the boys' team in order to let the girls win, or be kicked out from the competition altogether—preferably both. One day in the library, I made sure to talk as loudly as possible with the other boys in order to penalize the team. Instead of deducting points, the teacher loudly scolded me in front of the class: "I've never had to do this before, but I'm kicking you out of the game." She was trying to humiliate me; the girls snickered at me and the boys sarcastically, gleefully groaned. I was both pleased and annoyed. My desk was moved to the center of the classroom, between the two groups. But I did not feel between them—rather, I felt entirely outside. I should have been in another classroom.

I was defined by my gender ambiguity and had no friends for long periods of time. The unintelligibility of my gender along with my explicit refusal to label myself as a girl or boy infuriated classmates, particularly the young cis men who would berate me while trying to get an answer about what I was. When asked if I was a boy or a girl, I would simply respond "no" and attempt to walk away. They would, in turn, hurl slurs at me. "It," "She-li," and "Tranny" quickly became my second names. The harassment went on for years as I continued to withdraw socially.

My parents were finally ready to support me at the age of thirteen, although it came with the condition of normative expression and a straightforward, predetermined end point. I was fortunate that they took me to a Gender Spectrum Conference[1] at fifteen that allowed me to better navigate transitioning. However, as with many trans youth,

---

1. Gender Spectrum is an annual conference for young people and their families to learn about gender.

the opportunity came with a feeling of deep and lasting indebtedness to them as well as the abdication of control over *how* I transitioned.

I felt compelled to only wear clothes designated for women, often with bright, frilly colors. It didn't feel right to present exclusively feminine, but I didn't yet know of any category that fit me, and the rest of my town did nothing to help the situation. The gender binary operates in unique ways in rural communities. I found it ironic that some of the cis girls on the other team proudly labeled themselves tomboys, associating with the "cow culture" that held social status among us. While their expression was masculine (and arguably gender nonconforming), they were celebrated for their strength. This was the paradox of being a trans person assigned male at birth living in a rural community: masculinity is one's social standing, yet femininity and womanhood were the only ways to legitimize my own gender. As has been noted since the 1990s, the accessibility of *nonbinary, genderqueer,* or other genders that transcend the limitations of queer and transgender normativity has historically been restricted to only a privileged few. If I were to be believed that I was not a boy, then I had to be a gender-conforming girl.

When I began seeing a therapist, I pretended to be straight and gender conforming for fear that I would be denied treatment. Being a woman (or any gender) felt like pretending already, so what difference did it make to pretend to be straight on top of that? Truth was already subjective. My classmates, teachers, and family had been denying my gender for so long, they had caused my sense of self to feel so inauthentic, that it didn't matter anymore how I defined myself. Self-determination was not an option.

After a few weeks of therapy, my parents allowed me to see a doctor at the nearest transgender clinic, which was a four-hour drive away. Again, I was met with rejection for any gender nonconformity that did not fit the established guidelines of (binary) transgender health. I only wanted to go on hormone blockers to stop the remainder of puberty, but I did not want to take estrogen. My doctor wouldn't allow it. As a young rural trans person assigned male at birth, my access to health care and discourse on identity was very limited. Scared that this was my only opportunity to obtain medical treatment, I opted to go on spironolactone, testosterone inhibitor, as well as estrogen. The only alternative was to have my gender and identity completely delegitimized and be denied access to health care altogether. I figured womanhood was "close enough."

This social and medical regulation experienced by many young trans people affected the course of my life and shaped my identity. While I now present gender nonconforming, I still have a surge of fear when explaining my gender to others—a remnant of the traumas from the rural community I grew up in. This is the fault not of any one individual but of a collective culture that polices intersectionally marginalized trans people.

Over time, as I gained resources and independence, I began to rethink non/binary and transition categorically. "Transwoman" embodies my narrative much more closely than other labels and, as with many trans people assigned male, my gendered experience was largely shaped by my transness and gender nonconformity. This part of my identity is inseparable (and without space) from its proximity to womanhood. Yet I do not consider "woman" alone to accurately delineate my gender. Had I been treated differently during this critical period of psychological development during elementary and middle school, I have no doubt I would identify as nonbinary. Yet I reject the term "nonbinary" due to its role in maintaining the dominance of metropolitan individuals assigned female within the trans community. I also reject the term "binary" because my narrative does not fit that of binary bodies, nor does my presentation or lived experience.

I consider myself neither binary nor nonbinary. My current gender nonconformity now largely defines the circumstances of my identity as someone who is often antagonized on the street for my gendered ambiguity. Perhaps my ability to adapt denotes a privilege of being able to live comfortably within this liminal space. Although after years of transitioning, I still find myself asking the question, "where does that leave me?"

Interrogating the role of non/binary in my own life leads to a critical discussion of identity capital within the trans community: Does the formation of binary gender identities through coercion not posit access to nonbinary as a form of power? While both are subjugated through the gender binary, identities labeled as binary hold no material power over those identifying as nonbinary. Trans scholars, writers, and community members have long noted the relationship between exclusivity and these particular identities. In the essay "End of Genderqueer," published in 2006, genderqueer author Rocko Bulldagger reflects upon the inaccessibility of labels outside the binary during the 1990s and early 2000s.[2] "Genderqueer" was categorically exclusive to young, metropolitan, wealthy, white people assigned female while this same category espoused the superiority of genders outside the binary. Bulldagger remarks:

> I saw a drag king in Philly whose entire shtick consisted of asserting that no one could possibly understand hir complicated gender identity. Between being tragically misunderstood, perpetually on the cutting edge, and more radical than everyone else, when do genderqueers have time to connect with others? (I would feel more sympathetic if I weren't actively being excluded and looked down upon.) Before somebody even has a chance to be interested, they are dismissed as ignorant or convicted on charges of a mistaken pronoun.[3]

Having cofounded the organization Trans Student Educational Resources[4] in 2011, I have worked with countless young trans women who recall the perpetual elitism and transmisogyny from both the nonbinary community and other trans people assigned male who have internalized it. I am no exception. When first transitioning, I was coerced into femininity by those around me, who were complimenting how well I "passed" and condescendingly pointing to anything I did that they deemed not feminine enough. My entire gendered performance and aesthetic were under close scrutiny by other trans women. Did I put on too much eyeliner? I was trying too hard. Was I wearing a men's shirt? Then I was not truly a trans woman and only pretending. We unfortunately reproduce our continual inspection of one

---

2. Rocko Bulldagger, "The End of Genderqueer," in *Nobody Passes: Rejecting the Rules of Gender and Conformity*, ed. M. B. Sycamore, 137–48 (Berkeley: Seal Press, 2006).

3. Bulldagger, 146.

4. Trans Student Educational Resources is an organization dedicated to transforming the educational environment for trans and gender-nonconforming students. As of 2017, it is the only national organization run by trans youth in the United States. See more at www.transstudent.org.

another, adopting the rhetorical practices of "clocking"[5] from cisgender individuals. This led me to initially have a more gender-conforming presentation despite wanting to cut my hair short and wear clothes designed for cisgender men.

My forced reflection of cisgender women's standards of fashion also meant that I could not participate in the social economy established by the queer and assigned-female trans community, which privileges those who exert a specific masculinity (labeled androgyny on white, mostly assigned-female bodies). I was deigned too outwardly gender conforming to "understand" queer oppression. Simply due to my appearance, I was assumed to have only a simplistic grasp of the discourse on gender generated by this same nonbinary assigned-female community. My queerness was *nothing*: shortly after entering college, I was scolded by a peer for not knowing a *true* queer experience because I was perceived as straight in public—a debatable accusation when one is coming from a rural location where "passing" is negated by knowledge of the intimate life stories of everyone else in the community. Is this not what the queer/trans community should be moving away from? When I entered spaces that centered these bodies (which are not difficult to find at queer and transgender events), I would receive glares from other people in the room for the unusual presence of a body assigned male. The culture of elitism around the aesthetic of androgyny and nonbinary identity is disenfranchising at best.

When I entered college, I decided to take on an aesthetic that had the consequence of allowing me to "pass" as a nonbinary person assigned female. I was thin, white, and "androgynous," meaning that my appearance led to exclusion from trans women's spaces. This is the conflict of being a queer, gender-nonconforming trans woman: embracing masculinity was necessary for participation in queer social economies but would exclude me from transfeminine circles.

---

5. "Clocking" or "reading" are commonly used terms among trans women denoting that one is recognized as being trans, specifically recognized for being assigned male at birth. In practice, clocking operates to materially regulate the transgender aesthetic through humiliation. By verbally naming one's sex assignment, the one who is being read is coerced to further conform to corporeal norms in order to avoid being "read."

Who is able to access non/binary and who benefits from its proliferation? The accessibility of identity and labels is a heavy weight;
many trans people assigned male are excluded from queerness and
social spaces that center more privileged bodies within the trans
community. The worst forms of violence in the trans/nonbinary/
gender-nonconforming community are experienced not by white nonbinary people assigned female at birth but by women of color, who are
labeled as binary and excluded from queer/trans spaces.[6] This latter
group receives not only the most physical violence, but also nonphysical,
interpersonal, and social brutality.[7] When nonbinary identities are idol-
ized as the postmodern, fashionable, or intellectual, who is left out?
Imagining gender in terms of relational power reveals a need to rethink
where we invest our community's resources.

Admittedly, the newfound visibility of genders outside the binary
has dramatically changed and made all identities more accessible. Nevertheless, the sentiment and positionality have largely remained intact,
which punishes people of color, those assigned male, and rural people
for "reinforcing the gender binary." In reality, these identities are largely
constructed through pathology and preexisting narratives that assume
we exist in ways that we often transcend.[8] It is better to understand
that all trans people are undermining the gender binary in distinct
ways. Even when we internalize the binary and reproduce gender normativity, we cannot reproduce the binary itself. The gender binary
establishes an a priori system of gender stability, ignoring the possibility of transition. The rapid expansion of transgender, nonbinary, and
queer identities in recent years requires that we rethink these identity
categories altogether.

Sharing our narratives has been the tradition of the transgender
community in expanding discussions about our lives in order to radically reshape the movement for decades. While there have been thousands of published transgender narratives, the accounts of many trans

---

6. Che Gossett, "We Will Not Rest in Peace: AIDS Activism, Black Radical-
ism, Queer and/or Trans Resistance," in *Queer Necropolitics*, ed. J. Haritaworn,
A. Kuntsman, and S. Posocco, 31–50 (New York: Routledge, 2014).

7. b binaohan, *Decolonizing Trans/Gender 101* (Biyuti Publishing, 2014).

8. Eli Erlick, "Depathologizing Trans," in *The Remedy: Queer and Trans
Voices on Health and Healthcare*, ed. Z. Sharman (Vancouver, British Columbia:
Arsenal Pulp Press, 2016).

youth—rural, nonbinary, assigned male—are too often disregarded. Critically rethinking the geography, racialization, and gendering of nonbinary along with other identities outside of "male" and "female" creates a space for the rest of us whose stories are overlooked. From here, we can move toward imagining a revolutionary future of transgender liberation, where all trans people are free to be ourselves.

Acknowledgments

Like many of the people in these stories, this book went through its own five-year transition, and we could not have imagined the end result. Our collaboration was sparked by Zander Keig, editor of the anthology *Letters for My Brothers*. Following in its spirit, we set out to showcase our nonbinary siblings, who in turn pass along their wisdom to the next wave of gender explorers. We are sincerely grateful to Jenn Perillo and Stephen Wesley, our former and current editors at Columbia University Press. We are also deeply indebted to all the authors who shared their lives with the world.

Over the years that this book came together, I have lived in different cities, held different jobs, and hit the normal bumps and struggles of life. The work of the book could not have happened without the support I received in all areas of my life. I'd like to thank my dear friend Xander Karsten, my friend and genderqueer tutor Liat Wexler, my therapist Maegan Willan, and my family, biological and chosen. Most of all, I would like to thank my coeditor Micah, whose determination and hard work never wavered and finally carried this incredible anthology to fruition.

—SCOTT

In addition to my spouse and family, others who made this book a reality include Marlo Mack, aka gendermom, Eli Erick, and Charlie Blotner for pretending to be my friends; KJ Cerankowski and anyone who ever gave me publishing advice; and of course, my coeditor and coqueer Scott Duane. Lastly, this book is for my blog readers, who continually demanded representation for nonbinary people, and whose outpouring of appreciation kept me going.

—MICAH

Further Reading

BOOKS

Bornstein, Kate. *Gender Outlaw: On Men, Women and the Rest of Us*. 1st Vintage Books ed. New York: Routledge, 1995.

Bornstein, Kate, and S. Bear Bergman. *Gender Outlaws: The Next Generation*. Berkeley: Seal, 2010.

Erickson-Schroth, Laura, ed. *Trans Bodies, Trans Selves: A Resource for the Transgender Community*. Oxford: Oxford University Press, 2014.

Hoffman-Fox, Dara. *You and Your Gender Identity: A Guide to Discovery*. New York: Skyhorse, 2017.

Iantaffi, Alex, and Meg-John Barker. *How to Understand Your Gender: A Practical Guide for Exploring Who You Are*. London: Jessica Kingsley, 2017.

Mardell, Ash. *The ABC's of LGBT+*. Coral Gables: Mango Media, 2016.

McNabb, Charlie. *Nonbinary Gender Identities: History, Culture, Resources*. London: Rowman and Littlefield, 2017.

Nestle, Joan, Clare Howell, and Riki A. Wilchins. *GenderQueer: Voices from Beyond the Sexual Binary*. New York: Alyson, 2002.

Reiff Hill, Mel, and Jay Mays. *The Gender Book*. Houston: Marshall House Press, 2013. www.thegenderbook.com.

Richards, Christina, Walter P. Bouman, and Meg-John Barker. *Genderqueer and Non-Binary Genders*. New York: Palgrave Macmillan, 2017.

Stryker, Susan. *Transgender History*. Rev. ed. Berkeley: Seal, 2009.

ONLINE RESOURCES

Deutsch, Madeline B., ed. *Guidelines for the Primary and Gender-Affirming Care of Transgender and Gender Nonbinary People*. 2nd ed. Center of

Excellence for Transgender Health, University of California, San Francisco, June 2016. www.transhealth.ucsf.edu/guidelines.

Gender Neutral Pronoun Blog, a comprehensive guide about gender-neutral pronouns and how to use them. https://genderneutralpronoun.wordpress.com.

Genderqueer Identities provides awareness, information, and resources for genderqueer, nonbinary, questioning, and gender-nonconforming people and their allies. http://genderqueerid.com/gq-links.

Genderqueer.me, an online resource about transgender health and the nonbinary community. http://genderqueer.me.

Trans Lifeline is the first and only suicide hotline exclusively by and for trans people. www.translifeline.org or 1-877-565-8860.

Trans Student Educational Resources is a youth-led organization for trans and gender-nonconforming students. www.transstudent.org.

Trans WHAT? A gentle introduction to trans identities for allies. www.transwhat.org.

FOR PARENTS AND ALLIES

Angello, Michelle, and Ali Bowman. *Raising the Transgender Child: A Complete Guide for Parents, Families, and Caregivers.* Berkeley: Seal, 2016.

Brill, Stephanie, and Lisa Kenney. *The Transgender Teen: A Handbook for Parents and Professionals Supporting Transgender and Non-Binary Teens.* Berkeley: Cleis, 2016.

Ehrensaft, Diane. *The Gender Creative Child: Pathways for Nurturing and Supporting Children Who Live Outside Gender Boxes.* New York: The Experiment, 2016.

Stork, Kelly. *The Gender Identity Workbook for Kids: A Guide to Exploring Who You Are.* Oakland, CA: New Harbinger, 2018.

Tarney, Julie. *My Son Wears Heels: One Mom's Journey from Clueless to Kickass.* Madison: University of Wisconsin Press, 2016.

ORGANIZATIONS

Gender Odyssey is a trans-led organization providing trainings for trans youth inclusion in schools, as well as two annual conferences for transgender children, young adults, their families, and the providers that care for them. www.genderodyssey.org.

Gender Spectrum provides resources and trainings, as well as an annual conference in Moraga, California, for families with trans kids. www.genderspectrum.org.

Trans Youth Family Allies helps parents and family members navigate their children's transition, from school bathrooms to legal name changes. www .imatyfa.org.

CHILDREN'S BOOKS

Broadhead, Talcott. *Meet Polkadot.* Olympia: Danger Dot, 2013.

Hall, Michael. *Red: A Crayon's Story.* New York: Greenwillow, 2015.

Pessin-Whedbee, Brook. *Who Are You? The Kid's Guide to Gender Identity.* London: Jessica Kingsley, 2016.

Savage, Sarah, and Fox Fisher. *Are You a Boy or Are You a Girl?* London: Jessica Kingsley, 2017.

Silverberg, Cory. *Sex Is a Funny Word: A Book About Bodies, Feelings, and YOU.* New York: Triangle Square, 2015.

Contributors

ABIGAIL is a writer who has also worked in elementary education and marketing. She lives with her husband and three teenagers in Maryland.

KAMERON ACKERMAN is a radio DJ and janitor from upstate New York. He and his spouse are collaborating on a podcast called *this is what gender sounds like*. More of his writing can be found at www.janitorqueer .com. His love of sneakers and beverages knows no bounds.

GENNY BEEMYN, PhD, is director of the Stonewall Center at UMass Amherst and the coordinator of Campus Pride's Trans Policy Clearinghouse. They are the author of *A Queer Capital: A History of Gay Life in Washington, D.C.* and, with Sue Rankin, *The Lives of Transgender People*. Genny's latest work is the edited volume *Trans People in Higher Education*.

SAND C. CHANG, PhD (they/them), is a Chinese American nonbinary psychologist, educator, and advocate from Oakland, California, who works at NCAL Kaiser Permanente Transgender Services and in private practice. Outside of their professional work, Sand is a dancer, avid foodie, and pug enthusiast.

SUZI CHASE is a writer, educator, and transgender activist. She writes from Maryland.

NINO CIPRI is a queer and transgender/nonbinary writer, educator, and editor. They're often on Twitter @ninocipri talking about strange narrative forms and cats.

CK COMBS is trans and genderqueer and lives in his hometown of Olympia, Washington. He serves the community as a board member for Pizza Klatch, a nonprofit providing support and advocacy for LGBTQ+ youth. A childhood of daydreaming led him to become a writer, though he's camouflaged himself as a software developer to make a living.

JULES DE LA CRUZ, MPA, is a semiretired thirty-year law enforcement/ security professional now dabbling in passions such as wearing hats and maintaining pressed penny and Zoltar machines. Most importantly, Jules is now embarking on becoming a foster parent.

AUBRI DRAKE, MSW, MLS, is a nonbinary writer and researcher. Their work has been featured in *Ethnicity and Health*, *Library and Information Science Research*, and *The Naked I* at 20% Theatre Company, Twin Cities. Aubri is also a long-distance backpacker and photographer, and loves to share adventures on their *Transcending Mountains* blog.

SCOTT DUANE is a queer trans guy in his thirties living in Oakland, California. He thinks that storytelling is a powerful medium for change, especially in marginalized communities. When he's not writing stories, Scott writes code for a tech company in San Francisco.

BRIAN JAY ELEY is a marshmallow soft butch, genderqueer femme from Houston, Texas, living in Seattle, Washington. They are a rapper, producer, DJ, host, dancer, and podcaster, dedicated to social justice but still goofy and weird. You can find their music, as *Brian is Ze*, on Bandcamp and social media.

AVERY ERICKSON is a licensed acupuncturist, herbalist, and holistic primary care provider, and is especially interested in the spiritual empowerment of trans, nonbinary, and gender-nonconforming people. They have lived in San Francisco for some time, and have now retreated to the Southwest to commune with nature as they enter the next cycle of their life.

ELI ERLICK is a PhD student in feminist studies at the University of California, Santa Cruz, where she researches the political philosophy of the transgender movement. She is also the director of Trans Student Educational Resources, a national organization dedicated to transforming the educational environment for trans students.

LEVI S. GOVONI is a transgender writer, photographer, and dad. He graduated with a JD from Western New England University School of Law in 2011 and served on the board of directors for True Colors, Inc., a nonprofit organization serving LBGTQ youth. He lives in Hartford, Connecticut.

FÉI HERNANDEZ is a spiritual, immigrant, trans nonbinary artist, performing poet, and youth educator residing in Inglewood. They are a VONA fellow currently working on a poetry collection and art project.

MICHAL "MJ" JONES is a black queer and nonbinary writer, activist, educator, and musician living in Oakland, California. A talented interdisciplinary writer of essay, poetry, and prose alike, their work has been featured at *Foglifter Press*, *Everyday Feminism*, *Black Girl Dangerous*, and *Wear Your Voice Magazine*. MJ is deeply committed to liberation struggles, youth empowerment, intergenerational movement building, and anti-oppressive education.

KATY KOONCE, LCSW, is a psychotherapist in Austin, Texas. She has served transgender communities since 1998, when she formed the first therapist-led transgender support group in central Texas. As the front man for the "silicone cock rock" band Butch County, Katy has shared her signature blend of nonbinary swagger with a variety of audiences—from swampy Southern honkytonks to San Francisco Pride.

JEFFREY MARSH is the author of the self-esteem classic *How To Be You*. They are the first openly nonbinary author with a big-five publisher, Penguin Random House. Their inclusive messages have garnered over 350 million views on social media. Jeffrey is a precepted facilitator in the Soto Zen tradition of Buddhism.

KORY MARTIN-DAMON works for the state of Washington's unemployment department as the interim supervisor of a small unit that offers additional funds for workers needing retraining. When she lived as a transman she helped organize Seattle's first FTM conference. She lives in Tukwila, Washington.

JAMIE PRICE is a genderqueer songwriter from Edmonton, Canada. They release music under the name *Must Be Tuesday*, and are the writer/composer of the musical *My Boyfriend's Girlfriend*. They also do voice acting on a variety of serial fiction podcasts.

MICAH RAJUNOV is a writer, researcher, and advocate. Since 2011 Micah has created community resources for nonbinary identities through the site *genderqueer.me*. Micah's personal transition story has been featured in mainstream publications as well as a full-length documentary. After growing up in Mexico City, Micah lived in Philadelphia and then San Francisco, and is now a PhD student at Boston University. Micah is also a rock climber and a closet idealist.

SINCLAIR SEXSMITH (they/them) writes the award-winning sex, gender, kink, and relationship blog at Sugarbutch.net. Their short story collection, *Sweet and Rough: Queer Kink Erotica*, was a 2016 finalist for the Lambda Literary Award, and their work is widely published online and in more than two dozen anthologies. They identify as a white, nonbinary butch dominant, a survivor, and an introvert.

S. E. SMITH is a Northern California–based writer and journalist. smith's work has appeared in *Rolling Stone, The Guardian, Time, Esquire, Al Jazeera, Vice,* and many other fine publications, along with numerous anthologies, including *(Don't) Call Me Crazy, Get Out of My Crotch!,* and *The Feminist Utopia Project*. smith's work focuses on intersectional justice issues, because liberation for some is justice for none.

CHRISTOPHER SOTO (b. 1991, Los Angeles) is a poet based in Brooklyn, New York. They are the author of *Sad Girl Poems* and the editor of *Nepantla: An Anthology Dedicated to Queer Poets of Color*. They cofounded the Undocupoets Campaign and worked to establish grants for undocumented writers. They received their MFA in poetry from New York University.

CAL SPARROW is an artist who enjoys creating sci-fi characters and stories that fill some of the voids in the media landscape. Friends have praised Cal for their very convincing human persona, but agree that they would make a better cat next time.

ADAM "PICAPICA" STEVENSON formally talked about androgyny under the name *PicaPica*. Adam now writes all about the eighteenth century under the name of *The Grub Street Lodger* and develops novels that no one wants to read.

ALEX STITT, LMHC, is a genderqueer mental health counselor specializing in identity acquisition and trauma therapy. A novelist, fire-dancer, and LGBTQ advocate, Alex is currently authoring *Acceptance and Commitment Therapy (ACT) for Gender Identity*.

RAE THEODORE is the author of *Leaving Normal* and *My Mother Says Drums Are for Boys*. Rae is president of the Greater Philadelphia chapter of the Women's National Book Association and is passionate about Wonder Woman comics, Joan Jett, and professional wrestling. Don't judge. She lives in Royersford, Pennsylvania, with her wife, kids, and cats, and is working on a book about love.

JACE VALCORE is a thirty-two-year-old genderqueer college professor and tango dancer. They believe in the power of education to change hearts and minds and hope for a future in which gender diversity is widely accepted and understood.

JAYE WARE grew up in a rural county in England, and is now living in a coastal town in Fife, Scotland. Ze is studying for a PhD, researching young people's perspectives on gender and sexual diversity within high schools. Jaye is a keen walker and loves exploring Britain's national trails.

MELISSA L. WELTER (ze/zir) is a genderqueer activist, writer, and educator from northern California. Ze is a contributor to *Arcane Perfection: An Anthology by Queer, Trans, and Intersex Witches*. Ze is passionate about creating spaces of justice, healing, and transformation for nonbinary and trans folx.

RIKI WILCHINS is a gender activist and author of five books on trans and genderqueer theory and politics. Riki's latest book is *Burn the Binary!* When not thinking deep thoughts about Judith Butler and heteronormativity, s/he is usually playing tennis or doing long-distance runs.

HAVEN WILVICH (they/them) is a transfeminine organizer and nonprofit admin in their early thirties, born and raised in the Seattle area. When they're not blogging about gender and building local nonbinary community, they spend their time cooking and cuddling with cute people and pets.